Bargain Hunter's SECRETS TO ONLINE $HOPPING

Michael Miller

que®
800 East 96th Street,
Indianapolis, Indiana 46240

Bargain Hunter's Secrets to Online Shopping

International Standard Book Number: 0-7897-3201-7

Library of Congress Catalog Card Number: 2004104257

Printed in the United States of America

First Printing: May 2004

06 05 04 4 3 2 1

Trademarks

All terms mentioned in this book that are known to be trademarks or service marks have been appropriately capitalized. Que Publishing cannot attest to the accuracy of this information. Use of a term in this book should not be regarded as affecting the validity of any trademark or service mark.

Warning and Disclaimer

Every effort has been made to make this book as complete and as accurate as possible, but no warranty or fitness is implied. The information provided is on an "as is" basis. The author and the publisher shall have neither liability nor responsibility to any person or entity with respect to any loss or damages arising from the information contained in this book.

Bulk Sales

Que Publishing offers excellent discounts on this book when ordered in quantity for bulk purchases or special sales. For more information, please contact

U.S. Corporate and Government Sales

1-800-382-3419

corpsales@pearsontechgroup.com

For sales outside of the U.S., please contact

International Sales

1-317-428-3341

international@pearsontechgroup.com

Associate Publisher
Greg Wiegand

Acquisitions Editor
Stephanie McComb

Development Editor
Kevin Howard

Managing Editor
Charlotte Clapp

Project Editor
Andy Beaster

Copy Editor
Mike Henry

Indexer
Mandie Frank

Proofreader
Jennifer Timpe

Technical Editor
Evan Schwartz

Publishing Coordinator
Sharry Lee Gregory

Interior Designer
Anne Jones

Cover Designer
Anne Jones

Page Layout
Bronkella Publishing

Contents at a Glance

Table of Contents

About the Author

Michael Miller has written more than 50 nonfiction books over the past 15 years. His books for Que include *Absolute Beginner's Guide to eBay, Absolute Beginner's Guide to Launching an eBay Business*, and *Absolute Beginner's Guide to Computer Basics*. He is known for his casual, easy-to-read writing style and his ability to explain a wide variety of complex topics to an everyday audience.

You can email Mr. Miller directly at `bargains@molehillgroup.com`. His Web site is located at `www.molehillgroup.com`.

Dedication

To my siblings Melanie and Mark, who benefit tremendously from my own online bargain hunting--especially at holidays.

Acknowledgments

Thanks to the usual suspects at Que, including but not limited to Greg Wiegand, Stephanie McComb, Kevin Howard, Andy Beaster, and Mike Henry.

We Want to Hear from You!

As the reader of this book, *you* are our most important critic and commentator. We value your opinion and want to know what we're doing right, what we could do better, what areas you'd like to see us publish in, and any other words of wisdom you're willing to pass our way.

As an associate publisher for Que, I welcome your comments. You can email or write me directly to let me know what you did or didn't like about this book—as well as what we can do to make our books better.

Please note that I cannot help you with technical problems related to the topic of this book. We do have a User Services group, however, where I will forward specific technical questions related to the book.

When you write, please be sure to include this book's title and author as well as your name, email address, and phone number. I will carefully review your comments and share them with the author and editors who worked on the book.

Email: feedback@quepublishing.com

Mail: Greg Wiegand
Associate Publisher
Que Publishing
800 East 96th Street
Indianapolis, IN 46240 USA

For more information about this book or another Que title, visit our Web site at www.quepublishing.com. Type the ISBN (excluding hyphens) or the title of a book in the Search field to find the page you're looking for.

INTRODUCTION

Online shopping is booming. Shoppers spent a record $93 billion online in 2003, an increase of 27% over previous year sales. In a single day in December, the Web's largest online retailer, Amazon.com, reportedly sold 2.1 million items—which translates to 24 items sold *every second.*

That's big.

And if you're one of the millions currently shopping online, you know how easy it is. Search for what you want, click the mouse a few times, enter your credit card number, and wait for the package to arrive. That's all there is to it—no special skills necessary.

But shopping online and finding bargains online are two different things. Anyone can shop, but it takes real talent to find the lowest prices available. If you know what you're doing, you can save a lot of money shopping at online merchants. The bargains are there for you to find.

Hunting for bargains is what this book is all about. Which sites have the lowest prices? Where can you find closeout and refurbished merchandise? What about buying used instead of new? And how can you reduce your total purchase price—including shipping and handling? Those questions and more are answered in *Bargain Hunter's Secrets to Online Shopping*—your one-stop resource to the world of online bargains.

How This Book Is Organized

Everything you need to know about online bargain hunting is contained in this book. The information is organized into three main sections:

- **Part I, "Online Shopping Secrets,"** presents the basics of online shopping: how online shopping works, how to shop safely, how to research your purchases before you buy, and the steps you need to take to become a savvy online shopper.
- **Part II, "Money Saving Secrets,"** shows you how to hunt for the best bargains online: how to find the lowest price, how to take advantage of online coupons and rebates, how to save money at online malls and catalog stores, how to look for closeout and overstock savings, how to find bargains on eBay, and how to shop smart at Amazon.com, the world's largest online retailer.
- **Part III, "The Bargain Hunter's Online Shopping Directory,"** shows you *where* to find the best bargains online—more than 1,000 of the lowest-priced online merchants are listed, along with bargain hunter tips for each site.

That last section takes up the entire last half of this book, and serves as your guide to the best bargains on the Web. The Web sites are organized into 35 product categories, so you can quickly find those merchants that offer the products you're looking for. I guarantee you'll have the pages dog-eared before your holiday shopping is done!

Conventions Used in This Book

I hope that this book is easy enough to figure out on its own, without requiring its own instruction manual. As you read through the pages, however, it helps to know precisely how I've presented specific types of information.

Web Page Addresses

As you might suspect, there are a lot of Web page addresses in this book. They're noted as such:

`www.molehillgroup.com`

Technically, a Web page address is supposed to start with `http://` (as in `http://www.molehillgroup.com`). Because Internet Explorer and other Web browsers automatically insert this piece of the address, however, you don't have to type it—and I haven't included it in any of the addresses in this book.

Special Elements

This book also includes a few special elements that provide additional information not included in the basic text. These elements are designed to supplement the text to make your learning faster, easier, and more efficient.

tip

A *tip* is a piece of advice—a little trick, actually—that helps you save money or better use a particular Web site.

note

A *note* is designed to provide information that's generally useful but not specifically necessary for what you're doing at the moment. Some notes are like extended tips—interesting, but not essential.

caution

A *caution* will tell you to beware of a potentially dangerous action or situation. In some cases, ignoring a caution could cause you significant problems or cost you money—so pay attention to them!

Bargain Hunter's Secret

In addition, I've identified the very best secrets for bargain hunters and labeled them with this Bargain Hunters Secrets icon. Look for these icons throughout the book—these secrets will definitely save you money when you're shopping online!

Let Me Know What You Think

I always love to hear from readers. If you want to contact me, feel free to email me at `bargains@molehillgroup.com`. I can't promise that I'll answer every message, but I will promise that I'll read each one!

If you want to learn more about me and any new books I have cooking, check out my Molehill Group Web site at `www.molehillgroup.com`. This is also where you'll find any corrections or clarifications to this book, which I'll post as necessary.

(Statistics courtesy ComScore Networks, Goldman Sachs, Harris Interactive, and Nielsen/NetRatings.)

I

ONLINE SHOPPING SECRETS

ONLINE SHOPPING 101

Shopping online is great. It's much more convenient than battling the crowds at a traditional shopping mall, and it's easier to find exactly what you want; the selection is almost limitless. Best of all, shopping online is a boon for bargain hunters. You won't believe the money you can save when you start scouring the Internet for bargains.

Before you can hunt for bargains online, however, you have to be comfortable with the whole online shopping experience. If you're already an experienced online shopper, good for you—you can probably skim the information in this chapter. But if you're just now venturing online and aren't sure what to expect, read on. This chapter will show you what you'll find when you visit an online retailer, and guide you through the entire online shopping and purchasing process.

How Online Retailers Work

At first glance, an online retailer is kind of like a traditional retailer, but without the "bricks and mortar" storefront. Online retailers, just like traditional retailers, offer various types of merchandise for sale; you browse through the merchandise (using your Web browser) until you find something you want, and then you make a purchase, typically using a credit card.

But that's where the similarities end.

Many online retailers actually *are* traditional retailers. (Some examples are Sears and Circuit City online.) That is, they operate real-world storefronts in addition to their online stores. From an operational standpoint, these traditional/online retailers (let's call them *dual-channel* retailers) are able to piggyback their online sales onto their traditional sales by putting up a Web site and setting up some sort of packing and shipping operation. They often pull sales from either channel from the same inventory.

note

In retailing parlance, each different type of customer you sell to is called a *channel*. Therefore, traditional storefront sales are one channel, and online sales are another channel.

Other online retailers operate solely online; they don't have a traditional retail presence. (Examples are Amazon.com and Buy.com.) These retailers do all their business online or over the phone. They don't display any stock to the public; all their inventory is in boxes in a warehouse. The operation consists of the Web site front end, one or more warehouses, and a packing/shipping operation.

From a customer's standpoint, if you're buying off the Web, it doesn't really matter what kind of "bricks and mortar" presence a retailer has. All that matters to you is how well the retailer's Web site is organized, what products it has in stock (and at what prices), and how fast it ships. You could care less about whether it has "real" stores, too.

Bargain Hunter's Secret

That is, unless you actually want to pick up in person what you ordered online. That's right, some online retailers offer the option of in-store pickup. That's helpful if you don't want to wait several days to receive your purchase. This type of in-store pickup option is typically offered by a dual-channel retailer; you place your order from the online store, but pick up your purchase from the real-world store. (This is one of the primary advantages of buying from a dual-channel retailer, as opposed to an online-only store.)

That said, most of your online purchases will be shipped to you. After you place your order, the online retailer processes your payment and then sends the paperwork (electronically) to its warehouse, where your order is picked and packed. Some retailers are faster at this than others; some can get your order out the door the same day, others take several days or a week for this part of the process. After your order has been boxed up, it's handed to a delivery service, typically the United States Postal Service, UPS, or FedEx. Then the shipment travels across the country, where it's delivered to your doorstep.

In most cases, you pay all shipping charges for what you order. Some retailers offer free shipping, either for orders over a certain dollar amount, or as part of a promotion, but most will charge you for shipping. Make sure that you factor that shipping cost into the total cost of your order; remember that if you bought the same item from a traditional retailer, you wouldn't be paying for shipping.

Bargain Hunter's Secret

That added shipping cost might be offset by a tax savings. Most online-only retailers don't have to charge sales tax, which can be a real savings if you live in a high tax state. On the other hand, dual-channel retailers have to charge sales tax on orders shipped to states where they have retail locations; so, if you buy from Sears online and you have a Sears store nearby, you'll be charged your normal state sales tax on your online order. (This is one of the primary disadvantages of buying from a dual-channel retailer.)

So, this is the way online retailing works. Some online retailers are very large, doing millions of dollars of business a day. Others are very small, essentially run by one or two people out of their garage or basement. And the great thing about buying online is that you might never know how big or how small the merchant is you're dealing with; even the smallest retailers can look big-time if they provide great service!

Understanding the Online Shopping Process

If you've never shopped online before, you're probably wondering just what to expect. Shopping over the Web is actually quite easy; all you need is your computer and a credit card—and a fast connection to the Internet!

Online shopping is pretty much the same, no matter which retailer you shop at. You proceed through a multiple-step process that goes like this:

1. **Find a product**, either by browsing or searching through the site.
2. **Examine the product** by viewing the photos and information on a product listing page.
3. **Order the product** by clicking a "buy it now" button on the product listing page which puts the item in your online shopping cart.
4. **Check out** by entering your payment and shipping information.
5. **Confirm your order**, and wait for the merchant to ship your merchandise.

Let's look at each of these steps separately.

Step 1: Find a Product

The first step in online shopping is the actual shopping. That means accessing a retailer's Web site and either browsing through different product categories, or using the site's search feature to find a specific product.

Browsing product categories online is similar to browsing through the departments of a retail store. You typically click a link to access a major product category, and then click further links to view subcategories within the main category. For example, the main category might be Clothing; the subcategories might be Men's, Women's, and Children's clothing. If you click the Men's link, you might see a list of further subcategories: outerwear, shirts, pants, and the like. Just keep clicking until you reach the type of item that you're looking for.

> **tip**
>
> Think of searching as power shopping—the online equivalent of walking right to the specific item you want to buy, with no distractions. Browsing is more like traditional shopping, where you look at a lot of different items before you make your choice.

Bargain Hunter's Secret

Searching for products is often a faster way to find what you're looking for—if you have something specific in mind. For example, if you're looking for a men's silk jacket, you can enter the words **men's silk jacket** into the site's Search box, and get a list of specific items that match those criteria. The only problem with searching is that you might not know exactly what it is you're looking for; if this describes your situation, you're probably better off browsing. But if you *do* know what you want—and you don't want to deal with lots of irrelevant items—then searching is the faster option.

Step 2: Examine the Product

Whether you browse or search, you'll probably end up looking at a list of different products on a Web page. These listings typically feature one-line descriptions of each item—in most cases, not near enough information for you to make an informed purchase.

The thing to do now is to click the link for the item you're particularly interested in. This should display a dedicated product page, complete with picture and full description of the item. This is where you can read more about the item you selected. Some product pages include different views of the item, pictures of the item in different colors, links to additional information, and maybe even a list of optional accessories that go along with the item.

If you like what you see, you can proceed to the ordering stage. If you want to look at other items, just click your browser's Back button to return to the larger product listing.

Step 3: Order the Product

Somewhere on each product description page should be a button labeled Purchase or Buy Now or something similar. This is how you make the actual purchase: by clicking the Buy Now button. You don't order the product just by looking at the product description; you have to manually click that Purchase button to place your order.

When you click the Purchase or Buy Now button, that particular item is added to your *shopping cart*. That's right, the online retailer provides you with a virtual shopping cart that functions just like a real-world shopping cart. That is, each item you choose to purchase is added to your virtual shopping cart.

After you've ordered a product and placed it in your shopping cart, you can choose to shop for other products on that site or proceed to the site's checkout. It's important to note that when you place an item in your shopping cart, you haven't actually completed the purchase yet. You can keep shopping (and adding more items to your shopping cart) as long as you want.

You can even decide to abandon your shopping cart and not purchase anything at this time. All you have to do is leave the Web site, and you won't be charged for anything. It's the equivalent of leaving your shopping cart at a real-world retailer, and walking out the front door; you don't actually buy anything until you walk through the checkout line.

Step 4: Check Out

To finalize your purchase, you have to visit the store's checkout. This is like the checkout line at a traditional retail store; you take your shopping cart through the checkout, get your purchases totaled, and then pay for what you're buying.

The checkout at an online retailer typically consists of one or more Web pages with forms you have to fill out. If you've visited the retailer before, the site might remember some of your personal information from your previous visit. Otherwise, you'll have to enter your name, address, and phone number, as well as the address you want to ship the merchandise to (if that's different from your billing address). You'll also have to pay for the merchandise, typically by entering a credit card number.

The checkout provides one last opportunity for you to change your order. You can delete items you decide not to buy, or change quantities on any item. At some merchants, you can even opt to have your items gift-wrapped and sent to someone as a gift. All these options should be somewhere in the checkout.

You might also have the option of selecting different types of shipping for your order. Many merchants offer both regular and expedited shipping—the latter for an additional charge.

Another option at some retailers is to group all items together for reduced shipping cost, or to ship items individually as they become available. Grouping items together is attractive cost-wise, but you can get burned if one or more items is out-of-stock or not yet available; you could end up waiting weeks or months for those items that could have been shipped immediately.

tip

The better online retailers will tell you either on the product description page or during the checkout process whether or not an item is in stock. Look for this information to help you decide how to group your items for shipment.

Step 5: Confirm the Order

After you've entered all the appropriate information, you're asked to place your order. This typically means clicking a button that says Place Your Order or something similar. (I told you it's easy!) You might even see a second screen, asking you whether you *really* want to place your order, just in case you had second thoughts.

After your order has been placed, you'll see a confirmation screen, typically displaying your order number. Write down this number or print out this page; you'll refer to this number in case you ever need to contact customer service. Most online merchants will also send you a confirmation message via email, containing this same information.

And that's all there is to it. You shop, you examine the product, you place an order, you proceed to checkout, and then you confirm your purchase. It's that easy!

Online Shopping Step-by-Step: A Visit to a Typical Online Retailer

Let's get a little hands-on experience with the online shopping process by looking at a typical session at a typical online merchant. For our example, let's go to Buy.com (a very typical merchant) and shop for a DVD player (a very typical purchase). You can play along at home by going to the Buy.com site, located at `www.buy.com`.

As you can see in Figure 1.1, the Buy.com home page is lot like what you see when you walk in the front door of a large traditional merchant. There's all sorts of stuff on sale, and lots of merchandise vying for your eye (and your purchase dollar). But don't be swayed by all this eye candy; you're looking for one thing in particular, and there's no point in getting distracted from this task.

FIGURE 1.1
The Buy.com home page—note the categories listed along the left side.

What you're interested in are the different categories of merchandise that Buy.com offers. Some Web sites list their categories on tabs along the top of the home page; Buy.com lists its categories along the left side of the page. Because we're shopping for a DVD player, we'll click the **Electronics** link in the Office and Electronics section.

You're now taken to Buy.com's Electronics page, shown in Figure 1.2. Think of this as walking into the electronics section of a major department store. There are a lot of specials displayed here, typically those items currently on promotion or that the site is trying to push for one reason or another. Again, don't be swayed by these specials; go directly to the list of subcategories on the left side of the page, and click the **DVD Players** link.

Buy.com now displays its DVD Players page, shown in Figure 1.3, with a number of Hot Buys featured. It's okay to peruse these specials, but you want to look at *all* the DVD players offered, not just those on promotion. That means you need to click through to one last subcategory; click the **Single Disc** link on the left side of the page.

FIGURE 1.2

Buy.com's Electronics section—subcategories are listed along the left side.

FIGURE 1.3

The DVD Players page—one more subcategory to go!

Now we're finally where we want to be! Figure 1.4 shows Buy.com's Single Disc DVD Players page. All the single-disc DVD players that Buy.com offers are listed here. (Actually, there are two pages worth of listings; click the Next link to see the second page.) As you can see, you don't get a lot of details on this page. To learn more about any particular product, you have to click the link for that product.

FIGURE 1.4

Viewing all of Buy.com's single-disc DVD players.

For our example, let's say you're interested in item number 5, the JVC XVN44SL Progressive Scan DVD Player for $89.99. Click the link and you'll see the product page shown in Figure 1.5. There are lots of details here, from a product description and warranty info to technical specs and customer reviews. (See the list of links along the left side of the page.) You can even view a larger photo of the product by clicking the Larger Image link.

note

Note the category tree at the top of each Buy.com page. This is a navigational aid that shows you exactly where you are in the category hierarchy—in this case, **Home ⇢ Electronics ⇢ DVD Players ⇢ Single Disc.** You can click a link to move back up the categories.

FIGURE 1.5
Viewing product details for the selected item.

You read the details. You look at the picture. You evaluate the price. You like what you see. This is exactly what you where looking for, so go ahead and place your order—click the Buy Now button.

Buy.com now places this item in your *shopping basket*—this site's term for the ubiquitous online shopping cart—and displays the Shopping Basket page, shown in Figure 1.6. If you want to shop for more items, click the Continue Shopping button and you'll be whisked back to the main site. If this is all you want to buy, click the Checkout button to proceed to the checkout.

Now Buy.com displays the Welcome to Checkout page shown in Figure 1.7. If you've shopped here before, enter your email address and password; this will take you to the checkout page, with your personal information already entered for you. If you're a new customer, you'll need to enter this information manually, so click the Continue to Checkout button to proceed.

FIGURE 1.6

The contents of your shopping basket.

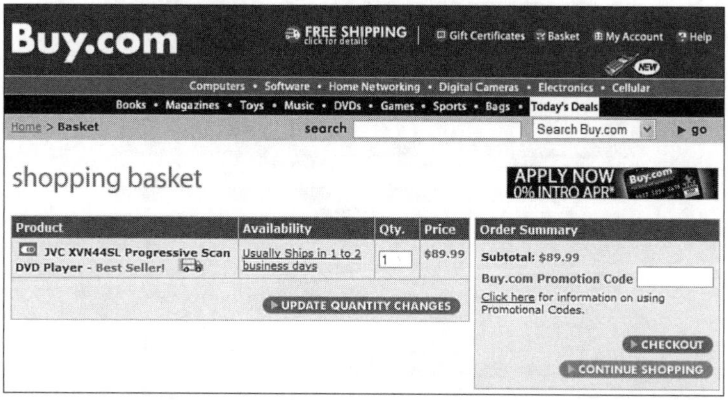

FIGURE 1.7

Getting ready to check out.

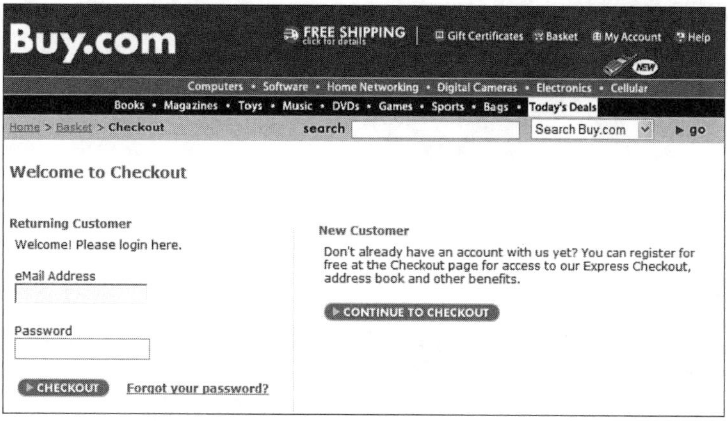

As a new customer, Buy.com needs you to enter the typical name, address, and phone number information, which you do on the First Time Customers page shown in Figure 1.8. Work your way down the page, making sure that you fill in all the required fields (those marked with an asterisk).

At the bottom of this page is the Payment Method section, shown in Figure 1.9. Let's assume that you're paying by credit card; select the type of card, and then enter your card number and expiration date. Click Continue when you're ready to proceed.

tip

You might be tempted to enter a phony email address so that you won't be added to anybody's spam list. That's actually a bad idea; you need to enter your real email address so that the site can contact you if there are any problems or delays with your order.

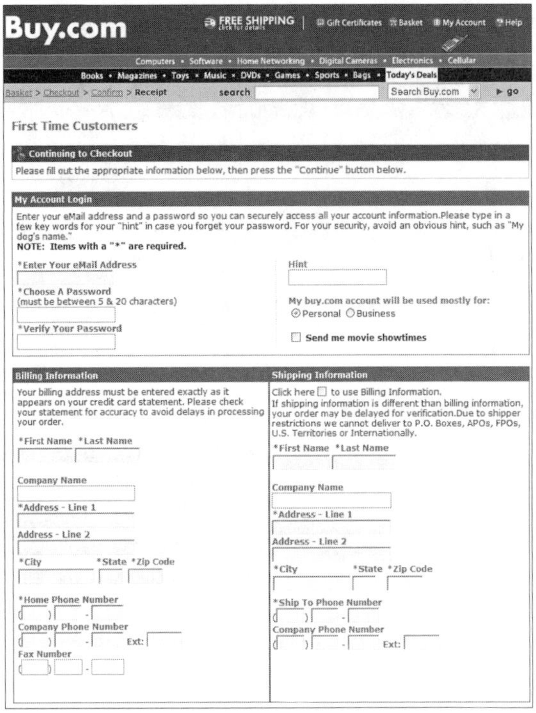

FIGURE 1.8

Entering your shipping information.

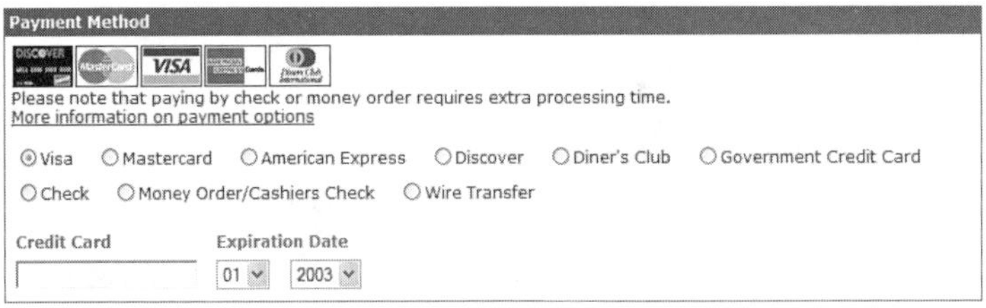

FIGURE 1.9

Entering your credit card information.

Buy.com now processes all this data and displays a confirmation page. Print this page for your records, and you're done. You should receive your new DVD player within the next week or so.

Paying for Your Purchase

During that shopping example we kind of skipped over the payment particulars. Which begs the question: When you're shopping online, how can (and should) you pay?

Almost all online retailers accept payment by credit card. Larger retailers will accept credit cards directly; some smaller retailers will accept credit cards via PayPal, which is a third-party electronic payment service. (Don't worry; dealing with PayPal is a snap. You give PayPal your credit card number, and then PayPal pays the retailer.)

Some online retailers also accept payment by check or money order. This is a hassle, however, because you have to place your order online, get instructions from the retailer, and then send your payment via snail mail. Your order isn't shipped until your payment is received—and, in the case of personal checks, until your check clears the bank. Paying in this fashion can delay your shipment by anywhere from one to three weeks.

Few, if any, online retailers accept payment by cash. This is more for your protection than any other reason. It's a really dumb idea to send cash through the mail. Cash is easily lost or stolen, and you have no way of tracking it after you've sent it. Take my advice: Don't pay by cash. Ever.

My recommendation is to do all your online shopping via credit card. There are a number of reasons for this.

First, it's the way most online shoppers pay, and what most online retailers expect. The whole online shopping process is built around credit card payments, so when you pay by plastic, everything goes smoothly.

Second, it's fast. You place your order, you enter your credit card number, the order is confirmed, and your product ships—just like that. There's no delay waiting for your payment to be received or your check to be cleared. Most credit card purchases are processed the same day—if not the same hour.

Third, it's safe. Yeah, you've heard horror stories about credit card theft and fraud, but the reality is that your credit card company is working overtime to protect you against this type of problem. In fact, if you check with your card company, you'll find that you're protected against credit card theft above a minimal amount; if your card number is stolen, you might be on the hook for $25 or $50, but the credit card company eats any amount more than that. In addition, if you have a problem with the order (like you never receive the item, or it breaks, or whatever), you can have your credit card company stop payment to the retailer. The credit card

note

Even though most online retailers accept credit cards, not all retailers accept all types of credit cards. MasterCard and Visa are almost universally accepted, but fewer retailers accept American Express and Discover, in part because of the higher fees these companies charge merchants. Make sure that the retailer accepts your particular card before you complete your purchase.

companies always work to your benefit, which can be a real lifesaver when you have a genuine dispute.

So, when you're ready to go online shopping, make sure that your credit card is at hand. It's the only way to pay!

What to Expect After the Sale

If nothing else, shopping online is quick. You can most often find what you want and place your order in just a few minutes. But what happens after you make that last mouse click?

Confirming Your Order

The first thing that happens, as I've noted, is that you'll probably get a confirmation email from the merchant. Print this out and keep it for your records; it should contain the order number, which you might need if problems arise.

The confirmation email might also contain shipping information and, in some cases, a tracking number for your order. If not, there might be a link back to your personal account page at the retailer's site, where this shipping and tracking info might be displayed.

Tracking Your Number

If you get a tracking number, you can use it to track your shipment. You might be able to link directly to the shipping service's tracking page, or you might have to manually enter the tracking number there. In any case, being able to track your shipment enables you to know when you can expect to receive the package at your door.

If you need to enter a tracking number manually, here are the addresses for the major shipping services' tracking pages:

- United States Postal Service: `www.usps.com/shipping/trackandconfirm.htm` (shown in Figure 1.10)
- UPS: `www.ups.com`
- FedEx: `www.fedex.com`

Go to the appropriate page, enter the tracking number, and view the progress of your shipment.

FIGURE 1.10

Tracking your shipment via the U.S. Postal Service.

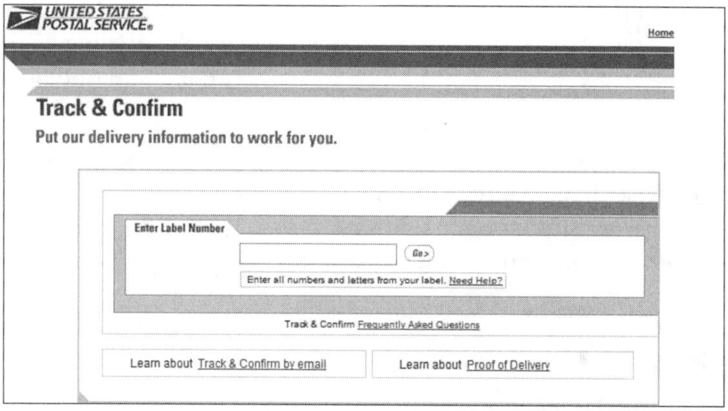

Receiving Your Order

What you do next is the hard part—you wait. Although it's nice to get that immediate gratification from shopping *right now* online, you don't get the same immediate gratification in terms of actually receiving what you purchased. Depending on the speed of the retailer and the shipping method chosen, you might have to wait anywhere from a few days to a few weeks to receive your order. Try to be patient.

When you receive your order, open the box and check through all the contents. There's probably a shipping receipt somewhere in or on the box, so check the contents against the receipt. Some retailers will break large orders into multiple shipments, so you might have more than one package to deal with—often shipped at different times from different warehouses. Make sure that you got everything you ordered, and that it's all in good condition.

Dealing with Problems and Backordered Merchandise

If you have any problems with what you ordered, this is where you need that order number the company gave you during checkout. You'll need to contact the retailer via the company's Web site, via email, or via phone (look for a phone number on the invoice), and tell the company what's wrong. Most retailers have a separate customer service department that does nothing but handle problems and requests like this.

A different situation exists if something you ordered wasn't currently in stock. If an item was *backordered*, that means the retailer was out of stock on that item, and has to wait for more to be delivered from the factory. Reputable retailers will try to provide some estimate of when you might receive the item, but remember—the company might not have any control over the situation. If the manufacturer in Minsk doesn't make another delivery for six months, that's how long you'll have to wait for your order. Fortunately, most retailers give you the option of canceling backordered items, so if you have to wait too long, you can bail out and order again at a later date.

Finally, there's always the potential for things to break. Most new merchandise you purchase should be covered either under a store warranty or under the manufacturer's warranty. If you're not sure what to do with malfunctioning or defective merchandise, contact the retailer's customer service department for instructions.

What's Next: Is It Safe?

Is online shopping safe?

Yes.

But that's a too-short answer to what is actually a somewhat complicated question. Turn to Chapter 2, "Shopping Safely—and Securely," to learn more about protecting yourself when you're shopping online.

SHOPPING SAFELY—AND SECURELY

Experienced online bargain hunters know that shopping online is every bit as safe as shopping in the real world. That's not to say that every transaction is 100% safe from fraud or other problems; nothing's that assured. But you shouldn't have any qualms about shopping online or providing your credit card information to pay for a purchase over the Web—as long as you take a few common-sense precautions.

Why Online Shopping Is (Generally) Safe

Some Internet newbies have reasonable concerns about whether the information they provide online is secure. They fear that once their credit card numbers are in cyberspace, anyone can grab them. Some users fear that information will be hijacked between themselves and the retailer's Web site; other users fear that the Web site itself can be hacked and the numbers stolen.

The reality is that both these fears are real, but overblown.

Yes, it's possible for a dedicated hacker to intercept the transmission of private information over the Internet. However, this type of illicit activity is extremely rare because it's extremely difficult. If someone wants to steal a few credit card numbers, it's easier to use a low-cost radio scanner to listen in on cordless phone calls, or to go dumpster-diving for carbons behind a local restaurant. Hacking into secure Internet transmissions is a lot more work.

As to stealing credit card numbers from Web site databases, it happens—although rarely. In almost all cases, security breaches of this magnitude are implicitly the cause of the site itself for not having adequate security measures on hand. In other words, it's not because of anything your or other users might do.

Know, however, that such hacks are rare, and becoming even less prevalent as online shopping sites enact ever more stringent security measures. Also know that your credit card company bears the brunt of any fraudulent activity perpetrated on your account; you might be liable for a small amount (typically $50), but anything more than that amount is the credit card company's responsibility.

The bottom line is that providing your credit card information to a secure Web site is much safer than handing your credit card to a complete stranger dressed as a waiter in a restaurant or giving it over a cordless phone. In addition, all major credit card companies limit your liability if your card gets stolen, whether that's on the Web or in the so-called real world. So, go ahead and use your credit card online—there's nothing to worry about!

Typical Online Shopping Problems—And How to Deal with Them

All that said, you can still encounter problems when shopping online. Most of these problems are the same type you encounter when shopping in the real world—and how you deal with them is equally similar.

Missing Orders

Probably the most common problem is not receiving what you ordered—or at least not receiving it when you expected to receive it. Most shipping problems can be solved with a little patience. That's because it's most often true that when a retailer says the package is in the mail, it actually is. So, give the order a few more days to arrive before you start getting worried.

Many online and mail-order retailers make the waiting process a little easier by making it possible for you to track your package from their warehouse to your front door. As explained in Chapter 1, "Online Shopping 101," you might receive a tracking number in a confirmation email, or be able to access this number on the Web site's account information page. You can then plug the number into the tracking service provided by the shipping service (USPS, UPS, FedEx, and so on), and determine exactly where your package is at this moment.

If you determine that your order really isn't on the way, it's time to contact the merchant's customer service department, which you can typically do via email or via a link on the retailer's Web site. Include your order number and email address in any such correspondence, and provide as much other information about your order as possible.

At this point, the retailer is likely to tell you that the item you ordered is either (1) backordered, (2) sold out, (3) discontinued, or (4) already shipped to you. If it's one of the first three alternatives, the merchant should provide you with the option of either waiting until more items come in stock (if, in fact, more will) or canceling your order. If you cancel your order, you should have the option of receiving a full refund, although some merchants will only offer a store credit against future purchases. (I don't like the store credit option, but this should be stated beforehand in the merchant's returns policy—more on this later in this chapter.)

What do you do if the retailer says the item was shipped several weeks ago, but you still haven't received it? What we have here is a lost package. In this situation, the retailer should work with you to help locate the package, either via tracking number or some other mechanism. Lesser merchants will say it's not their fault the package got lost and wash their hands of it; if this happens to you, you know you don't want to buy from that retailer again. Better merchants will go out of their way to make things right, sometimes to the extent of shipping another item to you at their expense. Although you shouldn't expect this kind of largesse, you should insist that the retailer help track down the missing shipment from its end, instead of just blowing you off.

Unwanted or Defective Merchandise

Another common problem occurs when you receive an item that you don't want—something you didn't order, something you don't like, or something that's defective. Again, this is a job for the retailer's customer service department; email or phone the retailer to ask for a returns authorization and instructions on how to ship back the item.

If you're lucky, this returns process should go off without a hitch; the smoothness of this process is a sign of a well-oiled retailer. But it helps to be prepared ahead of time, which means familiarizing yourself with the site's returns policy *before* you place your order. (A little late now, I know.) This is important because different retailers handle returns in different ways.

Some retailers will happily accept returns for any reason and give you a full refund. (The refund might include the original shipping charges in addition to the cost of the product—although you shouldn't expect this.) Other merchants will accept your return, but only offer a store credit in return. Still others will let you exchange a defective product for another similar item, but limit their exposure to this. And then there are those retailers that don't accept returns at all—all sales are final. (This can also happen at full-service retailers, in regards to close-out or distressed merchandise.) This is why you need to be familiar with the returns policy beforehand: so you'll know just what you can return, and what kind of refund you can expect.

One good thing about purchasing online is that you generally don't have to have a copy of the original sales receipt to return the merchandise, as you would with a traditional retailer. That's because all your paperwork is electronic, and should be in the retailer's computers. The retailer knows who you are without you having to prove it.

Unresponsive Merchants

Okay, you have a problem and you've contacted the retailer. In most cases, things get worked out from there. But what happens if the retailer refuses to help—and won't refund your money?

If you paid by credit card, your next step is to contact your credit card company. (The phone number should be on your monthly invoice.) Inform the company of your situation, and request a credit for the purchase amount. The credit card company will now contact the retailer to get its side of the story. More often than not, the retailer will respond to this pressure by offering to make things good. But even if the retailer stands firm, you'll be better off, because the credit card company will likely stop payment to the merchant and credit your account for the amount of the transaction. Credit card companies are very aggressive on behalf of their customers, all to your benefit.

Ongoing Disputes

If you didn't pay by credit card or if your credit card company refuses to credit your account, all is not lost. At this point, you can engage a dispute resolution service to mediate your issue with the retailer.

One of the most popular dispute resolution services is SquareTrade (`www.squaretrade.com`). As you can see in Figure 2.1, this site settles disputes through a two-part process: *dispute resolution* and *mediation*.

FIGURE 2.1

Mediate your disputes at SquareTrade.

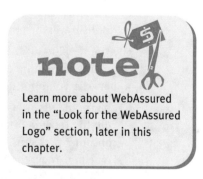

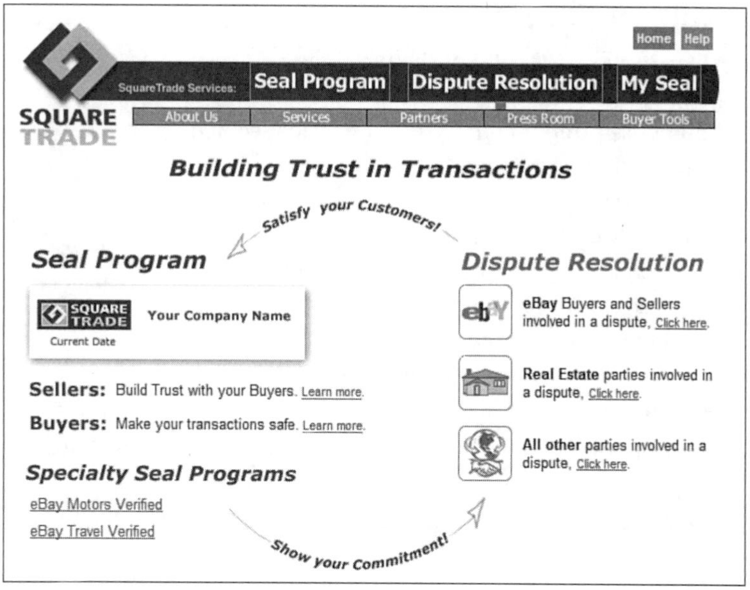

You start out with what SquareTrade calls online dispute resolution; this free service uses an automated negotiation tool to try to get you and the merchant to neutral ground. Communication is via email; the process helps to cool down both parties and enable you work to out a solution between the two of you.

If you and the merchant can't work things out in this manner, you have the option of engaging a SquareTrade mediator to examine the case and come to an impartial decision. This mediation service will cost you $20, and both parties agree to abide with the results. If the SquareTrade mediator says you're owed a refund, the merchant has to pay you. If the representative says there's no basis for your claim, you have to stop complaining.

Similar mediation services are offered by WebAssured (if the merchant is a member) and the American Arbitration Association (`www.adr.org`).

Protecting Yourself from Online Fraud

Fraud definitely exists on the Internet. You can have your credit card information stolen, or send money to a "retailer" who is nothing more than a scam artist. It is, however, easy to protect yourself from this kind of online fraud—as long as you use common sense.

> **note**
>
> Learn more about WebAssured in the "Look for the WebAssured Logo" section, later in this chapter.

Beware Online Scams

One of the basic rules of the Internet is to never enter your credit card for anything other than a purchase—and then only if the site has secured transaction processing. Some sites (particularly those offering adult content) will ask for a credit card to "validate" your ID or age. This is the sure sign of a potential rip-off. *Never* provide your credit card numbers in situations like this! Anyone who gets your credit card information *will* use that information—and charge your card!

note

Learn more about secured transactions in the "Look for a Secure Site" section, later in this chapter.

You should also beware of sites that offer what turn out to be pyramid schemes and multi-level marketing (MLM) plans. If you're not sure whether or not an offer is legitimate, check out the Scam Busters Web site (`www.scambusters.org`). Scam Busters lists the most widespread ongoing scams, so you'll know what offers to avoid.

Reporting Fraudulent Business Practices

When you think you're a victim of online fraud, it's time to call in the authorities. If you've had your credit card numbers ripped off, your first call should be to your credit card company. If your card has seen unauthorized use, the credit card company can put a stop to all future purchases and cap your losses, typically at the $50 level.

If you've had a large amount of money ripped off, you should also contact your local police department. In addition, if mail fraud is involved (which it is if any part of the transaction—either payment or shipping—was handled through the mail), you can file a complaint with your local U.S. Post Office or state attorney general's office.

Online, you can register complaints about individual merchants at the National Fraud Information Center (`www.fraud.org`), which is a project of the National Consumers League. This site will transmit the information you provide to the appropriate law enforcement agencies.

Another place to file a complaint is with the Better Business Bureau. The BBB OnLine Complaint System (`complaints.bbb.org`) can help facilitate communication between you and the merchant, and possibly get your dispute resolved.

You should also file a complaint about any fraudulent online business transaction with the Federal Trade Commission (FTC). Although the FTC doesn't resolve individual consumer problems, it can and will act if it sees a pattern of possible law violations. You can contact the FTC online (`www.ftc.gov/ftc/consumer.htm`) or via phone (202-382-4357 or toll-free at 877-FTC-HELP) .

Twenty Tips for Making Online Shopping Even Safer

Even though the potential for fraud exists, you shouldn't fear online shopping; the incidence of problems of any sort is extremely low. Still, there are several steps you can take to improve the security—and the success—of your online transactions. Read on to discover some tips to make your online bargain hunting as safe as possible.

Tip #1: Trust Your Instincts

Here's the number-one rule for shopping online: Trust your instincts. If something smells fishy, avoid it. If you're not comfortable shopping at a specific Web site, then don't. Determine your own level of risk for shopping online, and be your best guide.

Tip #2: Shop with Merchants You Know

One of the easiest ways to increase your online safety is to shop only at established and familiar companies. Although it's not a given, it's likely that L.L. Bean's Web site will be more secure than the site for Billy Joe Bob's Online House of Chewing Tobacco. If it's a retailer you've heard of, it's probably legitimate.

Size is also something to look for. The big online-only retailers are just as reputable as big "bricks-and-mortar" retailers, offering safe payment, fast shipping, and responsive service. Most of the smaller merchants on the Web are equally safe, although they might not have the same level of customer service as the big sites. Although it's difficult to judge the size or stability of any online retailer (any size business can hide behind a fancy Web page), chances are if you use a site that's big enough to accept credit card payments, you're in safe company.

Tip #3: See What Other Customers Have to Say

When you're bargain hunting online, it's likely that you'll find some of the lowest prices at merchants you haven't shopped with before. How do you know whether you're dealing with a reputable online retailer—or one that's likely to rip you off?

One of the better ways to check up on an unfamiliar merchant is to read what others have to say about that retailer. Fortunately, there are several Web sites, such as BizRate (`www.bizrate.com`) and ePublicEye (`www.epubliceye.com`), that offer either professional site ratings or reviews by the site's customers. You can read more about these retailer review sites in Chapter 3, "Researching Your Purchases Before You Buy."

Tip #4: Check for Customer Complaints

If a retailer has a lot of complaining customers, there's probably a reason for it. Fortunately, you can use the Web to check for retailers that have a lot of complaints pending.

When it comes to checking for complaints, I like the Complaints.com Web site (`www.complaints.com`). This site, shown in Figure 2.2, is all complaints, all the time—the perfect place to find out what kind of beefs customers have against a particular merchant or with a specific product. To see what complaints are filed against a specific retailer, enter the merchant's name in the search box and then click the Search All Complaints button.

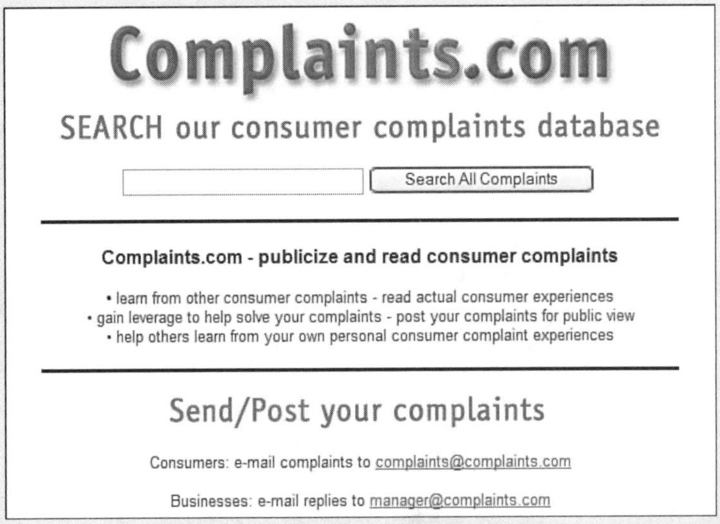
Complaints.com
SEARCH our consumer complaints database
Search All Complaints
Complaints.com - publicize and read consumer complaints
• learn from other consumer complaints - read actual consumer experiences
• gain leverage to help solve your complaints - post your complaints for public view
• help others learn from your own personal consumer complaint experiences
Send/Post your complaints
Consumers: e-mail complaints to complaints@complaints.com
Businesses: e-mail replies to manager@complaints.com

FIGURE 2.2
Search an online database of customer complaints at Complaints.com.

Of course, you can also use Complaints.com to register your own complaints about problem merchants. To post a compliant, just put it in an email addressed to `complaints@complaints.com`. If you include the address of the merchant you're complaining about in the body of your message, Complaints.com will forward your complaint for you; naturally, all complaints you file will be made available for public viewing by Complaints.com users.

You can also check out a retailer's reputation with the Better Business Bureau (`search.bbb.org`), which registers complaints filed by customers against specific businesses. As you can see in Figure 2.3, you can search the BBB database for reliability reports on more than two million different businesses.

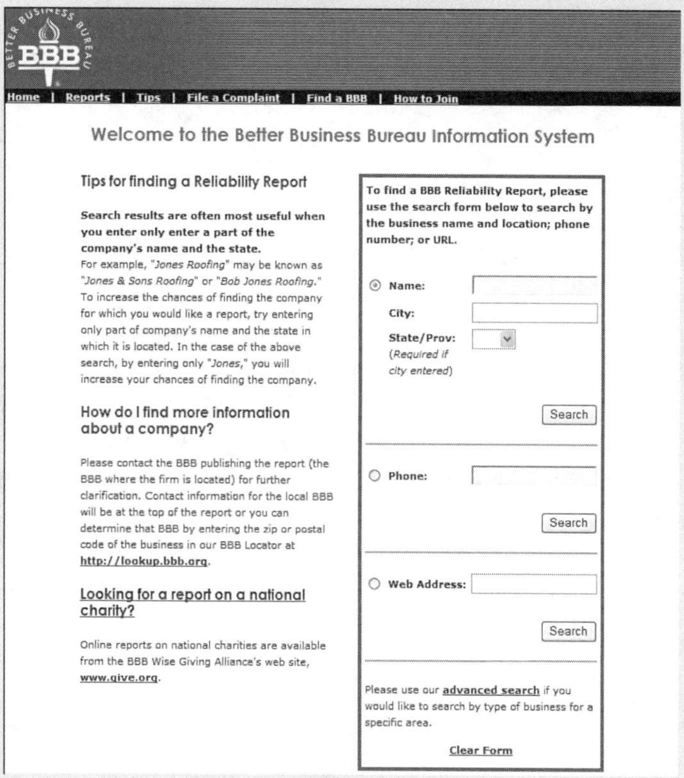
BETTER BUSINESS BUREAU
BBB
Home | Reports | Tips | File a Complaint | Find a BBB | How to Join
Welcome to the Better Business Bureau Information System
Tips for finding a Reliability Report
Search results are often most useful when you enter only enter a part of the company's name and the state.
For example, "Jones Roofing" may be known as "Jones & Sons Roofing" or "Bob Jones Roofing." To increase the chances of finding the company for which you would like a report, try entering only part of company's name and the state in which it is located. In the case of the above search, by entering only "Jones," you will increase your chances of finding the company.
How do I find more information about a company?
Please contact the BBB publishing the report (the BBB where the firm is located) for further clarification. Contact information for the local BBB will be at the top of the report or you can determine that BBB by entering the zip or postal code of the business in our BBB Locator at http://lookup.bbb.org.
Looking for a report on a national charity?
Online reports on national charities are available from the BBB Wise Giving Alliance's web site, www.give.org.
To find a BBB Reliability Report, please use the search form below to search by the business name and location; phone number; or URL.
Name:
City:
State/Prov:
(Required if city entered)
Search
Phone:
Search
Web Address:
Search
Please use our advanced search if you would like to search by type of business for a specific area.
Clear Form

FIGURE 2.3
Search for a Better Business Bureau reliability report on a specific online merchant.

Another place to check for complaints against a retailer is with the attorney general's office of the state where the seller is located. View a contact list for the various states' attorneys general at the National Association of Attorneys General (`www.naag.org`).

Tip #5: Look for the WebAssured Logo

Many quality online retailers subscribe to the WebAssured (`www.webassured.com`) service. To display the WebAssured logo, shown in Figure 2.4, a merchant has to agree to a high level of conduct encompassing accurate delivery, ethical advertising, full disclosure of product information, fast response to customer complaints, and consumer privacy.

As a consumer, you can use the WebAssured site to search for approved online merchants, request merchant background reports, file complaints about questionable retailers, and engage WebAssured's Automatic Dispute Resolution Service (AdDResS).

FIGURE 2.4
WebAssured merchants "deliver what we promise and promise only what we can deliver."

Tip #6: Look for a Secure Site

Data sent over the Internet can be picked off by dedicated hackers—unless that data is handled by a secure server. Secure transactions of this sort employ a technology called Secure Sockets Layer (SSL) that encodes information sent over the Web, using a form of digital encryption. If both your browser and the Web site feature SSL security, you know that your transaction has been encrypted and is secure.

Most major shopping sites feature SSL-encrypted ordering and checkout. You'll know you're using a secure site when the little lock icon appears in the lower part of your Web browser, as shown in Figure 2.5. (Don't expect to see this icon on regular shopping pages; on most sites, only the checkout pages are encrypted in this fashion.) If a site's ordering process isn't encrypted, don't shop there.

FIGURE 2.5
When this icon appears in Internet Explorer, you're shopping securely.

In addition, many secure sites are authenticated by a company called VeriSign (`www.verisign.com`). If a site displays the VeriSign Secure Site seal, shown in Figure 2.6, you can be assured that ordering is performed over a secure server.

FIGURE 2.6
The VeriSign Secure Site seal ensures secure transactions.

Tip #7: Look for Real-World Contact Info

Here's a piece of advice I always follow: Shop at only those sites that have real-world contact information. Let's face it, if something goes wrong with your order, you're going to need to contact somebody. Beware of sites that don't even include an email contact address, and try to target sites that prominently list their phone number (toll-free, ideally), fax number, or street address for post-sale support. Personally, I won't shop at merchants that don't provide a phone number. There has been the rare occasion where something has gone wrong and I need to talk to a real honest-to-goodness human being; as far as I'm concerned, no phone number, no order.

Tip #8: Make Sure That the Retailer Is Still in Business

You probably don't have to worry about Amazon.com or Nordstrom.com going belly up, but when you're dealing with smaller online merchants, there's sometimes a thin line between being in and out of business. If you visit a Web site that looks like it hasn't been updated for a while, fire off an email (or make a phone call) to see whether you get a response. If you don't, the merchant has probably closed its doors.

Tip #9: Check the Returns Policy

This tip falls under the heading of "no surprises." Before you place your order, find out what you have to do if you're dissatisfied with a purchase at this site. How easy is it to return an item? Who pays for the return shipping—you or them? Can you expect a full refund or just a store credit? Under what circumstances will the store *not* accept a product return? If there is no returns policy to be found, skip this site.

Tip #10: Check the Warranty

If you're buying new goods, make sure that they're fully covered by the manufacturer's warranty. Some online merchants sell closeout or "gray market" items that don't come with a standard warranty, leaving you on the hook if the item goes bad. (In addition, many authorized service centers won't work on items sold on the gray market.) Unless you're getting a *really* good deal, look for a merchant that offers authorized goods with a full factory warranty.

If you're buying used merchandise, find out what kind of warranty the goods come with. If an item is sold as is, you have no recourse if it's somehow defective.

Tip #11: Read the Privacy Policy

It's important to know what a merchant will do with the personal information you provide. Is your information secure, or will the merchant sell your info to telemarketers and spammers? The way to find out is to read the site's *privacy policy*, which should tell you how the site intends to use the information you provide.

A store's privacy policy is typically accessed from the "about" page, or sometimes in the fine print at the bottom of the home page. This statement will lay out (often in legalistic detail) just what the site can and will do with the personal information it collects.

You can also look for seals from privacy enforcement organizations, such as TRUSTe (`www.truste.org`) and BBBOnLine (`www.bbbonline.org`). These seals, like the ones shown in Figure 2.7, ensure that the site follows basic privacy guidelines.

FIGURE 2.7
Look for these seals to guarantee the privacy of your personal information.

Tip #12: Don't Provide Any More Information Than You Have To

While we're on the subject of privacy, you can limit your exposure by providing only information that's absolutely necessary. When it comes time to place your order, you're presented with a large form to fill out before you can complete your purchase. In most cases, you don't have to fill out every blank on the form. Essential fields should be indicated in some fashion; you'll have to fill them out. Other fields are optional and are typically used to collect information that can be sold to marketing companies. (Be especially wary of fields that ask about your hobbies or likelihood to purchase items in the near future.) To keep as much information private as possible; fill in only those blanks that are required by the site.

In particular, you should never provide your Social Security number to an online retailer. (Online banks and brokerages are exceptions to this rule, of course.) There's no reason why an online retailer needs anything more than your name, address, email address, and maybe your phone number to do business with you—along with your credit card number, of course, for payment purposes. *Never* give out your Social Security number needlessly!

Tip #13: Safeguard Your Password

Some online retailers offer rapid checkout to repeating customers, assigning each customer a username (sometimes your email address) and password. If someone knows your username and password, they might be able to make purchases from the retailer without providing a credit number.

Obviously, the weak link in this process is the password. That's not because passwords are inherently nonsecure, but because most users choose passwords that are too easy to guess. (That's human nature, of course; if a password is hard to guess, it's also hard to remember—and we often compromise security for convenience.)

To create a password that can't easily be guessed, all you need to do is increase the length (eight characters is better than six) and include both letters and numbers—and special characters (!@#$%), if you're allowed. You should also use a combination of uppercase and lowercase letters if the account recognizes both cases. Even better, you should make sure that you don't use the same password on multiple sites; you should also change your passwords on a regular basis.

Tip #14: Pay by Credit Card

It's ironic that some people are afraid of paying via credit card online, when it's the credit card payment that provides the most security for your online transaction. When you pay by credit card, you're protected by the Fair Credit Billing Act, which gives you the right to dispute certain charges and limits your liability for unauthorized transactions to $50. In addition, some card issuers offer a supplemental online shipping guarantee that says you're not responsible for *any* unauthorized charges made online. (Make sure you read your card's statement of terms to determine the company's exact liability policy.)

If you're still uncomfortable sending your credit card information over the Internet, many online retailers let you call in your payment information over the phone. Look for a toll-free number somewhere on the checkout page.

And remember, if you can't get a retailer to refund your money for a bad transaction, you can dispute the charge to your credit card company. Chances are your credit card company will be able work things out with the retailer, and credit your account for the amount in question.

In addition, if you want your children to shop online and they're too young for their own credit cards, check out Visa Buxx (`www.visabuxx.com`), a parent-controlled online payment card just for kids. You can specify a variety of parental controls, including predetermined spending values and online transaction monitoring.

Tip #15: Keep Good Records

It's only good sense to keep printed copies of all the transactions you make online. If you get only an email confirmation, print out the email and keep it in a safe place. It's also good to print out your final checkout page from the merchant's Web site. You might need these records to prove malfeasance at some future point.

Tip #16: Don't Shop from Spam—Or Pop-Up Ads

When it comes to avoiding potential bad eggs, here's a good place to start. Never—I repeat *never*—click through a link from a spam email or pop-up advertisement. Although it's true that some legitimate retailers utilize these odious advertising methods, most spam and pop-up advertisers are as fly-by-night as your average transient driveway blacktop service. Avoid spam and pop-ups like the plague, and don't patronize their sponsors.

Tip #17: Determine Your *Total* Price—Including Shipping Charges

This is another "no surprises" tip. A site might offer the lowest prices around, but then tack on an exorbitant shipping and handling charge. (That's how some shady sites make their money.) The rule here is to always look at your *total* price, including shipping, handling, and any other miscellaneous charges. The site with the lowest product price isn't always the best deal!

Tip #18: Don't Let Yourself Be Unnecessarily Upsold

Many online merchants like to offer a lot of optional add-ons when it's time to check out. Gateway, for example, puts *four* separate pages of accessories and service plans in front of you before you can finalize your purchase. (See Figure 2.8 for an example of what I mean—notice the preselected "extended service plan.") In most cases, you don't need or want any of these items, so you should resist the urge to add on to your order. You should also make sure that none of these options are checked by default; don't buy anything you don't want to buy.

Another issue occurs with some electronics retailers, particularly in the photography segment. Many of these retailers will insist on calling you via phone to confirm your order. When they get you on the phone, they try very hard to sell you accessory packages (camera cases, batteries, you name it); some retailers might even refuse to process your order unless you sign up for these add-ons, or tell you that the item has suddenly gone out of stock. If a retailer tries to pull this scam on you, tell them you're not interested. If they persist, cancel your order and then hang up the phone. (And watch your credit card bill to make sure that you're not "accidentally" billed for the cancelled transaction!) You don't need to deal with these sleaze artists; spend a few bucks more to buy from a legitimate retailer.

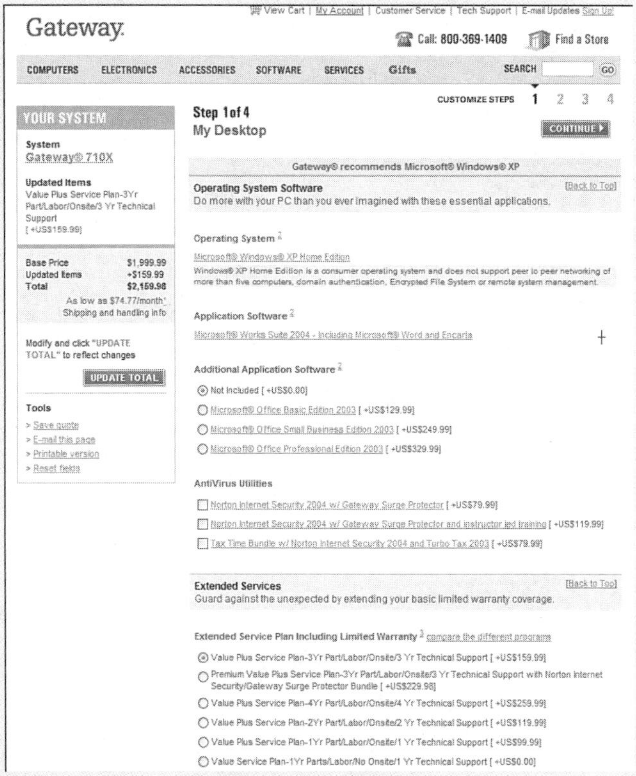

FIGURE 2.8
Don't order any add-ons you don't need!

Tip #19: Inspect Your Order After It Arrives

The right time to find out you have a problem with your order is just after it's delivered—not days or weeks later. As soon as the package arrives, open it up and inspect the merchandise. If something is missing or damaged, immediately contact the merchant for replacement or other restitution.

Tip #20: If It Sounds Too Good to Be True—It Probably Is!

Here's one last bit of common-sense advice. You'll find lots of incredible offers on the Web, most of which fall under the strict definition of that word—that is, they lack credibility. Do you really think you can get a brand-new Pentium 4 PC for less than $200? Or a flat-screen computer monitor for $29.95? Or a month's supply of Viagra for less than $10? Of course you can't. If the deal appears to good to be true, it probably is. Legitimate retailers will present legitimate offers. Don't get burned by dubious offers from shady retailers—let the buyer beware! For more tips on how to shop safely online, visit the Safeshopping.org Web site (`www.safeshopping.org`), sponsored by the American Bar Association.

What's Next: Protecting Yourself with Product Research

The information in this chapter should help you make safer purchases online. But you can make even better purchasing decisions by becoming an informed shopper. Learn how to make smarter purchasing decisions in Chapter 3, "Researching Your Purchases Before You Buy."

RESEARCHING YOUR PURCHASES BEFORE YOU BUY

Smart shoppers find better bargains. To be a smarter shopper, you need to do some homework before you fire up your credit card. That means researching the products you want to buy—and the retailers you want to buy them from.

Where to Find Product Information

Even if you never purchase anything online, the Web is a terrific resource for product information. You can find out a lot more about the products you're shopping for on the Web than you ever could in the real world. Think of the Web as a giant library of product specs and descriptions, and use that library to research your purchases before you buy.

Industry Web Sites

A good first place to start are the Web sites run by industry organizations, as well as the sites for industry-specific periodicals. These sites are useful sources of information about the general product category. You probably won't find product-specific information here, but you will find a lot of news and trend data.

For example, if you're looking for information about high-end home theater products, check out the Web site of CEDIA (www.cedia.net), the Custom Electronic Design & Installation Association. Also good in this instance are the sites for the electronics industry magazine *TWICE* (www.twice.com) and the consumer magazine *Home Theater* (www.hometheatermag.com).

For many product categories, there are also independent sites devoted to issues within the particular industry. For example, when it comes to home theater systems, you can't beat CineNow! (www.cinenow.com/us/), which features all manner of news and reviews. Also good is the Home Theater Forum (www.hometheaterforum.com), which hosts an active message board with lots of comments from audio and video aficionados. Both of these sites can help you fine-tune your next home electronics purchase.

Manufacturer Web Sites

After you've narrowed your shopping down to some specific models within a product category, your next step is to go straight to the horse's mouth—that is, to the manufacturer's Web site. Most manufacturers offer reams of useful product information on their Web sites; all you have to do is find it.

The first thing you need to do, of course, is find the Web site itself. You'd think this would be easy, but that isn't always the case. A good first step is to enter the manufacturer's name into a normal Web site address—that is, adding the name between a www. and a .com. So, if you're looking for Sony, try entering www.sony.com; if you're looking for Hoover, enter www.hoover.com.

You face a challenge when you're familiar with the brand but not necessarily the parent company. In some instances, there's actually a site for the brand, as with Levi Strauss' Dockers clothing brand (www.dockers.com). In other instances, you'll have to do some pre-homework homework to find out what company makes the product you're looking for.

When you get to the company's Web site, you have to drill down to that part of the site devoted to the product(s) you're shopping for. Most sites make this somewhat obvious, but if worse comes to worst, just enter the product name into the site's Search box.

tip

This process is slightly more difficult when you're dealing with a large global company that has offices in multiple countries; you might need to go to a global site and then click through to the U.S. site. For example, if you go to www.nikon.com, you find Nikon's global site; the company's U.S. site is actually www.nikonusa.com.

Most companies offer a lot of detailed information about each of the products they sell—but some don't. You'll find what you find. And don't be surprised if the company's Web site isn't fully up-to-date; it's quite common to discover that the product you're looking for is too new to be listed on a company's aging Web site. *C'est la vie.*

If you're lucky, you'll find everything from detailed product specs and pictures to warranty information and downloadable instruction manuals. For example, Fuji's Web site (`www.fujifilm.com`) offers product specifications, downloadable brochures and instruction manuals, zoom photos, and even video demos for Fuji's digital cameras, as you can see in Figure 3.1. This is a *great* source of pre-purchase information!

FIGURE 3.1
Detailed product information from Fuji's Web site.

Searching the Web

Whether you're searching for specific companies or general industry Web sites, it's time to turn to the searcher's best friend—the Internet search engine. Just go to Google (`www.google.com`) or any other major search site, and enter the name of the industry or product in which you're interested. The more general your query, the more general the sites you'll find; for information about a specific product, make sure that you enter the precise product name or number. It's amazing the information you can find when you look for it!

caution

Watch out for *sponsored links* in your search results. These are actually advertisements that other sites pay for to pop up when someone searches for a specific keyword. Fortunately, most search sites do a good job of identifying these paid results as just that, but make sure that you don't confuse them with the real results you're looking for.

Retailer Web Sites

Many online retailers offer detailed information about the products they sell. Going back to our home theater example, the online retailer Crutchfield (`www.crutchfield.com`) provides extremely detailed information about each of the products on its Web site, as you can see in Figure 3.2. In some cases, the merchant's Web site offers more info than does the manufacturer's site! Just remember, a retailer's site might offer information biased in favor of that retailer—but that's to be expected.

> **tip**
>
> Some retailers offer links to "similar items" on their product pages, which is a good way to compare other products you might be interested in.

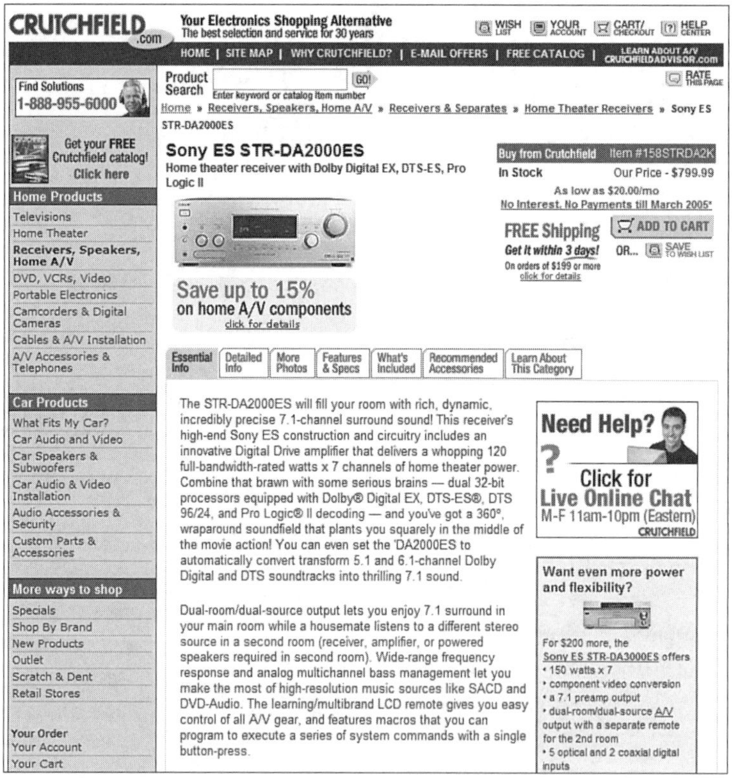

FIGURE 3.2
Many retailers, such as Crutchfield (pictured here), offer product specs and pictures.

Product Review Web Sites

For more objective information about a product, nothing beats the opinions of other users. The Web is a terrific forum for customer opinion; there are several sites that offer detailed customer reviews of just about any product you can imagine. Read on to learn more.

tip

Many price comparison sites, such as Yahoo! Shopping (`shopping.yahoo.com`), offer product reviews and buying guides, in addition to their featured price comparisons. Learn more in Chapter 5, "Hunting for the Lowest Price."

Reviewing Products Online

Bargain Hunter's Secret

Manufacturer-supplied specs are one thing; real-world reviews from a product's customers are another. I find it extremely useful to read what other users have to say about an item before I decide to buy. Your fellow consumers will give you the unvarnished pros and cons based on actual use, and tell you whether or not they think the product was a good deal.

There are many sites on the Web that provide forums for customers' product reviews. We'll look at some of the best of these sites here.

Amazon.com

Yeah, I know, Amazon.com is a retailer, not a product review site. But the fact remains: Amazon.com hosts one of the largest databases of customer product reviews on the Internet.

As you can see in Figure 3.3, almost all Amazon.com product pages include product reviews (typically provided by the manufacturer), editorial reviews (sourced from third parties), and customer reviews. The ones we're interested are the customer reviews, which are just what the name states—reviews of this specific product by Amazon.com customers.

When an Amazon.com customer writes a product review (and any customer can do so—it's not just for an elite group), he or she has to give the product a one-to-five star rating, along with the text review itself. The best and most frequent reviewers are accorded "spotlight review" status; these spotlight reviews are listed before the normal customer reviews. Amazon.com averages the star ratings for you, so you'll know up front the general consensus about any given product. Then it's time to read the reviews, which can range to detailed and well-informed to brief and goofy. (That's one of the things about reviews by real people—some are better at it than others.)

Bargain Hunter's Secret

I frequently use Amazon.com as a review source, even if I end up purchasing a product elsewhere. The user base is so large that you can find reviews about almost anything, and in general they do a good job of describing a product's strong and weak points. Plus, Amazon.com has one of the best site-specific search engines on the Web, so finding a particular product is often easier here than on other sites.

I
3

FIGURE 3.3

You don't have to buy at Amazon.com to take advantage of the site's customer product reviews.

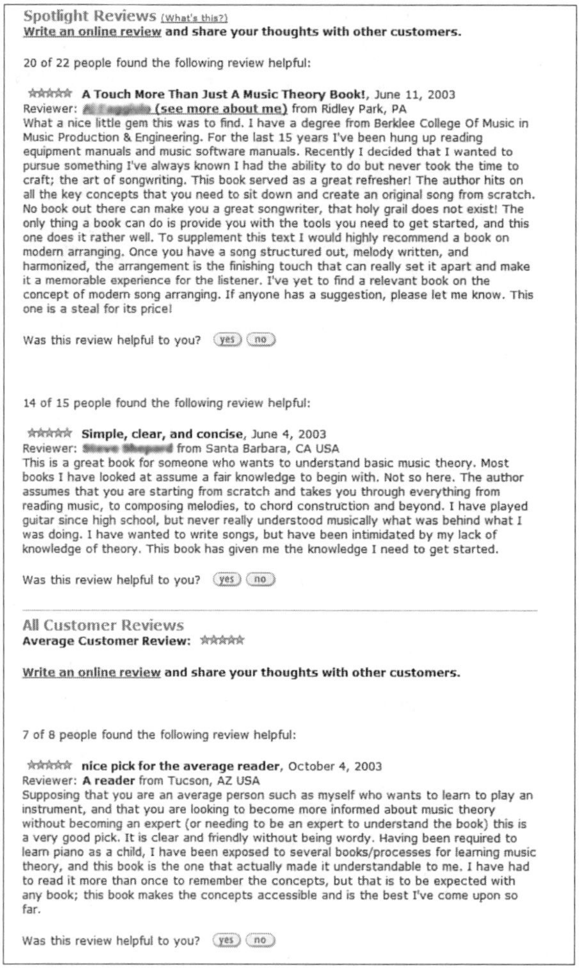

Spotlight Reviews [What's this?]
Write an online review and share your thoughts with other customers.

20 of 22 people found the following review helpful:

★★★★★ **A Touch More Than Just A Music Theory Book!**, June 11, 2003
Reviewer: ▓▓▓▓▓▓ **(see more about me)** from Ridley Park, PA
What a nice little gem this was to find. I have a degree from Berklee College Of Music in Music Production & Engineering. For the last 15 years I've been hung up reading equipment manuals and music software manuals. Recently I decided that I wanted to pursue something I've always known I had the ability to do but never took the time to craft; the art of songwriting. This book served as a great refresher! The author hits on all the key concepts that you need to sit down and create an original song from scratch. No book out there can make you a great songwriter, that holy grail does not exist! The only thing a book can do is provide you with the tools you need to get started, and this one does it rather well. To supplement this text I would highly recommend a book on modern arranging. Once you have a song structured out, melody written, and harmonized, the arrangement is the finishing touch that can really set it apart and make it a memorable experience for the listener. I've yet to find a relevant book on the concept of modern song arranging. If anyone has a suggestion, please let me know. This one is a steal for its price!

Was this review helpful to you? (yes) (no)

14 of 15 people found the following review helpful:

★★★★★ **Simple, clear, and concise**, June 4, 2003
Reviewer: ▓▓▓▓▓▓▓ from Santa Barbara, CA USA
This is a great book for someone who wants to understand basic music theory. Most books I have looked at assume a fair knowledge to begin with. Not so here. The author assumes that you are starting from scratch and takes you through everything from reading music, to composing melodies, to chord construction and beyond. I have played guitar since high school, but never really understood musically what was behind what I was doing. I have wanted to write songs, but have been intimidated by my lack of knowledge of theory. This book has given me the knowledge I need to get started.

Was this review helpful to you? (yes) (no)

All Customer Reviews
Average Customer Review: ★★★★★

Write an online review and share your thoughts with other customers.

7 of 8 people found the following review helpful:

★★★★★ **nice pick for the average reader**, October 4, 2003
Reviewer: **A reader** from Tucson, AZ USA
Supposing that you are an average person such as myself who wants to learn to play an instrument, and that you are looking to become more informed about music theory without becoming an expert (or needing to be an expert to understand the book) this is a very good pick. It is clear and friendly without being wordy. Having been required to learn piano as a child, I have been exposed to several books/processes for learning music theory, and this book is the one that actually made it understandable to me. I have had to read it more than once to remember the concepts, but that is to be expected with any book; this book makes the concepts accessible and is the best I've come upon so far.

Was this review helpful to you? (yes) (no)

ConsumerREVIEW.com

ConsumerREVIEW.com (www.consumerreview.com), shown in Figure 3.4, collects customer reviews from a bevy of specialty sites, detailed in Table 3.1. Users can write their own product reviews or search the site's formidable database of reviews.

note

Learn more about Amazon.com in Chapter 10, "Hunting for Bargains at Amazon.com."

Table 3.1 ConsumerREVIEW.com Specialty Sites

Site	Products Reviewed
AudioREVIEW.com	Audio equipment
CarREVIEW.com	New cars and accessories
ComputingREVIEW.com	Computers, PDAs, and other high-tech equipment
GolfREVIEW.com	Golf equipment
MtbREVIEW.com	Mountain bikes
OutdoorREVIEW.com	Snowboarding, skiing, fishing, and camping equipment
PCGameREVIEW.com	Computer games and accessories
PCPhotoREVIEW.com	Digital cameras
PhotographyREVIEW.com	35mm film cameras and equipment
RoadbikeREVIEW.com	Bicycles
VideogameREVIEW.com	Video games and consoles

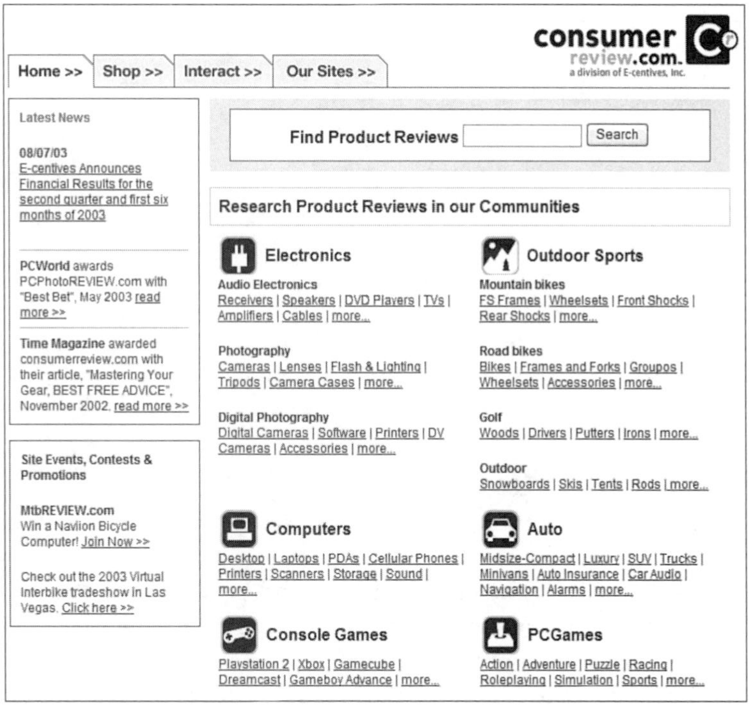

FIGURE 3.4
Product reviews in a variety of categories at ConsumerREVIEW.com.

You can browse the reviews in the various categories or search for reviews of specific products. The product review pages, such as the one shown in Figure 3.5, summarize the customer ratings, display detailed individual reviews, and enable you to vote on the usefulness of each review. The site also links to online merchants for immediate purchase of the items you're reading about.

FIGURE 3.5
A typical ConsumerREVIEW.com product review.

ConsumerReports.org

ConsumerReports.org (`www.consumerreports.org`), shown in Figure 3.6, is the online arm of the venerable *Consumer Reports* magazine, published by Consumers Union. This site, like the magazine, presents independent tests and reviews of all types of products, from automobiles to water heaters. Also useful are the numerous buyer's guides and multi-product comparisons, which can help you narrow down your product choices. Note, however, that you have to subscribe to the magazine to read the site's full reviews.

FIGURE 3.6
Product reviews for subscribers only from ConsumerReports.org.

ConsumerSearch

ConsumerSearch (`www.consumersearch.com`), shown in Figure 3.7, aggregates a variety of professional reviews about each product listed. That's right, these reviews aren't written by customers; they're written by professional reviewers, the guys you find writing for industry-specific magazines.

You start by browsing through a product category until you see a page that lists a number of different products. Next to each product is a one-paragraph summary of the available research; click the Full Story tab to read a more complete overview of the reviews. Click the All Reviews tab and you see summaries of the individual reviews, with the reviews themselves ranked by the site's editors, as shown in Figure 3.8.

Bargain Hunter's Secret

The ConsumerSearch site is a great place to get a handle on what various magazines and professional reviews are saying about the leading products in various categories. The site even includes summaries of print reviews that aren't available online. I find it quite useful to compare these different reviews; not all reviewers always like the same products.

FIGURE 3.7

ConsumerSearch: the site that reviews the reviewers.

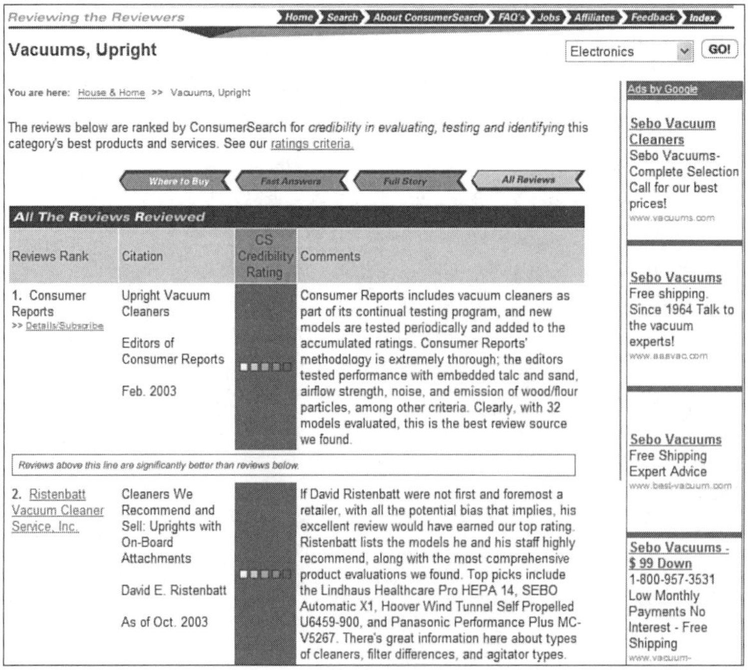

FIGURE 3.8

Comparing professional reviews at ConsumerSearch.

Epinions.com

Epinons.com (www.epinions.com) is my favorite product review site. What's great about this site is that users can write reviews about virtually anything—not just products, but also services, retailers, and locales. (For fun, check out the reviews of fast food restaurants!)

As you can see in Figure 3.9, the site organizes its reviews by category, which are accessible via a series of tabs at the top of the page. There are so many items reviewed, however, that you might be better off using the Search For box to search for items by specific product name or number.

FIGURE 3.9
One of the largest repositories of customer reviews on the Web: Epinions.com.

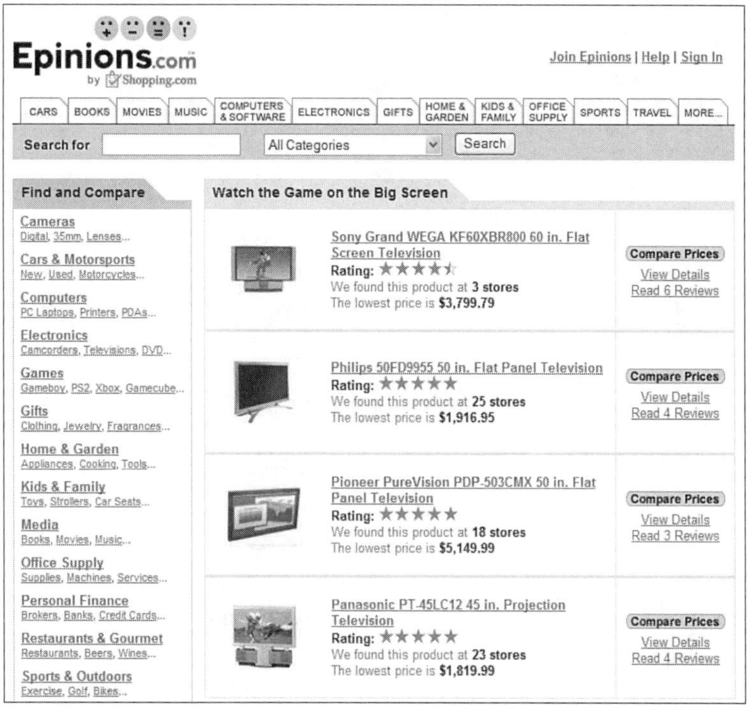

When you pull up a product page, you're greeted with a picture of the product along with links to manufacturer-supplied product details and any available customer reviews; the bottom of the page compares prices at various retailers. When you click through to a customer review page, such as the one shown in Figure 3.10, you'll most often find a series of considered, well-written reviews by people who take this responsibility quite seriously. You'll also find, at the top of the page, the overall average customer rating, as well as ratings for a variety of product attributes. It's a great way to find out just how a product is received in the real world by real users.

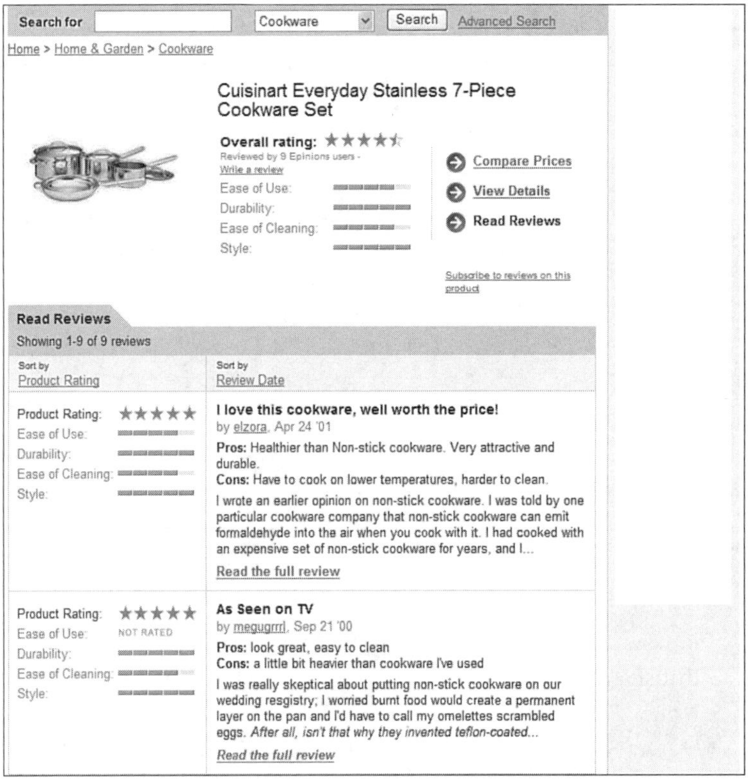
Search for
Cookware
Search
Advanced Search
Home > Home & Garden > Cookware
Cuisinart Everyday Stainless 7-Piece Cookware Set
Overall rating:
Reviewed by 9 Epinions users -
Write a review
Ease of Use:
Durability:
Ease of Cleaning:
Style:
Compare Prices
View Details
Read Reviews
Subscribe to reviews on this product
Read Reviews
Showing 1-9 of 9 reviews
Sort by Product Rating
Sort by Review Date
Product Rating:
Ease of Use:
Durability:
Ease of Cleaning:
Style:
I love this cookware, well worth the price!
by elzora, Apr 24 '01
Pros: Healthier than Non-stick cookware. Very attractive and durable.
Cons: Have to cook on lower temperatures, harder to clean.
I wrote an earlier opinion on non-stick cookware. I was told by one particular cookware company that non-stick cookware can emit formaldehyde into the air when you cook with it. I had cooked with an expensive set of non-stick cookware for years, and I...
Read the full review
Product Rating:
Ease of Use: NOT RATED
Durability:
Ease of Cleaning:
Style:
As Seen on TV
by megugrrl, Sep 21 '00
Pros: look great, easy to clean
Cons: a little bit heavier than cookware I've used
I was really skeptical about putting non-stick cookware on our wedding resgistry; I worried burnt food would create a permanent layer on the pan and I'd have to call my omelettes scrambled eggs. After all, isn't that why they invented teflon-coated...
Read the full review

FIGURE 3.10
Reading the detailed customer reviews at Epinions.com.

And here's a personal admission: I never make a major purchase without first checking out the customer reviews at Epinions.com. The site is *that* useful!

RateItAll

RateItAll (`www.rateitall.com`), shown in Figure 3.11, is a site where customers can rate a variety of products and services. It's not just limited to product ratings; you can also rate musicians, actors, colleges, baseball teams, drinks—you name it. Despite (or perhaps because of) the breadth of ratings here, RateItAll's product reviews here aren't near as extensive as those at Epinions.com and other larger sites. Although I sometimes find RateItAll interesting for its oddball review topics, to me it's less useful than some of the other major review sites.

tip

Epinions.com reviews are also featured at the Shopping.com price-comparison site, discussed in Chapter 5.

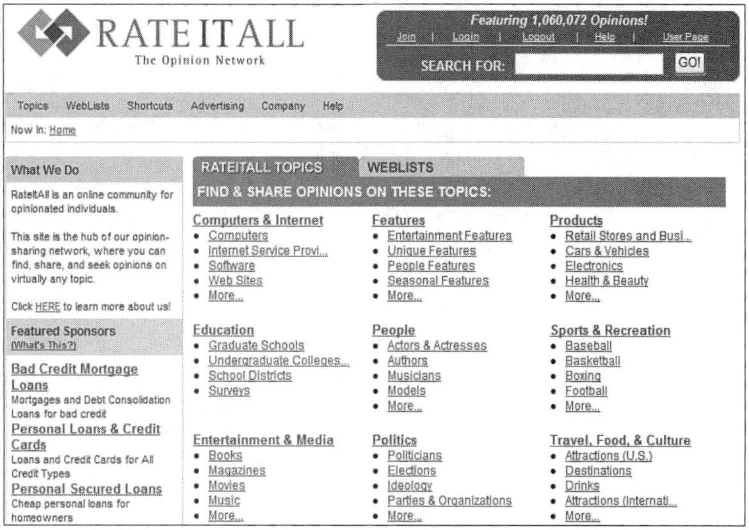

FIGURE 3.11
Find reviews of just about anything at RateItAll.com.

Review Centre

Review Centre (`www.reviewcentre.com`), shown in Figure 3.12, is unique in that it's a British-specific review site. It offers a great U.K.-specific perspective on products—which is especially useful if you live in England or are interested in British products. (And, as many products these days are sold globally, it's also useful if you *don't* live in the U.K.)

ReviewFinder

ReviewFinder (`www.reviewfinder.com`), shown in Figure 3.13, offers links to reviews of various types of electronic equipment: camcorders, computers, digital cameras, PDAs, video games, and so on. It's a good gateway to lots of other reviews across the Internet. In addition, the site also offers customer ratings of various online merchants, provided by PriceGrabber.com.

Product-Specific Review Sites

There are also many sites that offer reviews of specific types of products. These product-specific review sites are particularly prevalent in the electronics category. (Gadget geeks love to write about their gadgets!)

Table 3.2 shows some of these product-specific sites, by category.

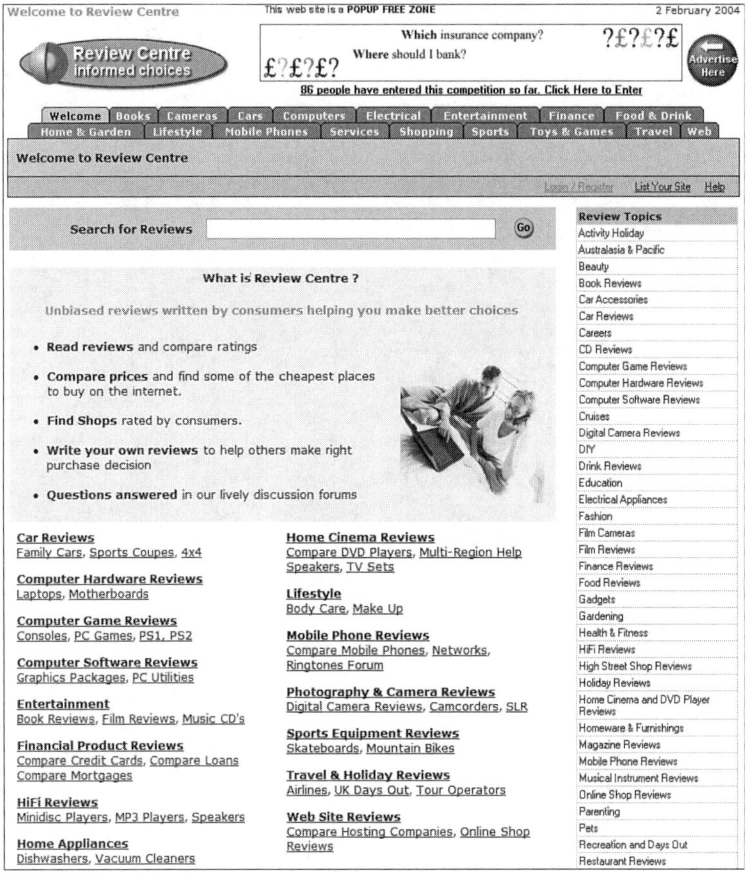

FIGURE 3.12
British product reviews at Review Centre.

Table 3.2 Product-Specific Review Sites

Category	Site	URL
Audio/Video Equipment	AudioREVIEW.com	www.audioreview.com
	AVguide.com	www.avguide.com
	eCoustics.com	www.ecoustics.com
	Plasma TV Buying Guide	www.plasmatvbuyingguide.com
Computers and Electronics	Ars Technica	www.arstechnica.com
	CNET Reviews	reviews.cnet.com
	ComputingREVIEW.com	www.computingreview.com
	ExtremeTech	www.extremetech.com
	The Gadgeteer	www.the-gadgeteer.com

Table 3.2 Continued

Category	Site	URL
	Maximum PC	www.maximumpc.com
	PC Magazine	www.pcmag.com
	Tom's Hardware Guide	www.tomshardware.com
Digital Cameras	DCViews	www.dcviews.com
	Digital Camera Resource Page	www.dcresource.com
	Digital Photography Review	www.dpreview.com
	Steve's DigiCams	www.steves-digicams.com

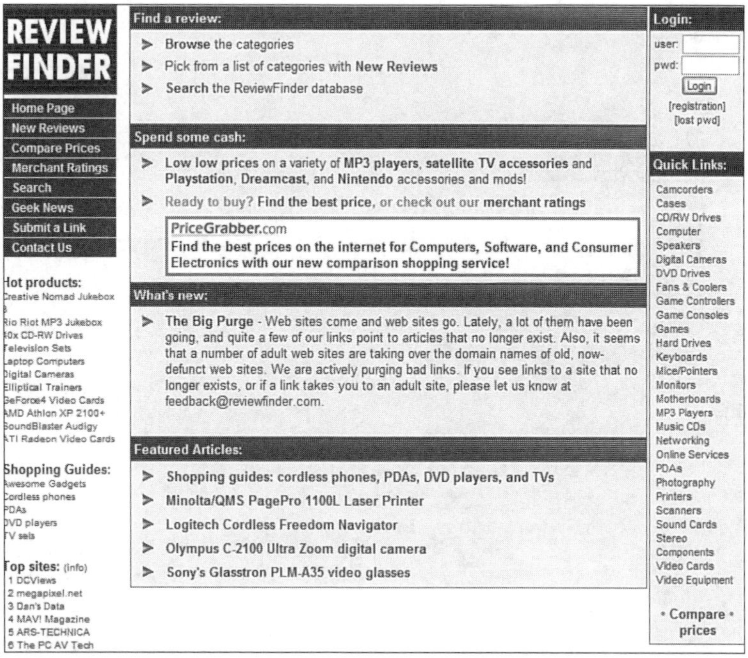

FIGURE 3.13
Use ReviewFinder to find third-party reviews of various electronic products.

Reviewing Online Retailers

Not surprisingly, the Web is also a great place to find out about Web-based retailers. Just as there are sites devoted to customer reviews of specific products, there are also sites devoted to customer reviews of specific retailers.

Being able to find out about an online retailer before you place your order will help you decide just where you want to shop. If you see a lot of negative customer reviews, you know to avoid a particular retailer; if you see a lot of satisfied customers, that's probably a good place to spend your money. And you can tell from the individual reviews just what a specific merchant is good or bad at. You might find one retailer has fast shipping but poor customer service, or another that offers extremely low prices but ships slow. Remember, it takes an informed shopper to find the best bargains—especially online!

tip

You can also research online retailers directly, by comparing returns policies, shipping charges, and so on—although you're likely to find much of this information in other customers' retailer reviews.

BizRate

BizRate (`www.bizrate.com`) is a price-comparison site that also offers one of the largest databases of store reviews on the Web; the site claims to have more than a million individual merchant ratings. To access BizRate's merchant reviews, click the Store Ratings link to view the page shown in Figure 3.14; from here you can browse stores by category.

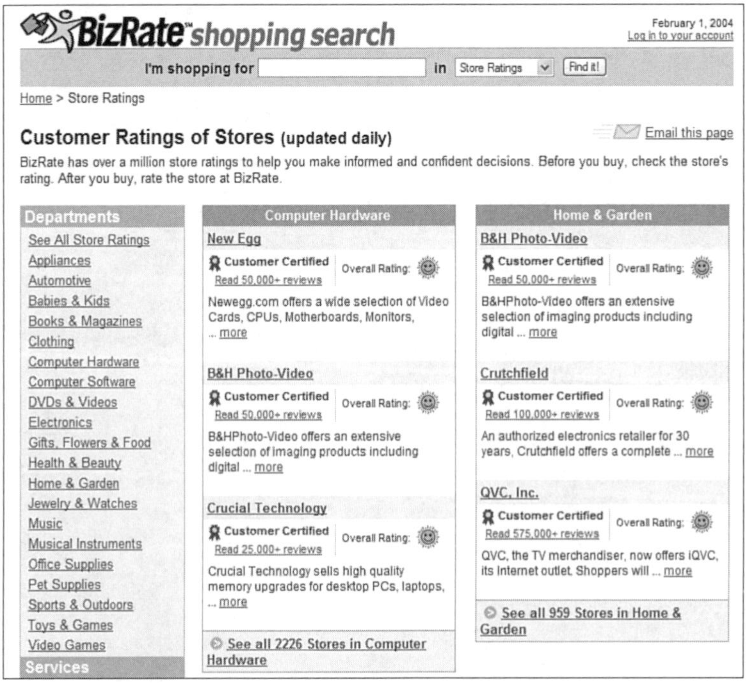

FIGURE 3.14
Online merchants rated at BizRate.

A typical BizRate store rating, such as the one shown in Figure 3.15, includes a rating summary (showing the percent of both positive and negative reviews) as well as detailed individual reviews by the merchant's customers. Customers rate each retailer on a number of different performance variables, including Would Shop Here Again, On Time Delivery, Customer Support, and Products Met Expectations. Some of the most popular stores have thousands of individual customer reviews on the BizRate site.

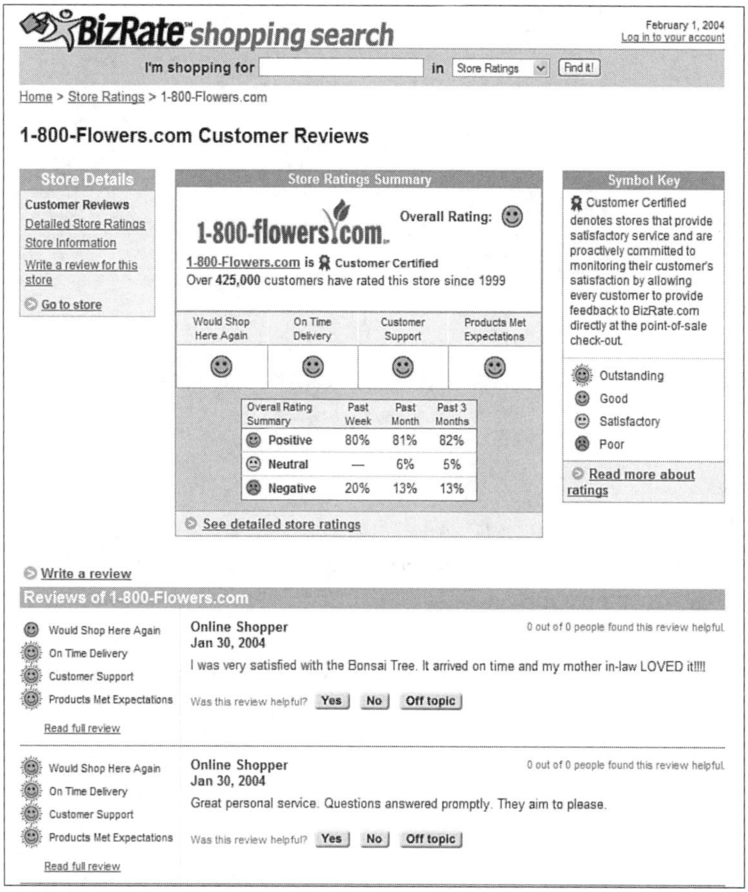

FIGURE 3.15
An individual BizRate merchant review.

ePublicEye

ePublicEye (`www.epubliceye.com`), shown in Figure 3.16, is another site that offers customer reviews of online merchants, as well as information about online fraud and scams. The ePublicEye database isn't quite as extensive as that at BizRate, although the information provided for each merchant is more detailed.

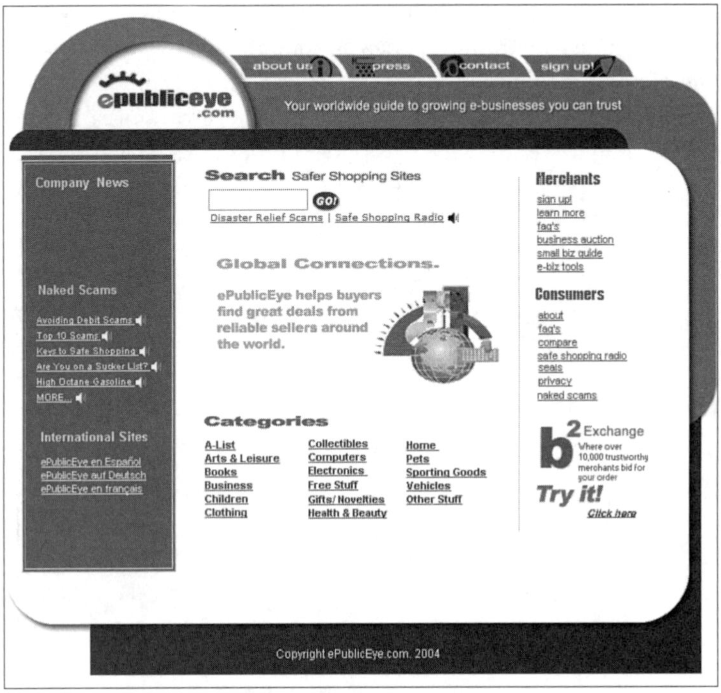

FIGURE 3.16
Even more customer reviews and ratings at ePublicEye.

You can browse sites by category or search for specific merchants. A typical merchant Report Card, such as the one shown in Figure 3.17, provides ratings for various performance categories (management accessibility, payment process, customer support, and so on), a listing of site features (including payment, delivery, and tracking methods), and a link to the individual customer reviews. Although the reviews here tend to be shorter than those at BizRate, the other site information provided paints a fairly complete picture of what you can expect when you shop at a given site. For that reason, I like to use ePublicEye in conjunction with BizRate; together, these two sites provide just about everything a savvy customer would need to know before starting to shop.

PlanetFeedback

PlanetFeedback (`www.planetfeedback.com/consumer/`), shown in Figure 3.18, is a bit different from the typical customer review site. With PlanetFeedback, consumers can both leave and read comments about a variety of online and traditional merchants. The letters you write—positive or negative—are posted publicly for all to read, and also forwarded to the retailer in question. It's a valuable service both for letter writers and for users wanting to know more about particular merchants.

FIGURE 3.17

A merchant Report Card at ePublicEye.

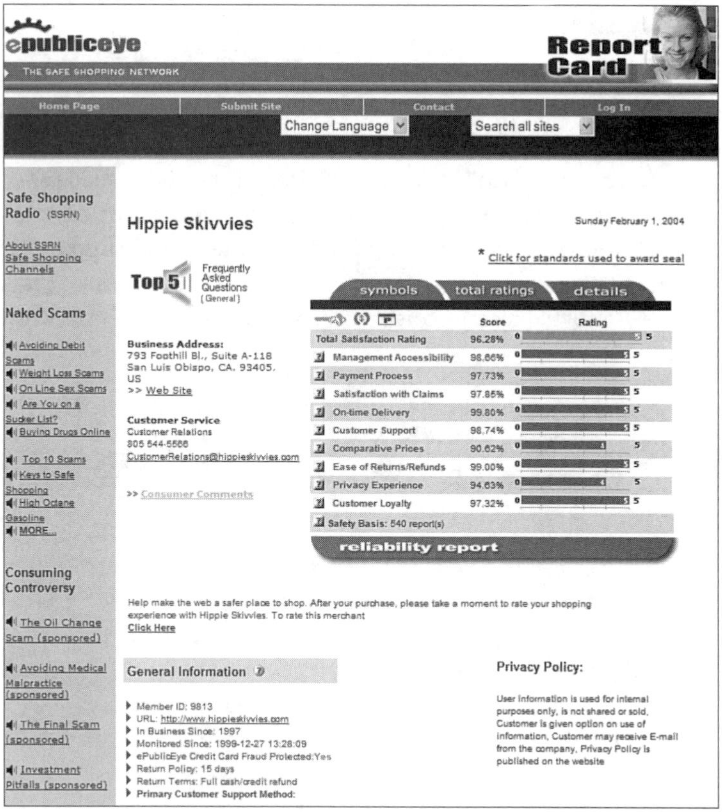

FIGURE 3.18

Praise or pan retailers at PlanetFeedback.

ResellerRatings.com

ResellerRatings.com (`www.resellerratings.com`) offers merchant reviews from its 120,000 registered members. Merchant reviews are organized by category, or you can search for specific merchants.

As you can see in Figure 3.19, reseller ratings are provided for both the past six months and for the merchant's lifetime. Resellers are rated on pricing, likelihood of future purchases, shipping and packaging, technical support, and return or replacement policy/performance. The individual customer reviews are a little short, but this site does provide a nice scorecard, especially for smaller or less-well-known merchants.

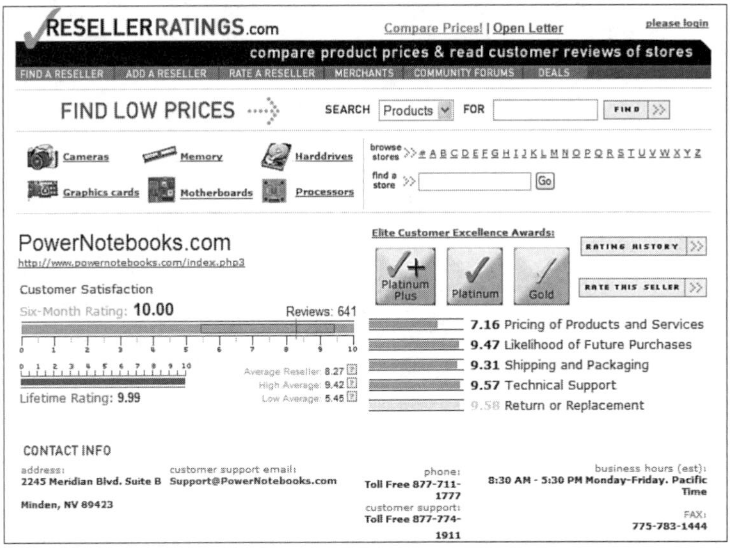

FIGURE 3.19
Reseller ratings at ResellerRatings.com.

SimplyQuick

SimplyQuick (`www.simplyquick.com`) is an interesting site in that it summarizes a lot of information and ratings provided by a number of other sites. As you can see in Figure 3.20, this information includes privacy and performance ratings from market research companies such as Gomez (`www.gomez.com`) and Forrester Research (`www.forrester.com`), along with brief comments on services offered. It's a good place to get a general picture of what you can expect from major online retailers.

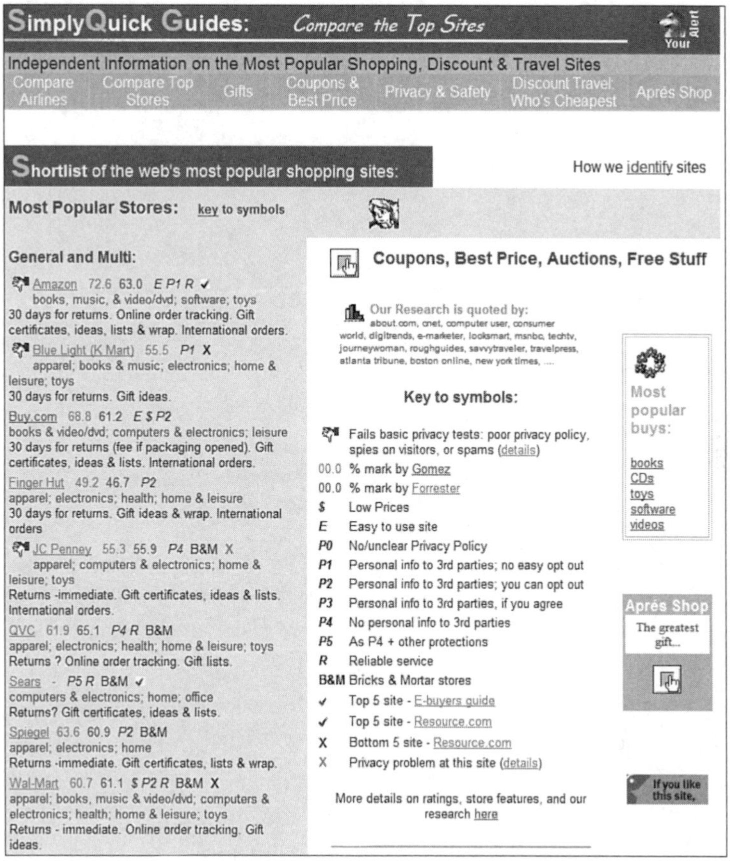

FIGURE 3.20
View performance and services in a nutshell at SimplyQuick.

What's Next: From Research to Bargain Hunting

Researching products before you buy is necessary homework for finding the best bargains on the Web. To learn all the steps involved in online bargain hunting, turn to Chapter 4, "Becoming a Savvy Online Shopper."

> **tip**
>
> In addition to the sites listed here, most price comparison sites also offer ratings or customer reviews of the merchants they link to.

BECOMING A SAVVY ONLINE SHOPPER

Finding the best bargains online requires both perseverance and a certain amount of savvy. The most successful online bargain hunters have a defined plan of attack that they use to track down the lowest prices and the best bargains available on any type of product they're shopping for. It's worth a few minutes of your time, before you start shopping, to put together your own personal bargain-hunting plan.

Step 1: Find the Lowest Price

The first—but not the only—step to getting the best deal online is to find the lowest price on the product you're shopping for. Although you can surf from site to site, tallying up the prices as you go, there are easier ways to compare prices on the Web.

Use a Price-Comparison Site

Bargain Hunter's Secret

The primary tool of the savvy online shopper is the price-comparison Web site. These sites, such as Shopping.com and PriceGrabber.com (shown in Figure 4.1), enable you to enter a product name or number, and then scour dozens of online retailers to see who's selling the item for the lowest price. It's a simple process to find the lowest prices out there, and then go directly to those merchants to complete your purchases.

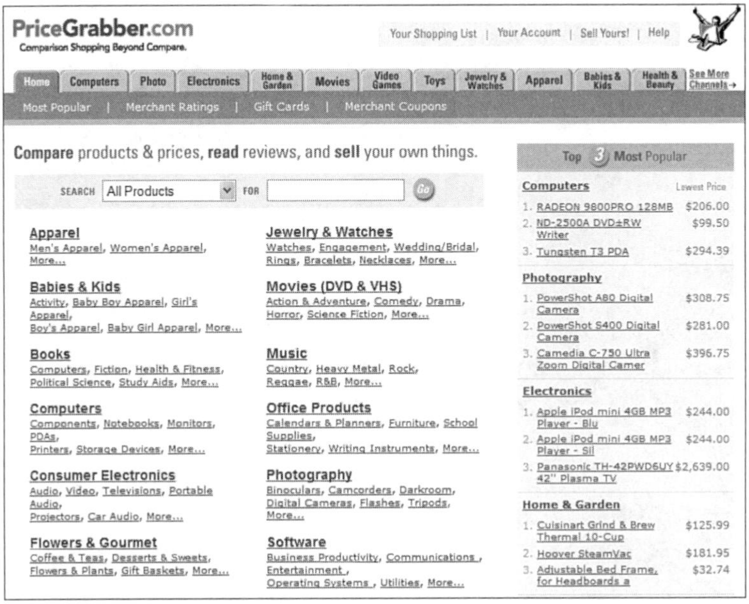

FIGURE 4.1
Use a price-comparison site such as PriceGrabber.com to find the lowest price.

As easy as this is, here's another tip: Don't stop with just one price-comparison site. As you'll learn in Chapter 5, "Hunting for the Lowest Price," you'll often find different prices at different sites—so it makes sense to comparison-shop the comparison shopping sites!

Check Competing Sites

It's a given that there's more than one online retailer selling what you want to buy. After you've found a merchant selling an item, surf over to its competitors and see what price they're charging. For example, if you find a book you want at Amazon.com, don't neglect to check out Barnes and Noble.com and Books-A-Million.com. Just because one store generally has the lowest price doesn't mean that it will *always* have the lowest price. Check the competitors!

Look for Sales

Online retailers are just like traditional retailers in that they frequently run sales and other special promotions, which can reduce the price of what you want to buy. To find out which merchants are running what promotions, turn to an online coupon/promotion site, such as DealofDay.com (shown in Figure 4.2) or

> **note**
> Learn more about using price-comparison sites in Chapter 5.

Specialoffers.com. These sites make it their business to know the ongoing promotions at major online retailers; stop here first to find out who's having a sale this week.

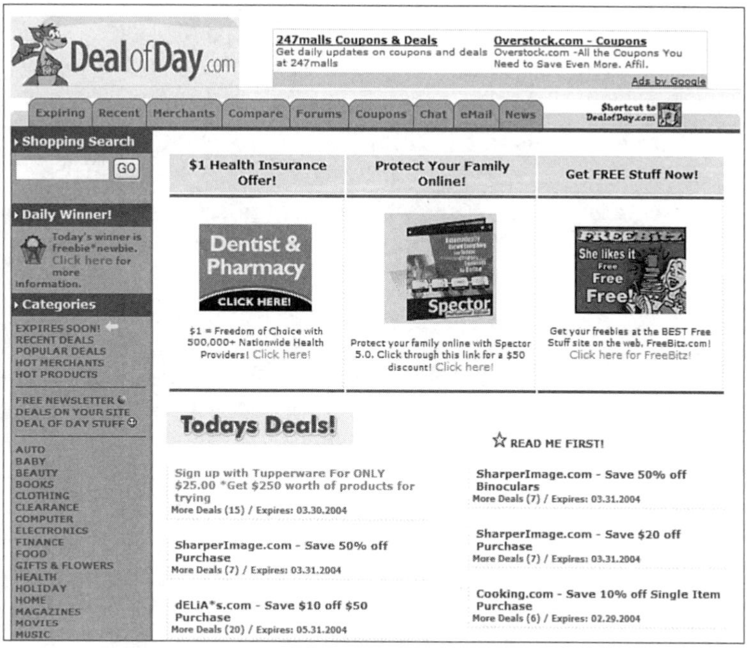

FIGURE 4.2
Look for online coupons and promotions at a site such as DealofDay.com.

Consider Buying Used or Refurbished Merchandise

Bargain Hunter's Secret

Sometimes you can save a few bucks by buying a used or refurbished item, instead of one new in the box. Amazon.com offers a "buy used" option for most of the products it sells, and you can find returned and refurbished items at the sites of many product manufacturers.

Know, however, that there are downsides to buying used merchandise. Although some refurbished items come with a "like new" warranty, many don't come with any warranty at all—and buying a used item as-is is a trifle risky.

So, before you take this route, make sure that you're okay with buying a used product. And if you don't want to buy a used item, don't get suckered into buying a refurbished item by mistake. Look out for shady retailers that sneak the refurbished line into the fine print. If a price looks abnormally low, make sure that you're really getting a new, in-the-box item, and not a damaged or refurbished one.

> **note**
>
> Learn more about online coupons and promotions in Chapter 6, "Hunting for Rebates, Coupons, and Promotions."

Consider an Online Auction

Speaking of used items, if that's what you're looking for, the best place to shop might be at an online auction site, such as eBay. eBay offers lots of used goods from individuals, as well as refurbished goods from major retailers and manufacturers. It's also a good source for brand new, in-the-box items; just be sure that you make a reasonable bid, and don't get caught up in a bidding frenzy!

> **note**
>
> Learn more about buying used and refurbished goods in Chapter 8, "Hunting for Closeout, Overstock, and Wholesale Bargains."
>
> Learn more about online auctions in Chapter 9, "Hunting for Bargains at eBay and Other Online Auctions."

Don't Forget to Shop Locally

With all this attention on finding the best bargains online, it's still possible to find terrific deals at traditional retailers. Don't automatically assume that the best deals are always available at online retailers; shop your local stores to see what their prices are, too.(And when you buy locally, you get the benefit of taking the item home with you—no waiting several days for shipment!)

Don't Obsess Over Pricing

The lowest price isn't always the best deal. If you're at all uncomfortable about buying at a particular online merchant, don't. It's okay to pay a little bit more for the peace of mind that comes from buying from a dealer you know and trust. It's the same online as it is in the "bricks and mortar" world: A dealer with quality service and a good reputation can command a premium price.

Step 2: Take Additional Savings

Okay, you've done your homework and found that one retailer offering what you want for the lowest price. Now it's time to try and knock a few more bucks off that price by using rebates, coupons, and other promotions.

Look for Manufacturer Rebates

Here's one you're familiar with from the "bricks and mortar" world. Let the product's manufacturer save you a few bucks by taking advantage of any available manufacturer rebates. It's quite common in some product categories to find the manufacturer offering a few bucks back when you fill in and mail back an official rebate form (along with appropriate proof-of-purchase, of course). Find the merchant offering the lowest base price on the product, and then use the rebate to lower your effective price that much more.

If you're not sure which manufacturers are offering what rebates, check out a rebate-tracking site, such as myRebates.com (shown in Figure 4.3) or rebatesHQ.com. These sites list current manufacturer rebates, enable you to print the official rebate forms, and even track the progress of your rebate claims.

note

Learn more about rebate-tracking sites in Chapter 6.

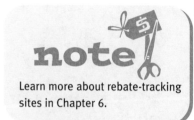

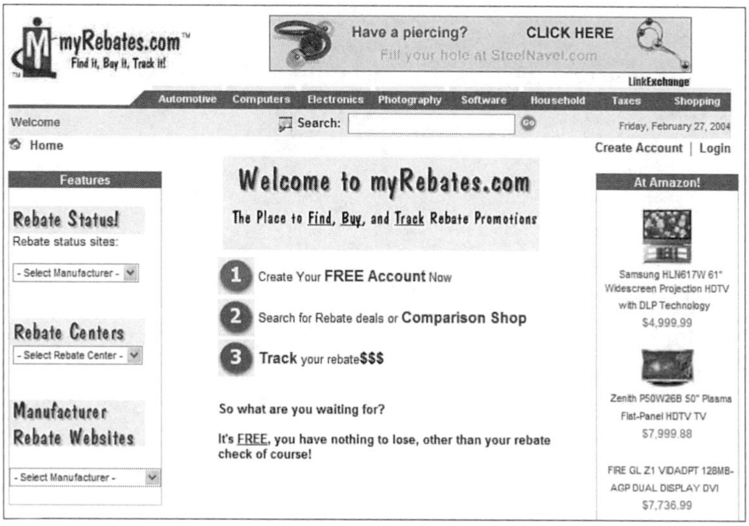

FIGURE 4.3
Use a rebate tracking site, such as myRebates.com, to find and track manufacturer rebates.

And don't forget to send in those rebate forms. Manufacturers count on a large percentage of customers never redeeming their rebates; you'd be surprised at how low most redemption rates really are.

caution

Watch out for sites that display misleading "after rebate" pricing. Although most retailers are fairly clear as to what their price is and what the rebate is, some merchants will display a big "after rebate" price, showing your net price—*not* what they're charging. Don't fall for this trap; you still need to find the lowest sale price, and *then* subtract the rebate amount.

Look for Online Coupons

Bargain Hunter's Secret

Just as traditional retailers and manufacturers try to entice you with dollars-off coupons, you can find similar coupons in the world of online retailing. The big difference between a traditional and an online coupon, of course, is that an online coupon isn't printed. Instead, you get a coupon code that you enter when you check out at a merchant's site.

There are numerous Web sites that track the online coupon offers from various manufacturers and retailers. Find the lowest price on a product and then apply any applicable coupon codes at checkout time; all the savings keep adding up!

note

Learn more about online coupons in Chapter 6.

Learn more about Amazon's Share the Love plan in Chapter 10, "Hunting for Bargains at Amazon.com."

Take Advantage of First-Time Customer Deals

Many online retailers offer special deals to first-time customers. You might get $10 off your first purchase, or a free gift, or something similar. Of course, you can be a first-time customer only once, but it's worth searching for this type of offer if indeed you're a newbie at a particular site. Look for these offers on the retailer's home page, or on a special offers or deals tab, or when you're checking out.

Take Advantage of Tell-a-Friend Promotions

Other merchants will pass on additional savings if you bring them additional customers. Amazon.com is notorious for this, with its Share the Love program. This program gives you a 10% discount if you provide a friend's email address at checkout—and if your friend purchases the same item within a week. If you're sure that your friends won't mind (although they probably will) and that they'll follow through and purchase the item you recommend, this is an interesting way to save a few bucks with every order.

Take Advantage of Cash-Back Purchasing Plans

Speaking of saving a few bucks with every order, several Web sites offer "frequent customer" plans that enable you to earn rebates for each purchase you make at participating retailers. These cash-back rebates are in addition to any other coupons and rebates you might earn. It's a sure-fire way to make your lowest price even lower—providing the online retailer participates in the program.

Step 3: Reduce Your Total Cost

The total price you pay is more than the price of the items you purchase; it also includes shipping charges, sales tax, and the like. So, the next step in your savvy shopping plan comes when you're ready to check out—and involves lowering these nonproduct costs.

Look for Free or Reduced Shipping Charges

The one drawback to shopping online is that the item has to be shipped to you—and shipping costs money. First, there's the actual shipping cost charged by UPS or FedEx or whatever service the merchant uses. Then there's the additional handling charge that most retailers tack on, ostensibly to cover the packing materials and the labor involved in picking and packing the order. If you don't watch it, these handling charges can really ding you.

note

Learn more about cash-back programs in Chapter 6.

Some less reputable dealers lure you in with an unusually low price on a product, and then sock it to you with an unjustifiably high shipping/handling charge. I was recently shopping for a DVD player, and found one merchant charging $10 less than any other online retailer. The catch? That retailer charged $24.95 for shipping/handling, when competitors were offering free shipping. So, I could "save" $10 on the product but end up spending a total of $15 more on the total order. Yikes!

What you want to look for are those merchants that offer some sort of deal on shipping. You might not be able to find out shipping charges until you enter a merchant's checkout, but that still lets you back out if the charges are too high. I like those merchants (such as Amazon.com and Buy.com, shown in Figure 4.4) that offer free shipping if your order is more than a certain dollar amount. Free shipping is the best deal there is!

FIGURE 4.4
Look for merchants, such as Buy.com, that offer free shipping.

Combine Orders for Lower Shipping Charges

Still on the subject of shipping charges, many sites offer two different options for shipping your order. You can choose to ship each item in your order individually; this will get you each item faster if one of the items is backordered or preordered, but cost you more in shipping costs. Or you can choose to combine all the items into a single shipment, which might (or might not) be slower, but will save you on shipping. Some sites

tip

Many price-comparison sites enable you to compare not only the base product price, but also the total price—including shipping/handling and taxes. When you're comparing prices, this total price is what you want to look at; you'll quickly rule out those merchants that sucker you in with a low price but try to make it back in shipping.

even let you combine multiple orders into a single order for shipping purposes—which could earn you free shipping, depending.

Pick a Slower—And Cheaper—Shipping Method

Bargain Hunter's Secret

Seeing a trend here? Some retailers offer yet another way to save money on shipping by choosing a slower shipping method. If you need to get the item right away, you can choose a faster and more expensive shipping option. But if you're in no hurry, choose the slowest method, and pay less—or, depending on the retailer, nothing at all.

Pick It Up Instead

Even better, if you're dealing with a dual-channel merchant (an online merchant with "bricks and mortar" locations) you might be able to cut out shipping charges completely by picking up the order yourself. This option has the advantage of getting you your order faster because many retailers let you pick up your merchandise within hours of placing your order. And because nothing gets shipped, there are no shipping/handling charges at all!

note

Of course, if you're buying from a merchant that lets you pick up the product, you'll probably be paying sales tax—which could wipe out your shipping savings.

Avoid Paying Sales Tax

Aside from shipping/handling, the other major nonproduct charge is sales tax. First, the good news—most online merchants don't charge sales tax. Now the bad news—if you buy from a dual-channel merchant that has locations in your state, it'll have to charge sales tax on your order.

Bargain Hunter's Secret

The logical conclusion, of course, is to avoid buying from those online merchants that have "bricks and mortar" stores in your area. If you get to the checkout page and find that there's a hefty sales tax added to your order, back up and shop elsewhere. You can save that 5%–10% by shopping at a retailer with similar pricing and no sales tax obligation.

Here's a good example. I live in the state of Indiana, which has a 6% sales tax. If I purchase a $200 MP3 player from Best Buy online, I have to pay $12 in sales tax. (That's because Best Buy has "bricks and mortar" stores in my state.) If I purchase that same MP3 player from Buy.com online (which doesn't have any "bricks and mortar" stores), I save that $12. As you can see, the larger your order, the more the sales tax savings matter.

Pay Your Credit Card Bill in Full Each Month

One last thing. Many unsavvy online shoppers end up paying more than they should by not paying their credit card bills in full every month. What's the point in saving a few bucks online when you give up 1%–2% a month in finance charges? Be smart and stay up-to-date on your credit card payments. Pay for your purchases in full every month and avoid those onerous finance charges!

Let's look at an example. You find a great deal on a computer that normally sells for $1600, but is available at your favorite online retailer for just $1500. You pay via credit card, but when the first bill comes, you don't have the cash to pay it in full. Instead, you decide to pay $100 per month—more than the minimum and enough to pay off your purchase in 15 months. Sounds like a plan, right?

But here's the problem: You forgot about the interest. Your credit card company charges an 18% annual rate, which translates into 1.5% per month on your current balance. I won't go into all the math here, but you end up paying more than $200 in interest before you get the PC paid off—which takes 18 months, not the 15 you originally thought. So, that $1500 computer actually costs you $1700, which is $100 more than the original $1600 price, not the $100 less you thought you were paying.

The moral of this story? Either pay your credit card bill in full when it first arrives or factor the interest charges into your total purchase price.

What's Next: How to Find the Lowest Prices

As you've learned, the first step towards becoming a savvy online shopper is to find those online retailers that offer the lowest prices. This is what online bargain shopping is all about, so turn to Chapter 5, "Hunting for the Lowest Price," to learn more.

II

MONEY SAVING SECRETS

5

HUNTING FOR THE LOWEST PRICE

Just a few short years ago, if you wanted to find the best bargains on the Web, you had to manually visit the sites of dozens of different online retailers—a very time-consuming process. Not so today because there are numerous sites that exist to automatically do this price comparison for you. Go to a price comparison site, find the product you want, and have the site return a list of merchants offering that product, along with current prices. Sort the list to find the merchant with the lowest price, and you're ready to buy—literally within seconds of starting shopping. It's the easiest way to hunt for bargains on the Web!

Comparing Products and Prices Online—Automatically

The most important development in the history of online shopping is the creation of the price comparison site. This is a site that uses software called a *shopping bot* (short for *robot*) to search a large number of online retailers for current prices on available products. This product and pricing information is used to create a large database that you, the consumer, can access at will. When you search a price comparison site, you're looking up the most recent pricing information in its database. In essence, you let the price comparison site do your shopping for you; all you have to do is evaluate the results.

How Price Comparison Sites Get Their Listings

The only glitch in this model is that most price comparison sites really don't compare prices across all online retailers. Instead, they build their price/product databases from product links submitted and paid for by participating retailers. That's right, most price comparison sites charge retailers to be included in their listings. The more retailers a site signs up, the more products there are for you to search through.

> **note**
>
> Retailers don't actually pay to have to their listings included on these sites; they pay only when a customer clicks their product listings. This is called a *pay-per-click* (PPC) model, and the individual fee is referred to as a *cost per click* (CPC). CPCs run anywhere from a nickel to more than a buck, depending on the site and the product category.

That said, these price comparison sites do appear to honestly present the lowest prices—from participating merchants, that is. The prices presented are legitimate, no matter who's paying what. The only thing is, it's possible that lower prices might exist at a retailer who doesn't sign on to a site's program.

The major exception to the paid inclusion model is Froogle, which you'll learn about in a few pages. Froogle searches all online retailers, and doesn't accept any paid listings. That makes Froogle's price comparisons just a tad more legitimate than those at other sites—even though, in practice, you end up getting pretty much the same results no matter where you search. (In the name of full disclosure, it should be noted that merchants can also submit their product listings to Froogle—they just don't have to pay for this privilege.)

How to Use a Price Comparison Site

The best price comparison sites offer more than just pricing information. These full-service sites enable you to sort and filter their search results in a number of different ways, and often include customer reviews of both the products and the available merchants. Some even enable you to perform side-by-side comparisons of multiple products, which is great if you haven't yet made up your mind as to what you want to buy.

As to *where* you want to buy, it's tempting to base your purchase decision solely on the lowest price. But there are other factors you should consider, such as

- **Product availability.** Does the merchant with the lowest price actually have the product in stock and ready to ship?

- **Shipping/handling costs**. Oftentimes the merchant with the lowest price also has the highest shipping costs. Look for merchants that offer free or low-cost shipping, and then compare the *total* price—the product price plus the shipping costs.
- **Product condition**. Some of these price comparison sites list not only new, in-the-box products, but also used or refurbished items. Don't fall for a super-low price on a refurbished product when what you really want is a brand-new one.
- **Sale or auction.** Some price comparison sites list not only items for sale from traditional retailers, but also items that individuals have for auction. Remember, bidding in an auction isn't the same thing as purchasing the item at retail—you have to wait for the auction the end, and your bid might not be the winning one.
- **Merchant reputation.** Not all online retailers are created equal. Some are actually bait-and-switch artists, or offer poor service, or take forever to ship, or otherwise promise to disappoint. Many price comparison sites also enable you to compare different retailers by reading reviews and ratings from previous customers. When you find a low price from a merchant you've never heard of before, take the time to read the customer reviews—and skip those merchants that rate poorly.

> **note**
>
> Learn more about shopping at online auctions in Chapter 9, "Hunting for Bargains at eBay and Other Online Auctions."
>
> To find more sites that provide reviews of online retailers, turn to Chapter 3, "Researching Your Purchases Before You Buy."

When it comes to price comparison sites, there are five that consistently attract the most consumer traffic: BizRate, Froogle, mySimon, Shopping.com, and Yahoo! Shopping. We'll look at each of these sites separately, and then provide a list of all the other price comparison sites available.

BizRate

BizRate (`www.bizrate.com`) is one of the oldest comparison shopping sites, founded way back in the stone ages of 1996. The site claims to index more than 30 million products from more than 40,000 different online retailers; it certainly is one of the most comprehensive comparison sites I've found.

Bargain Hunter's Secret

BizRate not only compares prices, it also offers customer reviews of the most popular products. The site's customer reviews extend to reviews of online retailers, as you learned back in Chapter 3. These product and merchant reviews make BizRate an extremely useful shopping comparison site.

The BizRate home page, shown in Figure 5.1, is your gateway to all the site's services. You can browse through the products in various categories by using the tabs along the top of the page, or search for specific products via the Search For box. Major product categories include Appliances, Automotive, Babies & Kids, Books & Magazines, Clothing & Accessories, Computer Hardware, Computer Software, DVDs & Videos, Electronics, Gifts, Flowers & Food, Health & Beauty, Home & Garden, Jewelry & Watches, Music, Musical Instruments, Office Supplies, Pet Supplies, Sports & Outdoors, Toys & Games, Video Games, and Travel & Leisure. (The merchant reviews are under the Store Ratings tab.)

FIGURE 5.1
Comparison shopping at BizRate.

Comparing Products

If you choose to browse through the categories, you'll soon find yourself at a category page like the one shown in Figure 5.2. This is a great way to shop when you're not sure what product you want, because BizRate offers a number of ways to fine-tune your purchase.

One of these options enables you to narrow your product selection by brand, product line within a brand, price range, and other product variables. For example, if you're shopping for digital cameras, you can narrow your search to cameras that offer a particular resolution range (in megapixels, of course) or specific features—digital zoom, installed memory, and so on.

After you've narrowed your search, BizRate then enables you to compare two or more different products. Just check the box next to a particular product, and then click the Compare button. The resultant page, shown in Figure 5.3, displays the selected products side-by-side with their features compared in tabular format. This is a terrific way to see how one product compares to another without having to click back and forth between the individual product pages.

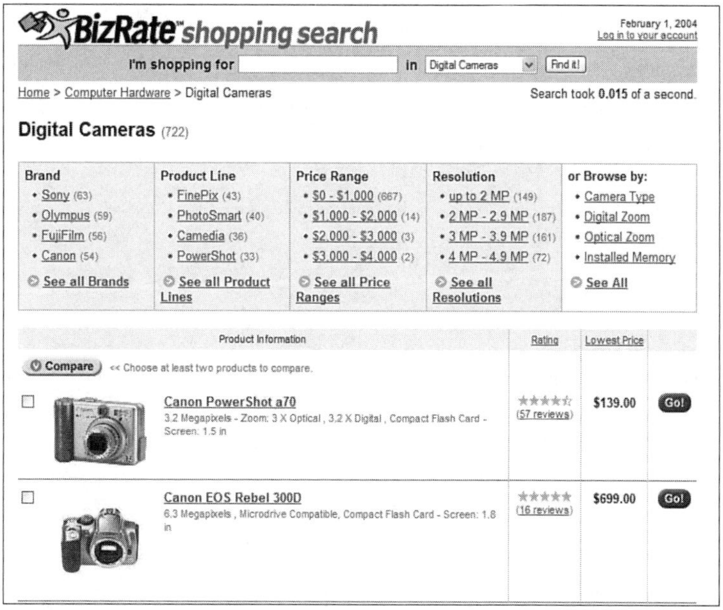

FIGURE 5.2
Shopping for products within a particular category.

FIGURE 5.3
Comparing multiple products side-by-side.

Naturally, when you find a product that meets your needs, you'll want to read more about that product and compare prices from different merchants. All you have to do is click the product name, and you'll be taken to a dedicated product page, which we'll discuss next.

Finding the Lowest Prices

When you land on a particular product page, like the one shown in Figure 5.4, BizRate displays a wealth of information. The very top of the page shows a picture of the product, along with brief product specs and the average customer rating. To view a more detailed product description, click the See Product Details link; doing so displays a page that lists a longer description and quite comprehensive product specs. To view the individual customer reviews, click the Read Reviews link.

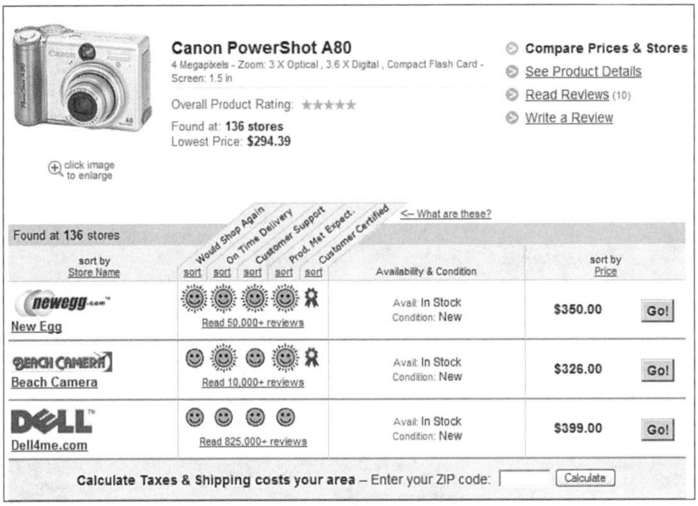

FIGURE 5.4

A typical BizRate product page.

At the bottom of the main product page is the price comparison data. For each store listed, you see the customer store ratings in four major performance categories, the availability and condition of the product at that store, and the store's current price. You can sort by any of these criteria by clicking the appropriate Sort By link at the top of any column. For example, if you want to sort by price, click the Sort By Price link.

When you first visit the site, BizRate lists the raw selling price at each store. Because the total price you pay depends on shipping costs (which vary widely from store to store) and taxes (which you might or might not have to pay), you can configure BizRate to display the total selling price by entering your ZIP code into the Calculate Taxes & Shipping Costs box.

tip

Don't ignore the store ratings. Your fellow customers can give you a heads-up in terms of what to expect from each listed merchant—so you can avoid those retailers that offer less-than-desired service.

I recommend you do this, and then resort the listings by price again. Because some stores offer free or reduced-price shipping, the lowest base price won't always be the lowest total price.

When you find a store that looks attractive to you, click the Go! button to go to that store. From there you can further evaluate the product and the merchant, and make your purchase if you want.

Hunting for Bargains

It's not just enough to find the lowest current prices. BizRate can also lead you to extra savings on selected products.

Bargain Hunter's Secret

When you're hunting for additional bargains, the first place to look is the Special Offers tab on BizRate's home page. This page lists all the special offers and product rebates offered by the merchants in BizRate's database. For example, on the day I checked, BizRate offered 1,370 special offers and 1,273 different product rebates—not a bad deal! The offers are organized by category; just click through to see what's available.

Bargain Hunter's Secret

You can also look for bargains on BizRate's product category pages. Scroll down to the Related Searches box, shown in Figure 5.5. Here you'll find links to coupons, rebates and incentives, and free shipping offers. Click each link to access each of these promotional offers.

Related Searches
Digital Cameras Store Coupons (37)
Related Searches
Recently Viewed Items
Digital Cameras Rebates & Incentives (35)
Free Shipping Offers
Shop by Store Name (274)

FIGURE 5.5
Finding all the bargains in a given product category.

Thoughts on BizRate

BizRate is a good, solid price comparison site. I particularly like the site's merchant reviews and ratings, which several other sites license separately. It's also one of the better sites in terms of finding additional bargains and promotions; most price comparison sites look at only price, not at discounts and rebates. BizRate is also a pretty good site for comparing different products, although that's not a unique feature these days.

My only problem with BizRate is that, unique among these major sites, it encourages advertisers to pay more for higher profile listings. This means that the merchants at the top of a search results list might not always be the best place to buy; they've paid extra for that position. This doesn't affect things when you sort the results by price, but the default positions can be a tad misleading. Know this before you shop here.

Froogle

Froogle (`froogle.google.com`) is the new shopping search engine from Google, the king of all Web search engines. Unique among the major price comparison sites, Froogle is completely objective; Froogle doesn't take money for its listings, instead sending its software to independently scour the Web for merchants and products.

There are two ways to use Froogle, as you can see in Figure 5.6. You can search for specific products or browse through general product categories. We'll look at each method in turn.

note

Froogle's name is a Googlized version of the word *frugal*.

FIGURE 5.6
Froogle—the Web's fastest shopping search engine.

Searching for Bargains

Because Froogle is an offshoot of Google, it's no surprise that it works so well as a product search engine. In most cases, all you have to do is enter a product name or number into the search box at the top of the home page, and then click the Search Froogle button. Froogle displays all matching products on a search results page, such as the one shown in Figure 5.7.

caution

Watch out for the "ads" on Froogle's search results page. These are the listings in the Sponsored Links section; they're not really search results, but rather listings paid for by Froogle's advertisers.

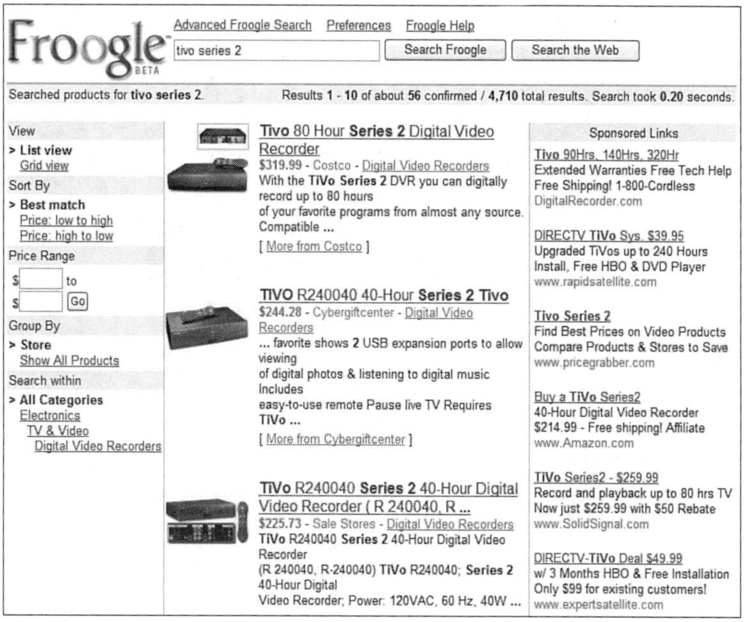

FIGURE 5.7
The results of a Froogle search.

From here you have a few options. By default, Froogle displays products in a simple list. If you prefer a grid-like display such as the one in Figure 5.8, click the Grid View link in the left column.

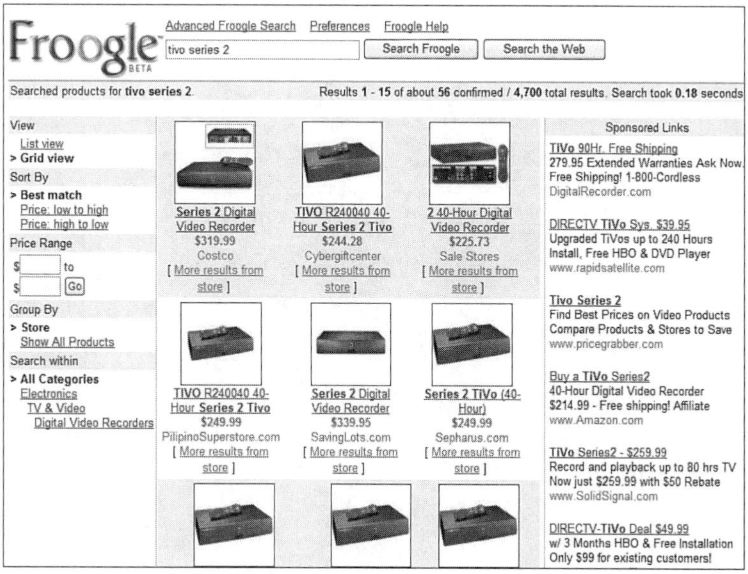

FIGURE 5.8
Products displayed in grid view.

Also by default, Froogle organizes its results based on customer demand. If you prefer to see all the products offered by a particular store, click the Show All Products link in the left column. You can choose to sort the products by price; click either the Price: Low to High or Price: High to Low links. You can also limit the listing to products within a particular price range; just enter the appropriate values in the Price Range boxes.

When you find a product you're interested in, just click the link. You'll be taken to that merchant's Web site, where you can learn more or place an order.

Advanced Searching

If you find that Froogle is returning too many (or too few) search results, you can use the Advanced Search page to fine-tune your query. When you click the Advanced Froogle Search link on Froogle's home page, you're taken to the Froogle Advanced Search page, shown in Figure 5.9.

FIGURE 5.9
Advanced Froogle searching.

Here you can select a number of different search parameters, including

- Find products that contain *all* the words you select.
- Find products that contain the *exact phrase* you enter.
- Find products that contain *at least one* of the words you enter.
- Find products *without the words* you enter.
- Display products within a specific price range.
- Display products where the words you enter occur in the product name, the product description, or both.
- Display products from a specific category only.

- Display your results grouped by store, or display all products.
- Display your results in list or grid view.
- Enable the SafeSearch filter, which blocks results containing adult content (great for when your kids are shopping).

You don't have to go to the Advanced Search page to fine-tune your search. For example, you can search for an exact phrase from the main search box by enclosing the phrase in quotation marks, like this: **"nikon coolpix 2100"**. You can also exclude a word from your search by using the "-" sign in front of the word. And, of course, you can change the way your results are displayed by selecting options on the search results page.

Browsing for Bargains

Many users are more comfortable browsing than searching, which is why Froogle offers a list of product categories on its home page—Apparel & Accessories, Arts & Entertainment, Auto & Vehicles, Baby, Books Music & Videos, Business & Industry, Computers, Electronics, Flowers, Food & Gourmet, Health & Personal Care, Home & Garden, Office, Sports & Outdoors, and Toys & Games. When you click through the categories and subcategories, you end up with a listing of products similar to a search results page, with the same display options.

Thoughts on Froogle

If all you want is the lowest price—without a lot of product comparison data—then Froogle is the site for you. Like its parent site, Google, Froogle is fast and extremely comprehensive; chances are you'll find several merchants selling the product you want, at the lowest price offered.

Bargain Hunter's Secret

The best thing about Froogle is that its listings aren't tainted by the pay-per-click model. Merchants can't buy their way into Froogle's listings; what you see are legitimate prices, found independently by Froogle's world-class search software.

I use Froogle when I know what I'm looking for but don't know where to find it. Because it doesn't depend on paid listings, the site typically returns more merchants selling any given product than any of the other price comparison sites.

> **note**
>
> For what it's worth, mySimon is part of the CNET network of sites, which also includes CNET Shopper.com.

mySimon

The mySimon site (`www.mysimon.com`) was one of the first price comparison sites on the Web. It's still one of the most popular, even though it doesn't search near as many merchants as some of the newer sites.

Searching and Browsing

As you can see in Figure 5.10, the mySimon home page enables you to search for specific products or browse through the major categories: Apparel & Accessories, Autos, Babies & Kids, Beauty & Health, Books, Computer Hardware, Digital Photography, Electronics, Flowers & Gifts, Food & Wine, Home & Garden, Jewelry & Watches, Movies, Music, Office Products, Personal Finance, Software, Sports, Toys & Games, Travel & Leisure, and Video Games.

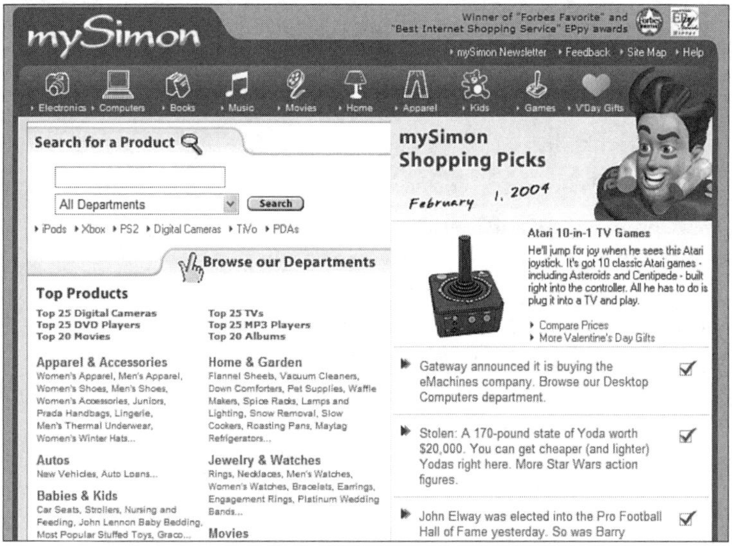

FIGURE 5.10
The mySimon home page.

Whether you search for an item or browse to it, mySimon will eventually display a complete product listing like the one in Figure 5.11. You can sort this list by merchant, brand, product, or price by clicking the link at the top of each column. Information about a merchant is available by clicking the Merchant Info link; this displays a Store Profile page that lists available services (but *not* customer ratings or reviews—the mySimon rating is actually somewhat useless). Click the Buy button to view the merchant's product page and make a purchase.

Thoughts on mySimon

To be honest, I find mySimon to be one of the least useful of the big price comparison sites. It doesn't offer any product comparison features, customer reviews, or detailed merchant ratings. To add insult to injury, in most categories, mySimon appears to have fewer merchants signed up than the other major price comparison sites. The end result is that you're less likely to find the lowest possible price out there—a definite drawback when you're trying to compare prices.

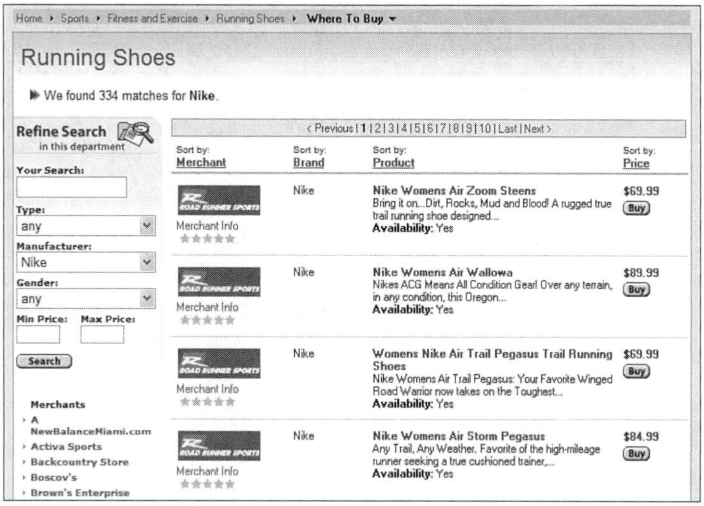

FIGURE 5.11
Comparing prices at mySimon.

All this said, mySimon remains a popular site among consumers—primarily because it's so easy to use. I don't like it, but you might.

Shopping.com

The new Shopping.com site (`www.shopping.com`) is a relaunched and revamped version of the old DealTime site, now incorporating customer reviews from Epinions.com (`www.epinions.com`). This makes Shopping.com perhaps the most fully featured price comparison site on the Web. You can use Shopping.com, shown in Figure 5.12, to compare different products, evaluate merchants, and then find the lowest price—all in one place.

> **note**
> Learn more about Epinions.com in Chapter 3.

Finding What You Want

Like all the other price comparison sites, Shopping.com enables you to either search for specific products or browse through major categories: Books, Clothing, Computers and Software, Electronics, Gifts, Health and Beauty, Home and Garden, Jewelry and Watches, Kids and Family, Movies, Music, Office, Sports and Outdoors, and Video Games. Whether you search or browse, you eventually end up at a product listing page like the one shown in Figure 5.13. From here you can filter the results by price, product type, brand, or other product attributes. You can sort the results by best matches (default), price, or product rating. (The product ratings are provided by the customers at Epinions.com.) You can also display the products as a grid rather than a list, by clicking the View as a Grid link.

FIGURE 5.12
One of the most full-featured price comparison sites—Shopping.com.

Comparing Products

When you're in the process of choosing a particular product, Shopping.com makes it easy to perform side-by-side product comparisons. Just check the Check to Compare boxes next to the items you're looking at, and then click the Compare Products button. The result is the type of comparison shown in Figure 5.14, with the features of each product displayed in tabular format.

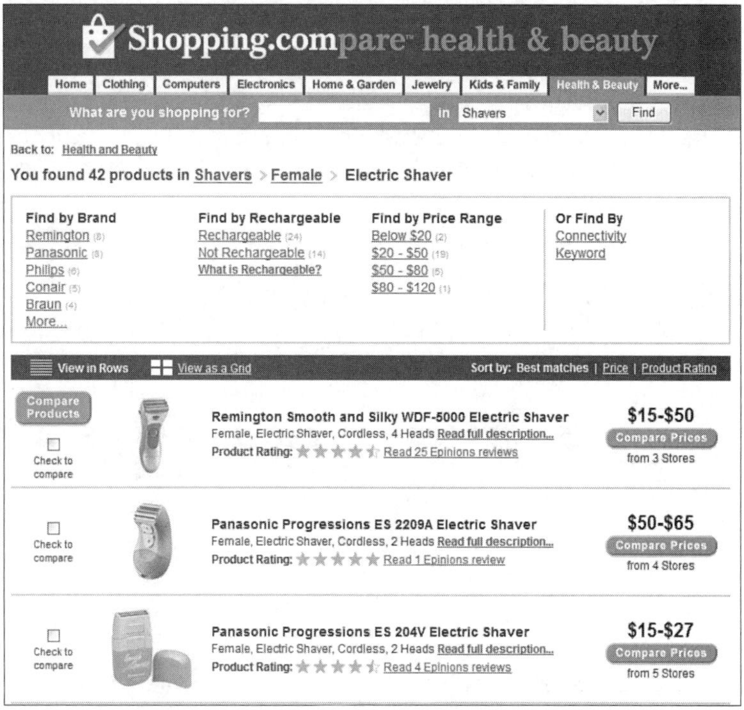

FIGURE 5.13
The results of a product search at Shopping.com.

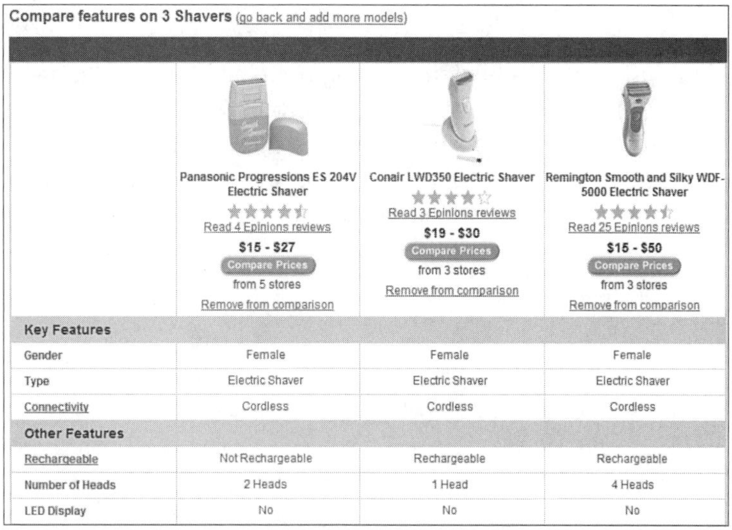

FIGURE 5.14
Comparing products side-by-side.

Part II
5

Learning More—And Making a Purchase

To learn more about a particular product, click the Compare Prices button. This displays a product page like the one shown in Figure 5.15. From here you can read detailed product information by clicking the See Full Specifications link or read customer reviews by clicking the Read Epinions Reviews link.

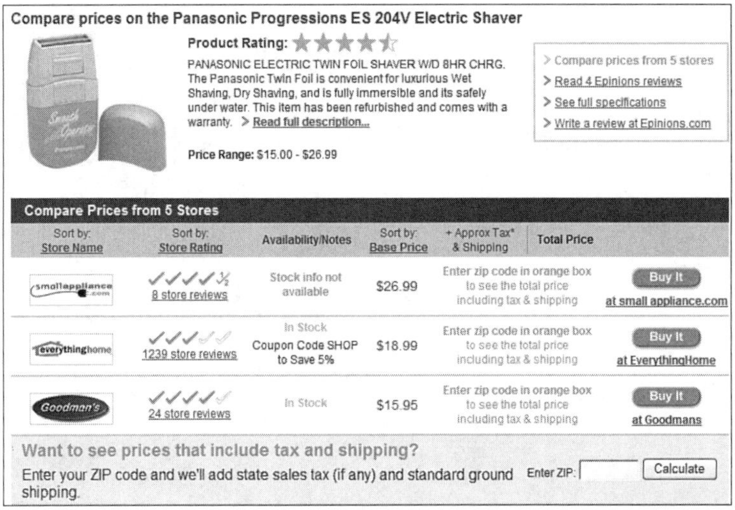

FIGURE 5.15
Comparing prices from different merchants.

Below the product picture is a listing of all stores carrying this product. You can sort this list by store name, store rating (from Epinions.com customers), base price, or total price. To see the total price (which includes shipping and taxes), enter your ZIP code into the Enter ZIP box, and then click the Calculate button. Obviously, total price is more important than base price because some merchants like to stick it to you when it comes to shipping and handling charges.

When you're ready to buy, click the Buy It button to go directly to the merchant's product page.

Thoughts on Shopping.com

I like Shopping.com—a lot. In part that's because it incorporates product and merchant reviews from Epinions.com, which is my favorite customer review site. But I also find the Shopping.com site extremely easy to use; I seldom have difficulties finding the products I want, as sometimes happens at other sites. And Shopping.com almost always presents the lowest prices on what I'm looking for, which obviously matters. It's a well-conceived site that works well—what more could you ask for?

Yahoo! Shopping

Yahoo! Shopping (`shopping.yahoo.com`) was recently revamped into one of the leading price comparison sites on the Web. Formerly, it was merely a large directory of online merchants; now it's a full-featured shopping search engine, complete with numerous product comparison features.

Different Ways to Shop

The Yahoo! Shopping home page, shown in Figure 5.16, offers several different ways to shop for any given product.

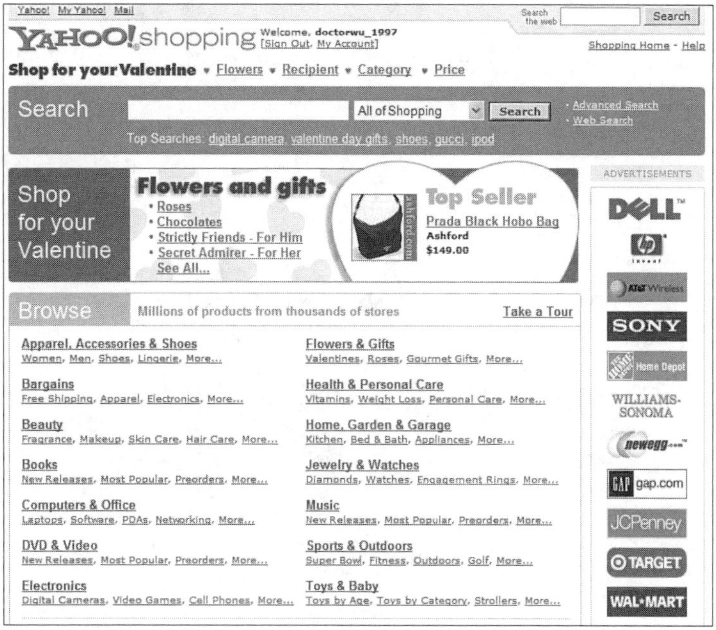

FIGURE 5.16
Shopping from the Yahoo! Shopping home page.

You can

- Search for a specific product by using the top-of-page Search box.
- Browse by major product category—Apparel, Accessories & Shoes, Bargains, Beauty, Books, Computers & Office, DVD & Video, Electronics, Flowers & Gifts, Health & Personal Care, Home, Garden & Garage, Jewelry & Watches, Music, Sports & Outdoors, and Toys & Baby.
- Browse all products of a specific brand by clicking the Shop by Brand link.
- Browse a specific store by clicking the Shop by Store link.

Shopping by Category

If you decide to browse through the categories, you'll land on a specific category page like the one shown in Figure 5.17. The site's category pages are like shopping gateways into a specific category, offering all manner of information and product reviews. You can also use this page to narrow your search by product type, brand, or price.

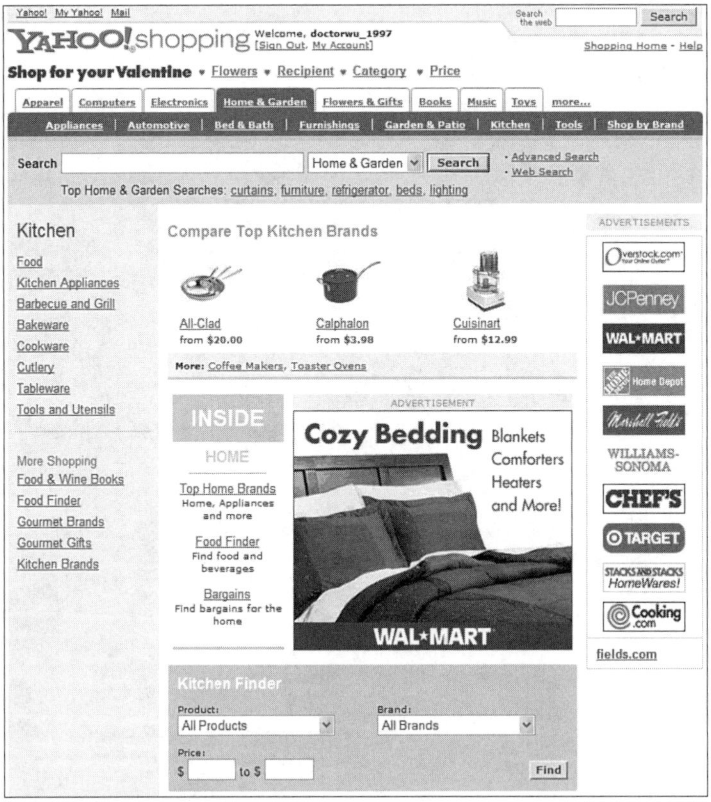

FIGURE 5.17
Find the product you want from a product category page.

Finding the Lowest Price

What happens next depends on what type of product you're looking for. In some categories, such as Home & Garden, you end up with a simple product listing like the one in Figure 5.18. Clicking a product listing takes you directly to the merchant selling that product; there's no way to obtain a more detailed product listing or to compare prices between merchants.

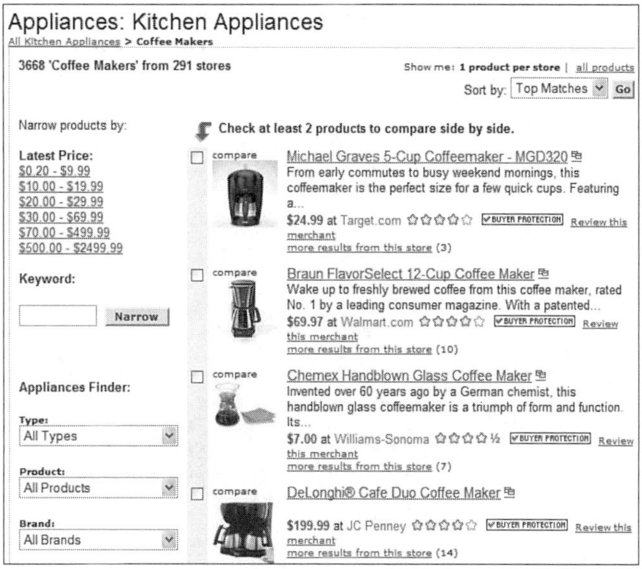

FIGURE 5.18
In some categories, Yahoo! Shopping offers simple product listings.

In other categories, such as Electronics, you see a product comparison page like the one in Figure 5.19. From here you have several options—to view more product information, click the Full Specifications and Description links; to read customer reviews, click the User Reviews link; to read outside reviews (when available), click the appropriate review link; and to view a buyer's guide (when available), click the Buying Advice link.

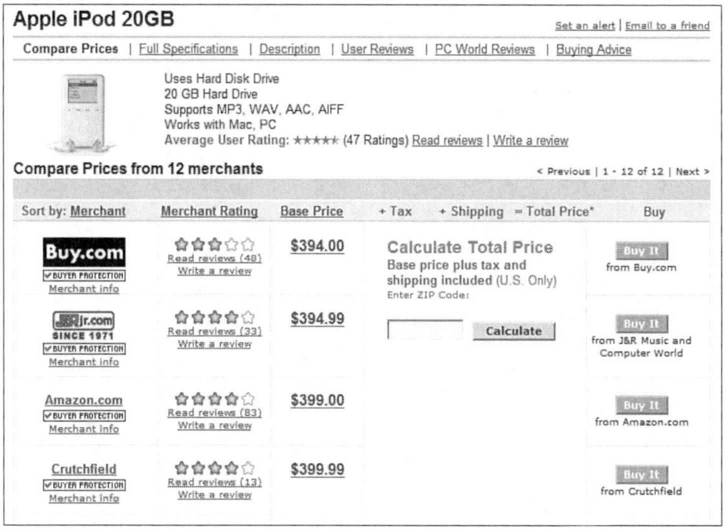

FIGURE 5.19
In other categories, Yahoo! Shopping offers more detailed information and comparisons.

If you see this full product comparison page, there's a list of merchants below the main product information. You can sort this list by merchant, merchant rating, base price, or total price (including shipping and tax). (To calculate the total price, enter your ZIP code into the Calculate Total Price box, and then click the Calculate button.) You can read what other customers have to say about any given merchant by clicking the Read Reviews link next to a merchant's name. Click the Buy It button to go to the merchant's site to make your purchase.

Comparing Products with SmartSort

There's another nifty feature of Yahoo! Shopping you might want to check out. For selected product categories—Cell Phones, Desktop Computers, Digital Cameras, Digital Video Camcorders, DVD Players, MP3 Players, Notebook Computers, Personal Digital Assistants, and Televisions—the site offers something it calls SmartSort. This feature enables you to interactively narrow down products that match your shopping criteria by using a series of slider controls.

You access SmartSort by clicking the Yahoo! SmartSort link on the Yahoo! Shopping home page. Select the category you're interested in, and you see a selection page like the one in Figure 5.20. The contents of this page differs by product, but basically it presents a series of product features, each accompanied by its own slider control. Use your mouse to adjust each slider according to how important that feature is to you; move the slider to the right if it's less important, or to the left if it's more important. You can also enter a target price range into the How Much Do You Want to Spend? boxes at the top of the page.

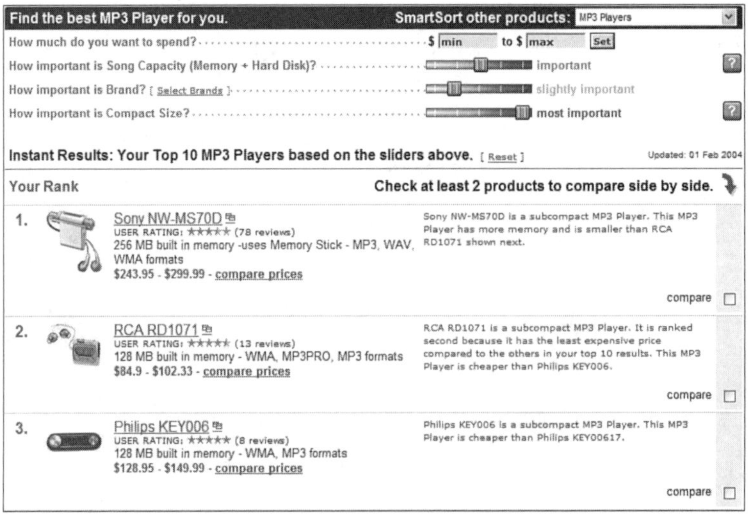

Find the best MP3 Player for you.
SmartSort other products: MP3 Players
How much do you want to spend?
$ min to $ max Set
How important is Song Capacity (Memory + Hard Disk)?
important
How important is Brand? [Select Brands]
slightly important
How important is Compact Size?
most important
Instant Results: Your Top 10 MP3 Players based on the sliders above. [Reset]
Updated: 01 Feb 2004
Your Rank
Check at least 2 products to compare side by side.
1.
Sony NW-MS70D
USER RATING: ★★★★★ (78 reviews)
256 MB built in memory -uses Memory Stick - MP3, WAV, WMA formats
$243.95 - $299.99 - compare prices
Sony NW-MS70D is a subcompact MP3 Player. This MP3 Player has more memory and is smaller than RCA RD1071 shown next.
compare
2.
RCA RD1071
USER RATING: ★★★★★ (13 reviews)
128 MB built in memory - WMA, MP3PRO, MP3 formats
$84.9 - $102.33 - compare prices
RCA RD1071 is a subcompact MP3 Player. It is ranked second because it has the least expensive price compared to the others in your top 10 results. This MP3 Player is cheaper than Philips KEY006.
compare
3.
Philips KEY006
USER RATING: ★★★★★ (8 reviews)
128 MB built in memory - WMA, MP3 formats
$128.95 - $149.99 - compare prices
Philips KEY006 is a subcompact MP3 Player. This MP3 Player is cheaper than Philips KEY00617.
compare

FIGURE 5.20

Searching for products interactively with Yahoo! Shopping's SmartSort.

As you move the sliders, the site will display a list of matching products. The items on this list change every time you move a slider, so you can see how your criteria affect the available products. It's actually a fairly effective—and fun!—way to find the products you want.

Reading the Reviews

Yahoo! Shopping is also a good site for third-party product reviews. In particular, the site offers product reviews from *PC World* (computers and electronics products) and *Consumer Reports* magazines—although you have to subscribe to access these latter reviews.

Hunting for Bargains

Bargain Hunter's Secret

Like BizRate, Yahoo! Shopping also offers links to various retailer and manufacturer promotions and discounts—including those merchants offering free shipping. To hunt for these bargains, click the Bargains link on the Yahoo! Shopping home page. This takes you to the Bargains page, where you can browse the bargains available in various product categories.

Thoughts on Yahoo! Shopping

Yahoo! has done a pretty good job with its new Yahoo! Shopping site—or at least in some sections of the site. Before this latest overhaul, Yahoo! Shopping was nothing more than a collection of somewhat motley merchants; today, it's one of the better price and product comparison sites on the Web.

That's not to say that Yahoo! Shopping is perfect. It's apparent that some sections of the site (such as Electronics) have more product information and better price comparison functionality. If and when Yahoo! can roll out these features across the entire site, I'll like Yahoo! Shopping a lot better.

I also don't like the fact that if you use the search function, your results are often littered with listings from small Yahoo! Merchants and listings from Yahoo! Auctions listings. This means you have to sort out a bunch of nonretail results from the product listings—a tedious task, to be sure. I'd like Yahoo! Shopping a lot more if there were some way to exclude these often irrelevant or unwanted results.

Comparing the Price Comparison Sites

Now that you've learned a little about each of the major price comparison sites, the question still remains: Which of these sites can actually deliver the best bargains?

The answer to that question is a little tricky, for a number of reasons.

First, many of these sites search the same retailers, using similar search technology. Which means that you'll often find multiple sites delivering the same results—not a bad thing.

Second, and somewhat in contradiction to the first point, these sites don't *always* search the same retailer sites. Which means that you'll sometimes find wildly differing results, depending on which merchants are included in which price comparison database.

Third, not all the sites update their listings as quickly as the others. Which means that sometimes a fresher site will report a lower price than a site that isn't quite as up-to-date.

Fourth, these sites don't always judge prices by the same criteria. Yahoo! Shopping, for example, is prone to mix results from Yahoo! Auctions and used products from Yahoo! Merchants in with its standard product pricing, thus reporting a lower range of prices—even though it's not a head-to-head comparison with new, in-the-box product from legitimate retailers. Other sites don't always list results if a product is out of stock at a given retailer, thus excluding what might be a lower price from the results list.

And, to be honest, some of these price comparison sites are better at some categories than they are with others. mySimon, for example, is generally pretty good with clothing and electronics, but terribly lacking when it comes to books, movies, and music—as you'll see next.

A Spot Comparison

All that said, I thought I'd offer a brief spot comparison between these five sites. Note that this is literally a snapshot of results; I did one particular search on one particular day, so this isn't an extensive survey over an extended period of time.

I searched for six specific products:

- *Finding Nemo* DVD
- Hamilton Beach toaster, model 22415
- Kangol wool men's cap
- Panasonic DVD player, model S25
- Ugg women's boots
- Canon PowerShot A70 digital camera

The results are interesting, as you can see in Table 5.1.

Table 5.1 Selected Price Comparisons

Site	*Finding Nemo* DVD	Hamilton Beach Toaster	Wool Kangol Cap	Panasonic DVD Player	Women's Ugg Boots	Canon A70 Digital Camera
BizRate	$15.98 (Wal-Mart)	$17.37 (Bioarmed)	$36.00 (Karmaloop)	$69.99 (Etonics.com)	$100.00 (Nordstrom)	$224.99 (Radio Active Deals)
Froogle	$15.98 (Wal-Mart)	$12.13 (BuilderDepot)	$28.99 (Blair, Irvine Park)	$69.99 (Etonics.com)	$99.95 (Onlineshoes.com, Zappos.com)	$234.98 (Best Sale Pricing, Hot Buys Electronics)
mySimon	No matches	$23.96 (Celebrity Cookware.com)	$36.00 (Karmaloop)	$69.99 (Etonics.com)	$99.95 (Zappos.com)	$238.99 (Cameras and Electronics.com)
Shopping.com	$19.99 (Sears)	$14.99 (Kitchen Collection)	$28.99 (Irvine Park)	$69.99 (Etonics.com)	$115.90 (Nordstrom)	$245.00 (Inoax)
Yahoo! Shopping	$15.98 (Wal-Mart)	$17.37 (Bioarmed, igadgets)	$28.99 (Blair)	$69.99 (CompUSA, Etonics.com, HypAudio.com)	$99.95 (Nordstrom, Shoestoboot.com, Wavejammer.com)	$222.00 (Digital Gadgets)

Evaluating the Results

My first observation is that, more often than not, all five sites found the same low price—often at the same merchants. For example, all five sites found the Panasonic DVD player for $69.99 at Etonics.com; three of the five sites found *Nemo* for $15.98 at Wal-Mart.

Other times, it was quite obvious that the sites *weren't* searching the same merchants. Take the Kangol cap, for example. Froogle, Shopping.com, and Yahoo! Shopping found the item for $28.99 at either Blair or Irvine Park. BizRate and mySimon, however, didn't have these merchants in their databases, both reporting a higher $36 price at Karmaloop.

When it came to small appliances, like the Hamilton Beach toaster, the pricing was all over the board, from a low of $12.13 at Froogle to a high of $23.96 at mySimon. This example shows the wisdom of shopping at more than one price comparison site, just in case.

Finally, the camera category proved a tricky one to navigate. There are tons of photography retailers on the Web, and each price comparison site displayed results from dozens and dozens of different merchants. The lowest price was actually difficult to ascertain because some merchants listed refurbished products in their results, and some listed pricing after a manufacturer rebate. I tried to filter out the used products and post-rebate prices, but still found the price comparison difficult. That's because the lowest prices on this product came from retailers that I either have no experience with, or those that I know to practice bait-and-switch techniques or aggressive upselling. This is definitely one instance where I wouldn't automatically gravitate to the lowest price ($222 at Yahoo! Shopping), but instead would seriously consider the customer reviews of each merchant.

note

Interestingly, mySimon was unable to find any merchants selling the *Finding Nemo* DVD; this shows what happens when you have fewer merchants signed up for those paid listings.

Bottom line? Although you'll often find similar pricing at each price comparison site, this isn't always the case. It's probably worth your while to shop at more than one of these sites in order to find the very best deals.

Using Other Price Comparison Sites

Although the five sites we've looked at so far are the most popular price comparison sites, they're not the only such sites on the Web. In the name of completeness, let's take a very quick look at some of the other sites you can use to compare products and prices.

General Price Comparison Sites

BizRate, Shopping.com, and the other big sites enable you to shop for products across all major product categories. Here are some additional all-category price-comparison sites:

- AimLower (`www.aimlower.com`)
- BuyPath (`www.buypath.com`)
- CheapestRate.com (`www.cheapestrate.com`)
- CompareSite (`www.comparesite.com`)
- FindAll.com (`www.findall.com`)
- NexTag (`www.nextag.com`)
- PriceGrabber.com (`www.pricegrabber.com`)
- PriceSCAN.com (`www.pricescan.com`)
- PricingCentral.com (`www.pricingcentral.com`)

- RoboShopper.com (`www.roboshopper.com`)
- ShopSearchEngine.com (`www.shopsearchengine.com`)

Product-Specific Price Comparison Sites

If you're shopping for only one type of product, you don't necessarily need to navigate all the pages at a multi-category site; you might be better off using a site that compares prices on products within only a single category.

To that end, Table 5.2 presents some price comparison sites that specialize in specific categories of products.

Table 5.2 Price Comparison Sites for Specific Products

Site	URL	Books	CDs	DVDs & Videos	Video Games	Computers	Digital Cameras	Electronics
AAABookSearch	`www.aaabooksearch.com`	X	X	X	X			
Active Buyer's Guide	`www.activebuyersguide.com`					X	X	X
Best Web Buys	`www.bestwebbuys.com`	X	X	X			X	X
Bookfinder	`www.bookfinder.us`	X						
CNET Shopper.com	`shopper.cnet.com`					X	X	X
DVD Price Search	`www.dvdpricesearch.com`			X				
EveryBookstore.com	`www.everybookstore.com`	X						
MetaPrices	`www.metaprices.com`	X	X	X				
Price.com	`www.price.com`	X	X	X		X	X	X
PriceMix	`www.pricemix.com`							X
ShoppingAisles.com	`www.shoppingaisles.com`	X	X	X	X			
StreetPrices	`www.streetprices.com`				X	X	X	X
ValueCompare	`www.valuecompare.com`	X						

What's Next: Comparing Discounts and Promotions

As you've just learned, price comparison sites do a good job of finding the lowest prices available on the Web. But sometimes even lower prices exist, thanks to limited-time promotions, online coupons, and rebate programs. How do you find these special promotions and discounts? Find out in Chapter 6, "Hunting for Rebates, Coupons, and Promotions."

HUNTING FOR REBATES, COUPONS, AND PROMOTIONS

Finding a good price on a specific product isn't the only way to save money online. You can find even bigger bargains by taking advantage of cash-back purchasing programs, manufacturer rebates, and online coupons!

Finding—And Tracking—Traditional Rebates Online

You're probably familiar with traditional product rebates, where the manufacturer sends you a check after you purchase one of its products and fill in the appropriate forms. You can still get manufacturer rebates on purchases you make online, and even use a number of rebate-tracking sites to help you identify current rebate programs. Many of these sites provide manufacturer rebate forms you can print out to help claim your rebates, and enable you to track the progress of your rebate payment after you've mailed it in.

How Rebate-Tracking Sites Work

For example, rebatesHQ.com, shown in Figure 6.1, enables you to search for manufacturer rebates by either manufacturer or product category.

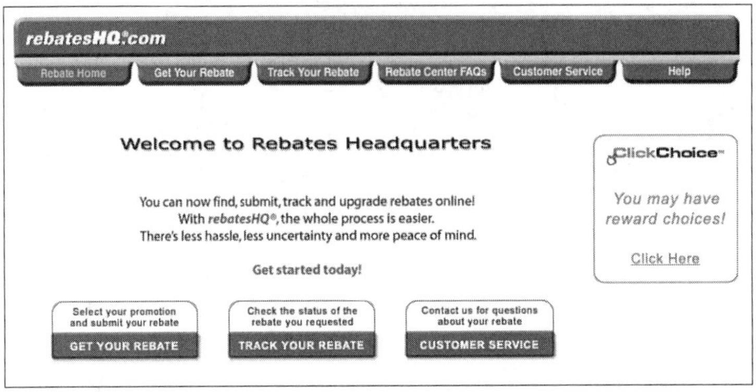

FIGURE 6.1
Use rebatesHQ.com to find and track product rebates.

To find out what rebates are available, select the Get Your Rebate tab. When the Get Your Rebate page appears, as shown in Figure 6.2, you have three ways to search. You can pull down the Search by Manufacturer list to see all rebates from a particular manufacturer; enter a product name or model number in the Search by Product box to search for rebates on a particular product; or pull down the Search by Category list to see all rebates offered in a particular product category.

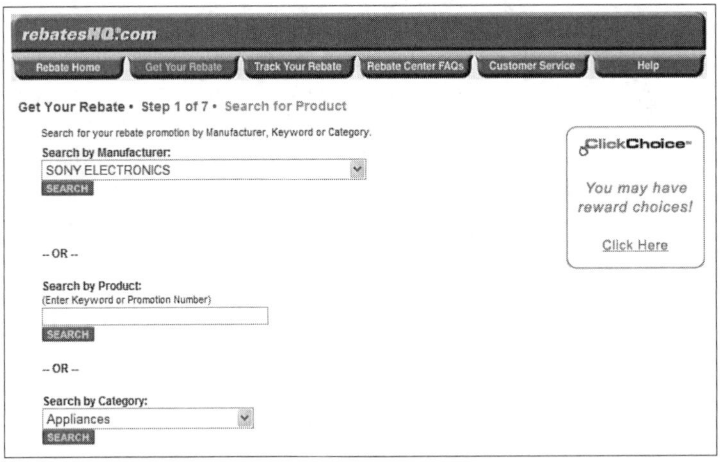

FIGURE 6.2
Searching for manufacturer rebates at rebatesHQ.com.

Click the appropriate Search button to proceed, and you'll see a list of all matching rebates, like that shown in Figure 6.3. Select a given rebate to view more details and fill out the rebate form online. (You'll still probably have to mail in your proof-of-purchase, however.)

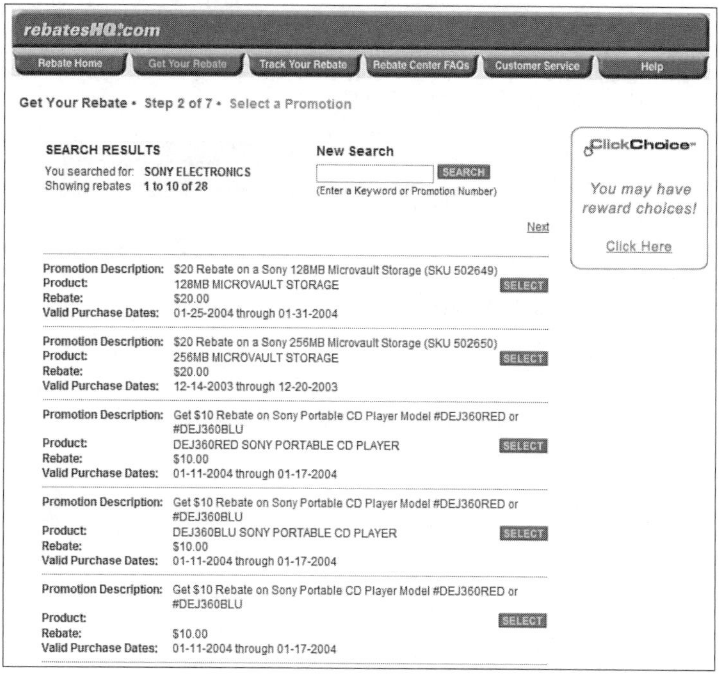

FIGURE 6.3
Viewing all rebates offered by a single manufacturer.

To track the progress of a rebate you've previously submitted, select the Track Your Rebate tab. When the Track Your Rebate page appears, as shown in Figure 6.4, enter either your rebate tracking number or your name and address. Click the Search button, and rebatesHQ.com will tell you what it knows about when you can expect your rebate check in the mail.

Finding Rebate-Tracking Sites

Here are some of the most popular sites for manufacturer rebates:

- myRebates.com (`www.myrebates.com`)
- RebateCatcher.com (`www.rebatecatcher.com`)
- RebatePlace.com (`www.rebateplace.com`)
- rebatesHQ.com (`www.rebateshq.com`)
- RefundSweepers (`www.refundsweepers.com`)

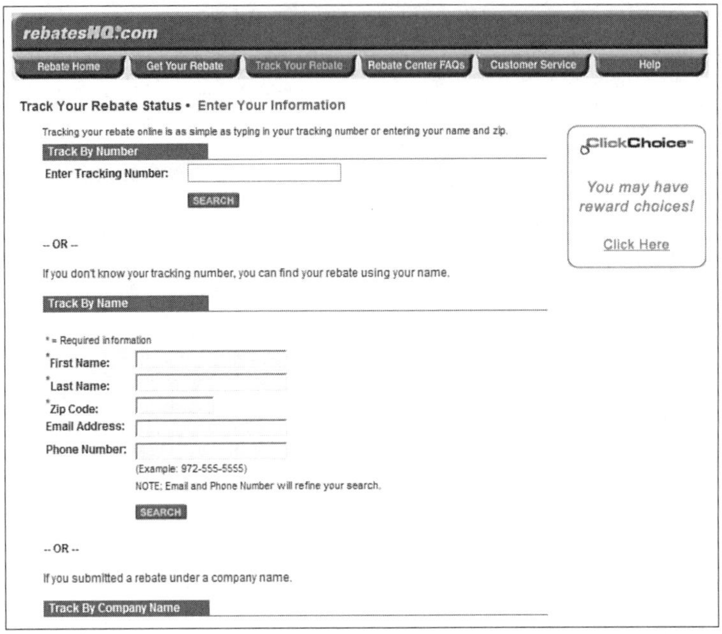

FIGURE 6.4
Tracking the progress of your rebate at rebatesHQ.com.

Getting Cash Back for Your Online Purchases

Wouldn't it be great to get paid for shopping? Well, there's another type of rebate you can take advantage of if you're a frequent online shopper. These are special cash-back purchasing programs, where you earn rebates whenever you shop at qualified merchants. These programs are free to join, and earn you bucks with every purchase you make.

How Cash-Back Programs Work

These online purchasing programs are offered by several different Web sites, all of which make special deals with a variety of online merchants. You have to sign up for the program (at no charge), and then you're directed to shop at participating online retailers.

> **note**
>
> Signing up for an online cash-back program is free of charge; all you have to provide is your name, email address, and street address. The cash-back site makes its money from a commission on the sales you make at participating merchants.

Bargain Hunter's Secret

Whenever you make a purchase from a participating merchant, you're rebated a specified percent of the purchase price. For example, if you sign up for the cash-back program at MoreRebates (shown in Figure 6.5), you can earn a 2% rebate on your purchases at Gateway, a

5% rebate on your purchases at Hammacher Schlemmer, and a 10% rebate on your purchases at Roses.com. You'll receive these rebates in the form of a check at some specified time in the future.

FIGURE 6.5
Sign up for the rebate program at MoreRebates.

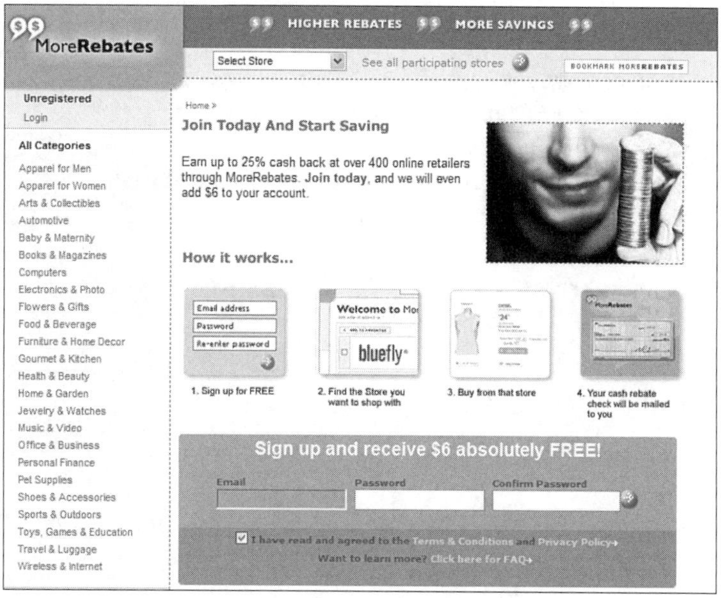

Making sure that your purchases are registered is typically as easy as going to the cash-back site before you start your shopping. Then you link to the retailer you want from the cash-back site; your purchases will then be automatically tracked for you.

Where to Find Online Cash-Back Programs

Most sites offering cash-back programs have deals with hundreds of different online retailers. And these are reputable programs, not the sort of fly-by-night sites that offer big promises in exchange for your (often paid) registration but deliver nothing in return. In fact, that's a good way to tell the good sites from the bad: Reputable cash-back sites don't charge a membership fee.

Some of the most popular of these cash-back sites include

- Ask Mr. Rebates (www.askmrrebates.com)
- Ebates (www.ebates.com)
- MoreRebates (www.morerebates.com)
- PayDrop.com (www.paydrop.com)
- QDeals.com (www.qdeals.com)

- RebateShare.com (www.rebateshare.com)
- Simple Rebates.com (www.simplerebates.com)

Using Online Coupons

Another good source of added savings are online coupons. Or, to be more accurate, online coupon *codes*, because there's really no way to use a printed coupon with an online merchant. What you get instead is a code you can enter when you check out at an online merchant; the coupon savings are deducted from your order when you check out.

note

Some online retailers refer to coupon codes as *promotion codes*. Different name, same deal—big savings for you!

These sites make their money when you use the coupon; the coupon/promotion codes link back to their site, so the merchant knows to pay a small commission on your purchase.

Where to Find Online Coupons

There are a large number of sites that specialize in online coupons.

Here are some of the most popular sites to find online coupons and promotions:

- About.com Coupons/Bargains (couponing.about.com)
- Bargain Boardwalk (www.bargainboardwalk.com)
- Bargain Shopping.org (www.bargainshopping.org)
- Bargain-Central (www.bargain-central.com)
- CouponMountain (www.couponmountain.com)
- Daily eDeals (www.dailyedeals.com)
- dealcoupon (www.dealcoupon.com)
- DealofDay.com (www.dealofday.com)
- dealsdujour.com (www.dealsdujour.com)
- eCoupons (www.ecoupons.com)
- eSmarts.com (www.esmarts.com)
- KovalchikFarms.com (www.kovalchikfarms.com)
- MyCoupons (www.mycoupons.com)
- RefundSweepers (www.refundsweepers.com)
- SlickDeals (www.slickdeals.net)
- Specialoffers.com (www.specialoffers.com)
- TotalDeals.com (www.totaldeals.com)

tip

Many of these sites also enable you to sign up for daily or weekly email newsletters that inform you the newest deals on the Web.

How to Apply an Online Coupon

How you apply an online coupon depends on which site you visit. Some online coupon sites totally automate the process; others just give you the coupon codes for you to apply on your own.

Using a "Click to Save" Coupon Site

Let's look at a more full-service site first. For our example, we'll use MyCoupons (`www.mycoupons.com`), although many other sites work in the same fashion.

As you can see in Figure 6.6, MyCoupons enables you to search for coupons by either product category or merchant. After you browse a bit and find a deal that you can't resist, you'll either see a page full of virtual coupons, like the one in Figure 6.7, or the site will open a pop-up window displaying a specific coupon.

FIGURE 6.6

Browsing for online coupons at MyCoupons.

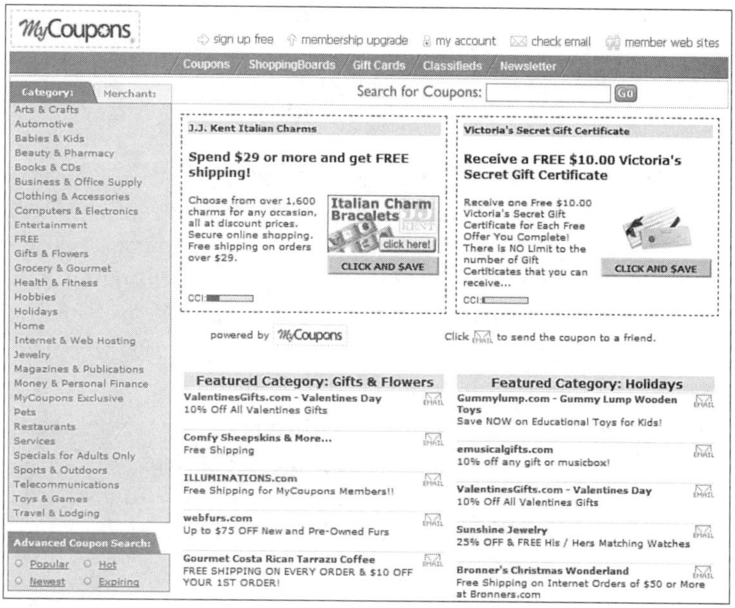

To use a coupon, all you have to do is click either the Click and Save or Redeem Coupon button, or click the coupon itself. This will take you directly to the participating merchant, where you can do your shopping and make your purchase. When you check out, the coupon savings is automatically applied to your order.

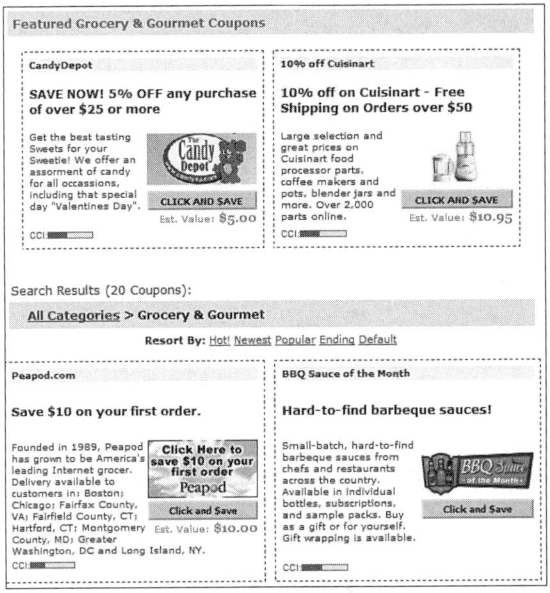
Featured Grocery & Gourmet Coupons
CandyDepot
SAVE NOW! 5% OFF any purchase of over $25 or more
Get the best tasting Sweets for your Sweetie! We offer an assortment of candy for all occassions, including that special day "Valentines Day".
CLICK AND SAVE
Est. Value: $5.00
10% off Cuisinart
10% off on Cuisinart - Free Shipping on Orders over $50
Large selection and great prices on Cuisinart food processor parts, coffee makers and pots, blender jars and more. Over 2,000 parts online.
CLICK AND SAVE
Est. Value: $10.95
Search Results (20 Coupons):
All Categories > Grocery & Gourmet
Resort By: Hot! Newest Popular Ending Default
Peapod.com
Save $10 on your first order.
Founded in 1989, Peapod has grown to be America's leading Internet grocer. Delivery available to customers in: Boston; Chicago; Fairfax County, VA; Fairfield County, CT; Hartford, CT; Montgomery County, MD; Greater Washington, DC and Long Island, NY.
Click Here to save $10 on your first order
Peapod
Click and Save
Est. Value: $10.00
BBQ Sauce of the Month
Hard-to-find barbeque sauces!
Small-batch, hard-to-find barbeque sauces from chefs and restaurants across the country. Available in individual bottles, subscriptions, and sample packs. Buy as a gift or for yourself. Gift wrapping is available.
Click and Save

FIGURE 6.7
Click a coupon to start saving.

Applying a Coupon Code Manually

Other online coupon sites simply provide you with the coupon code, which you then can apply yourself when you make a qualifying purchase. For example, Bargain Boardwalk (`www.bargainboardwalk.com`), shown in Figure 6.8, lists coupons in a variety of product categories and for a number of different merchants. Below each coupon listing is the coupon code; you enter this code when you make your purchase and check out at that merchant's site.

In the case of Bargain Boardwalk, when you click the coupon listing, a pop-up window (like the one in Figure 6.9) appears and displays the coupon code, and the main browser window takes you to the home page of the participating merchant. Keep the pop-up window open so that you can access the coupon code when you're ready to check out.

Using Printed Coupons Online

It's an odd fact of online shopping that traditional printed coupons often can't be applied online. This is a particular issue with online grocers; you're probably used to handing the grocery clerk a handful of coupons to apply against your purchase, which you can't do online. This might sometimes make your online purchase less of a deal than purchasing at a traditional store.

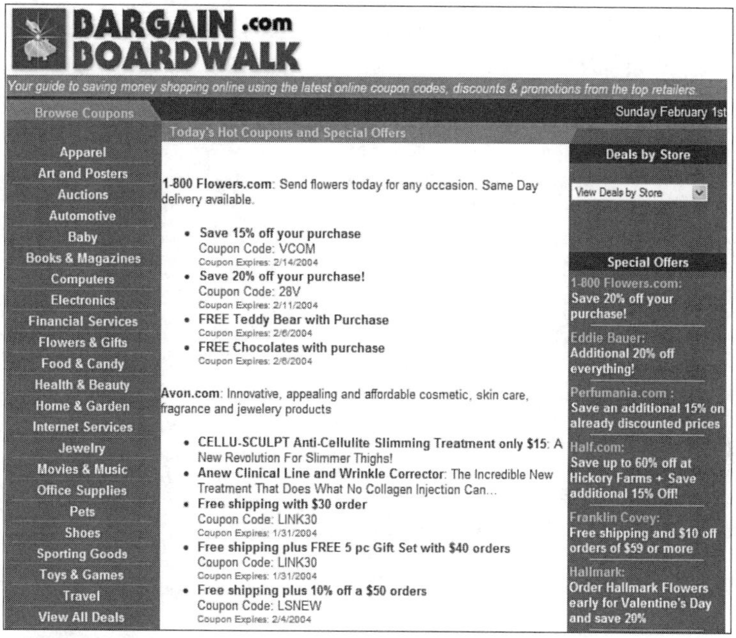

FIGURE 6.8
Browse the coupon listings at Bargain Boardwalk.

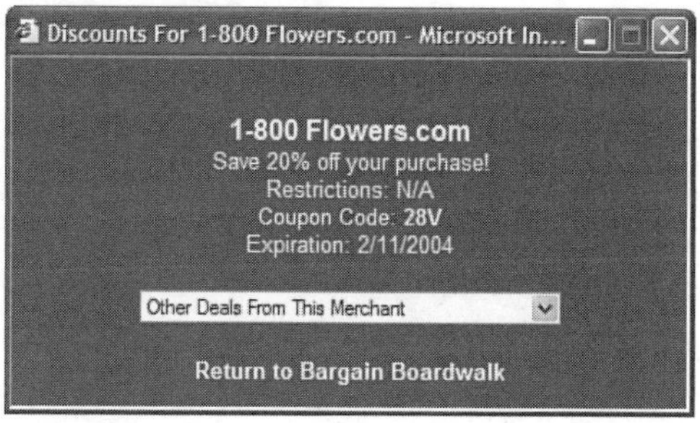

FIGURE 6.9
Access the coupon code from this pop-up window.

Bargain Hunter's Secret

That said, many printed coupons *can* be used at online retailers—especially coupons offered by dual-channel retailers, such as Office Depot or CompUSA. Look for a promotion code printed on the coupon, and enter that code when you check out at that retailer. It might not always work—but you don't lose anything by trying!

tip

Want to learn more about online coupons and rebates? Then check out the useful information at CouponsandRefunds.com (`www.couponsandrefunds.com`)—including a list of rebate clearinghouses and a large database of online coupon codes.

Searching for Free Shipping and Other Promotions

Many of the online coupon sites just mentioned also serve as guides to other types of online promotions—sales, discounts, free shipping offers, and so on. For example, if you go to Specialoffers.com and click the Free Shipping tab, you'll find a list of merchants offering free shipping on qualified orders, as shown in Figure 6.10.

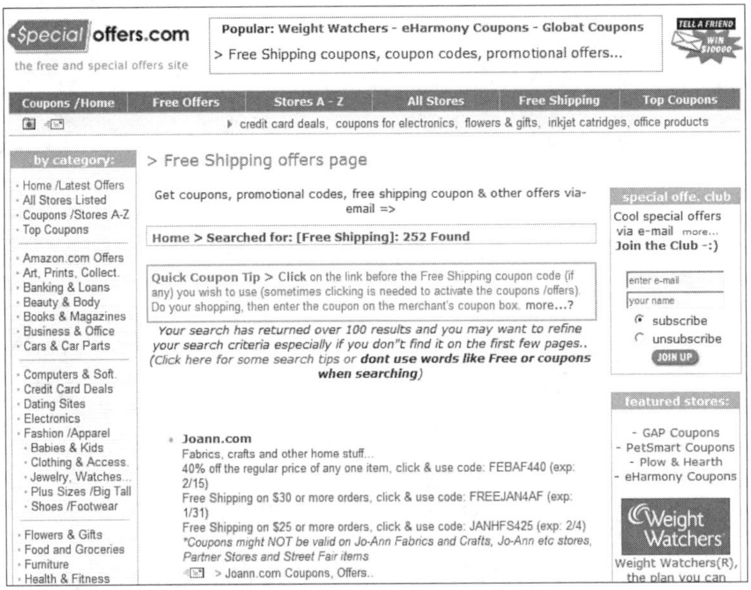

FIGURE 6.10
Searching for free shipping offers at Specialoffers.com.

Other online coupon sites list similar special offers mixed in with their coupon codes. When you're hunting for online bargains, it's a good idea to check these sites to find out what promotions are available where.

Searching for Other Free Stuff Online

If you don't mind sorting through a bevy of come-ons, it's even possible to find things for free on the Internet. Yes, most of this free stuff is tied into other offers, but still—free is good!

What kind of free stuff am I talking about? Well, there are contests, new customer giveaways (like the old 12 CDs for a penny deal), buy one/get one free deals, product samples, trial versions, and the like. (Figure 6.11 shows some of the free stuff available at Free-Stuff.com.)

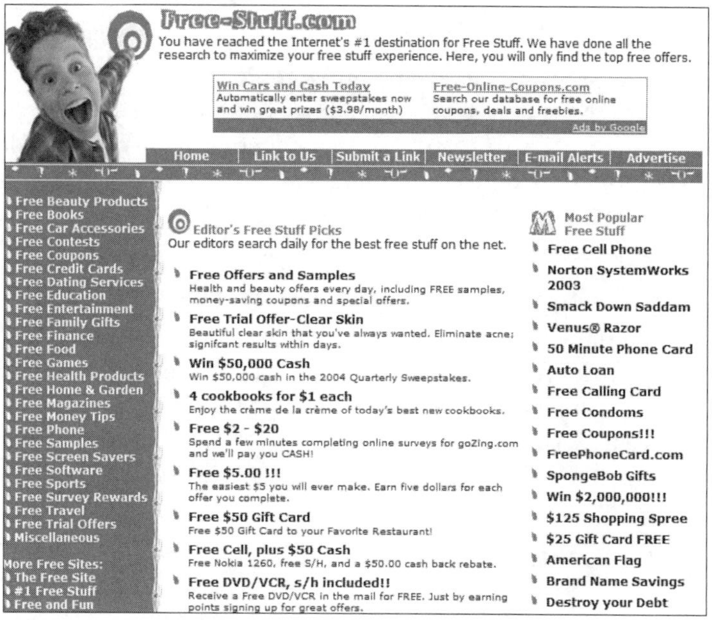

FIGURE 6.11

Find free stuff online at Free-Stuff.com.

Where can you find these free offers? Try these links:

- #1 Free Stuff (`www.1freestuff.com`)
- Best Free Stuff Online (`www.bestfreestuffonline.com`)
- Free-Stuff.com (`www.free-stuff.com`)
- FreeClutter.com (`www.freeclutter.com`)
- FreeShop.com (`www.freeshop.com`)
- Totally Free Stuff (`www.totallyfreestuff.com`)

When you're shopping these "free stuff" sites, be careful to read all the fine print. A lot of these free offers come with strings attached, so make sure of what you're getting before you sign up. At the very least, you'll be expected to provide some personal information—name, address, phone number—that could be used for future marketing purposes. You might also have to sign up for some program in order to get a freebie; these programs might have a monthly subscription price that kicks in after a few months at no charge. Remember, there are few free lunches in life, so it's *caveat emptor* as far as these free deals go.

Part II 6

Using the Web to Print In-Store Coupons

This book is about online bargain hunting, but that doesn't mean we can just ignore ways to use the Internet to save money at traditional merchants. Case in point: Web sites that enable you to print out traditional in-store coupons for everything from grocery items to fast food restaurants.

How to Print an Online Coupon

These in-store coupon sites, such as H.O.T! Coupons (shown in Figure 6.12) work by offering coupons that you can print out on your own computer printer. You typically have to enter your ZIP code (so that you'll see those coupons available for your area), and then choose a category or merchant. The coupon is then displayed onscreen, as shown in Figure 6.13; print the coupon on your computer printer and use it as you would any traditional printed coupon.

H.O.T!
COUPONS
your local coupon source
LOCAL SAVINGS - [HOME] [OFFICE] [TRAVEL]
Search
- For H.O.T! Coupons in your area!
Search by Zip Code
46032
GO!
Search by Geography
Alaska
GO!
ENTER YOUR CITY
Welcome to H.O.T! Coupons!
We are a leader in online coupons, saving you money on products and services you use everyday near your Home, Office or when you Travel. Just enter your zip code or city/state and click "GO!"
MONEY MAILER
"Like Getting Money In Your Mailbox"
Advertise with us to drive customers into your business everyday.
H.O.T! Coupons Savings Club
Join the Savings Club for your own personal coupon page and email with new coupons and special offers in your area.
About Us
Advertise on H.O.T! Coupons
Savings Club
FAQ's
Products & Services
Privacy Statement
Franchise Opportunities
Contact Us

FIGURE 6.12
Searching for printable coupons at H.O.T! Coupons.

Where to Find Printable Coupons

There are a number of sites that enable you to print in-store coupons on your computer. The most popular of these sites include

- CoolSavings.com (`www.coolsavings.com`)
- CouponCart.com (`www.couponcart.com`)
- CouponPages.com (`www.couponpages.com`)
- H.O.T! Coupons (`www.hotcoupons.com`)
- KEYCODE (`www.keycode.com`)
- ShoppingList.com (`www.shoppinglist.com`)

- SiteforSavings.com (www.siteforsavings.com)
- Valpack.com (www.valpack.com)
- ValuPage (www.valupage.com)

FIGURE 6.13
Print this coupon to use at a traditional retailer.

Finding "Bricks and Mortar" Sales Online

Just as you can use the Web to find and print coupons for use with traditional retailers, you can also use the Web to find the best deals at those "bricks and mortar" stores. SalesHound (www.saleshound.com), shown in Figure 6.14, lists advertised sales at hundreds of national and local retailers. All you have to do is enter your ZIP code, and SalesHound displays all the sales and deals it knows about in nearby stores, from CVS Pharmacy to Home Depot. It's a great way to do your shopping homework before you leave home!

FIGURE 6.14
Search for "bricks and mortar" sales with SalesHound.

What's Next: Where to Save Money on Your Online Purchases

Now that you know lots of ways to save money on your online purchases, it's time to find out just where the best bargains are. Turn to Chapter 7, "Hunting for Bargains at Online Malls, Catalogs, and Department Stores," to learn more.

7 HUNTING FOR BARGAINS AT ONLINE MALLS, CATALOGS, AND DEPARTMENT STORES

The Internet is filled with bargains—you just have to know where to look. When it comes to finding online retailers, you can look at an online mall, at an online department store, or in an online catalog. They're all good places to find online savings.

Bargain Hunting at Online Malls

There are untold thousands of merchants selling their wares online. Where most larger e-tailers have their own dedicated Web sites, many smaller merchants gather together under umbrella sites called *online malls*. These malls enable you to shop at each merchant individually, or search the entire mall for those products you want.

Bargain Hunter's Secret

One of the primary benefits of using an online mall is that you can often find smaller merchants that might not otherwise show up on your radar screen. Another advantage offered by some online malls is the ability to search all the merchants in the mall for particular items; that is, you don't have to visit each merchant separately to find the items you want.

General-Interest Malls

There are a ton of these virtual malls on the Web. The most popular type of online mall is just like a "bricks and mortar" mall in that it hosts merchants across all product categories—hundreds of them, big and small. (But there's no Orange Julius online—darn it!)

All of these malls operate in a similar fashion. For example, the InternetMall, shown in Figure 7.1, enables you to view stores by product category, or search for specific stores or products. When you select a product category, all the stores in the mall offering that type of product are listed; click the individual store link to go directly to that store.

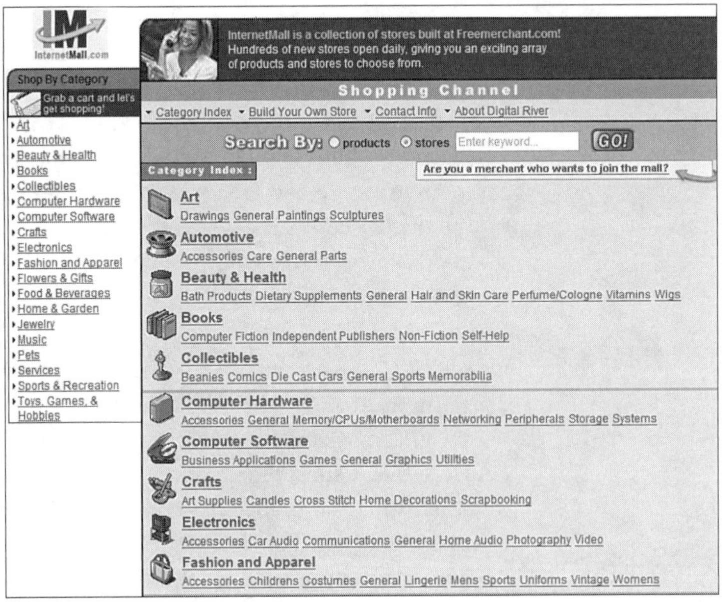

FIGURE 7.1
Shopping a variety of small merchants at the InternetMall.

With some online malls, participating stores are linked together in a common mall-wide shopping cart. If a mall features this type of common shopping cart, you can make purchases at multiple stores, but have to check out only once. Note, however, that this type of linkedcheckout is becoming less common as the stores themselves develop more independence.

Table 7.1 presents a short list of some of the most popular general-interest online malls.

Table 7.1 General Interest Online Malls

Mall	URL
@InterMall	www.1mall.com
ePlanetShopping.com	www.eplanetshopping.com
FingerTipShopper	www.fingertipshopper.com
Internet Store List	www.internetstorelist.com
InternetMall	www.internetmall.com
Shopping-Headquarters	www.shopping-headquarters.com
ShoppingAide.com	www.shoppingaide.com
SkyMall	www.skymall.com
WebSquare.com	www.websquare.com

Note that merchants aren't necessarily tied to just one mall. It's not unusual to find the same merchants at multiple malls. Still, you'll probably need to shop at more than one online mall to find all the merchants you're looking for.

note Yes, the online SkyMall is the same one you know from all those in-flight catalogs.

Specialty Malls

Other online malls are more focused in their appeal, grouping together merchants that offer products to a defined segment of the marketplace. Some of these specialty malls are shown in Table 7.2.

Table 7.2 Specialty Online Malls

Mall	URL	Description
African American Shopping Mall	www.aasm.com	Afro-centric products (shown in Figure 7.2)
Antique and Collectible Mall	www.tias.com	Antiques, art, and collectibles
Craft Ireland	www.craftireland.com	Irish gifts and crafts from more than 450 merchants
Crafty Crafters	www.craftycrafters.com	Crafts and artwork from 90 small merchants
digiCHOICE	www.digichoice.com	Customizable products, such as computers, furniture, and jewelry
Elegant-Lifestyle.com	www.elegant-lifestyle.com	High-end luxury items
Hippy Buggs Shopping Mall	www.hippybuggs.com	Merchants "with a hippy flair"
Jewelry Mall	www.jewelrymall.com	Jewelry

Table 7.2 Continued

Mall	URL	Description
OddSpot.com	www.oddspot.com	Unusual and hard-to-find products and services
Wired Seniors	www.wiredseniors.com	Merchandise and services of interest to the over-50 age group

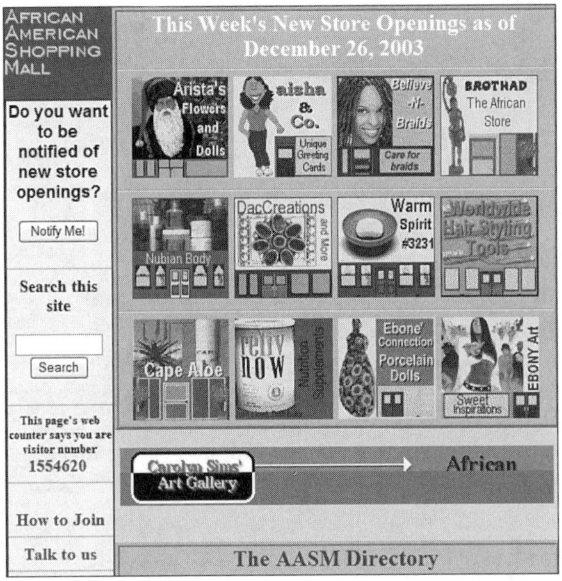

FIGURE 7.2
Shopping for Afro-centric products at the African American Shopping Mall.

Country-Specific Malls

Then there are the country-specific online malls, which present local merchants for shoppers outside the United States. Some of these malls will ship overseas, but in general these are retailers specifically for citizens of a given country.

For our Canadian shoppers, check out ShopStiX Consumer Mall (www.shopstix.com) and Cybershopping.ca (www.cybershopping.ca), both of which offer goods from Canadian online retailers. And if you're in the U.K., the top English online malls are Shopping A to Z (www.shoppingatoz.co.uk) and ShoppingTrolly.net (www.shoppingtrolley.net).

Bargain Hunting with Online Catalogs

Another popular type of online merchant is the online cataloger. These are traditional catalog or direct-mail merchants, such as L.L. Bean and Lands' End, who have migrated their operations—and their bargains—to the Web.

Shopping from a Catalog Merchant—Online

I really like online catalog merchants. In general, these merchants run extremely efficient operations, and are often easier to deal with than newer online-only retailers. That's because these folks have been doing the nonretail thing for years, and have it all down to a formula—detailed product descriptions, multiple product photos, streamlined ordering, efficient packing and shipping, and first-rate customer service (complete with toll-free phone numbers). Shopping at an online catalog merchant is just like purchasing from one of its catalogs; browse or search for the items you want, and then click a button to make your purchase. Unlike some other retailers, these sites offer few hassles and even fewer surprises.

Shopping from an online catalog is much like shopping from a printed catalog. Let's look at Lands' End, shown in Figure 7.3, as an example. The various product categories are tabbed across the top of the home page; when you access a category page, you see specific types of products listed down the left side of the page.

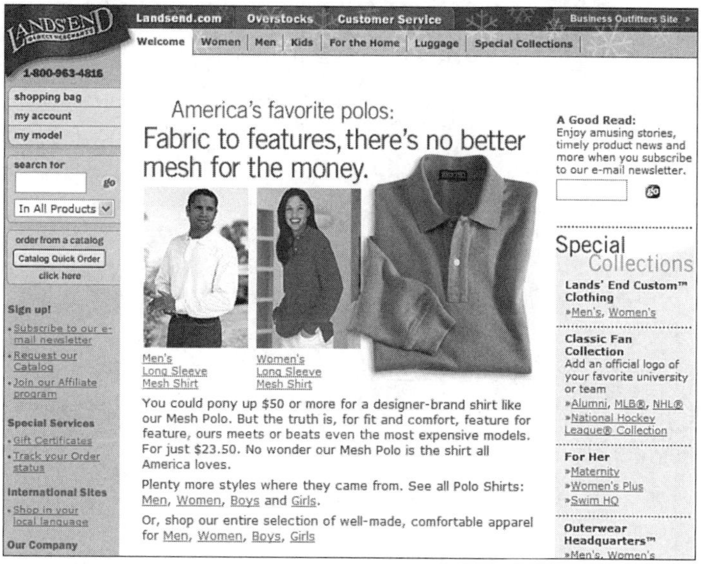

FIGURE 7.3
The online version of the Lands' End catalog.

When you click through to an individual item, you get a lot of detailed product information. As you can see in Figure 7.4, there's big picture of the product, accompanied by the same descriptive info found in the printed catalog. You can scroll down to the bottom of the page for even more information, or click the Try It On My Virtual Model link to see what the item looks like when actually worn. Click a color to see a larger color swatch, and then click a size and color to order the item. It's really quite easy, and Lands' End pulls out all the stops to make sure that you're comfortable with what you're buying.

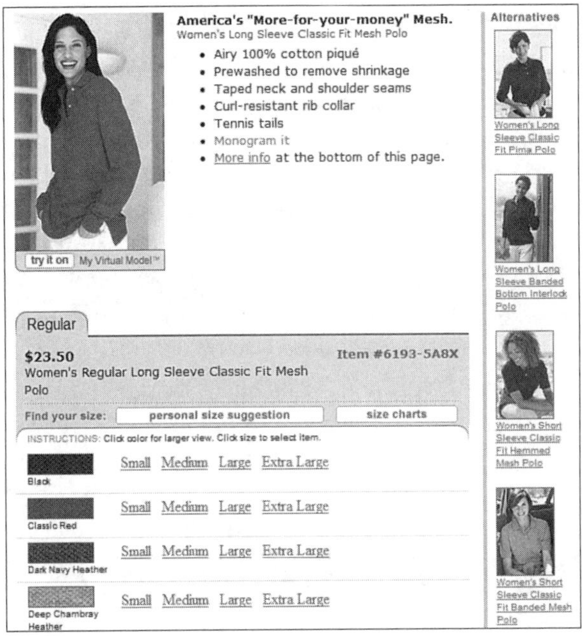

FIGURE 7.4 Shopping for individual products at Lands' End.

Most online catalogs operate in a similar fashion. The most popular of these online catalog merchants are listed in Table 7.3.

Table 7.3 Online Catalog Merchants

Merchant	URL
Crate and Barrel	www.crateandbarrel.com
Crutchfield	www.crutchfield.com
Eddie Bauer	www.eddiebauer.com
Hammacher Schlemmer	www.hammacher.com
Harry and David	www.harryanddavid.com
J. Crew	www.jcrew.com
J. Jill	www.jjill.com
L.L. Bean	www.llbean.com
Lands' End	www.landsend.com
Sharper Image	www.sharperimage.com
Spiegel	www.spiegel.com
Williams-Sonoma	www.williams-sonoma.com

For the best bargains at these sites, look for links to sale and clearance merchandise—or to the retailer's online outlet store. For example, the J. Jill site offers a Sale page, shown in Figure 7.5, where all items it has on sale are displayed—including end-of-season clearance items. Lands' End has a similar Overstocks page, which features closeouts and reduced-priced items.

FIGURE 7.5
Shopping for sale merchandise at J. Jill.

Searching for Print Catalogs Online

Despite the obvious appeal of online catalog sites, the printed catalog business is still quite healthy. Some consumers prefer shopping from a printed catalog, and ordering from a real live person over the telephone. If this is you, you can still use the Internet to obtain catalogs from most major catalog merchants.

There are a number of Web sites that either enable you to order your favorite catalogs online (for regular mail delivery) or view the printed catalogs on the Web. These sites are shown in Table 7.4.

Table 7.4 Print Catalog Sites

Site	URL
CatalogCity.com	`www.catalogcity.com`
CatalogDirect	`www.catalogdirect.com`
CatalogLink	`www.cataloglink.com`
Catalogs.com	`www.catalogs.com`
Google Catalogs	`catalogs.google.com`

My favorite of these sites is Google Catalogs, shown in Figure 7.6. This site works like the main Google search site in that you can either search for specific catalogs or products, or browse through the major product categories on the home page. Find a catalog you like, and you can read it online, as you can see in Figure 7.7; click the thumbnail image of a two-page spread to display it full-size onscreen.

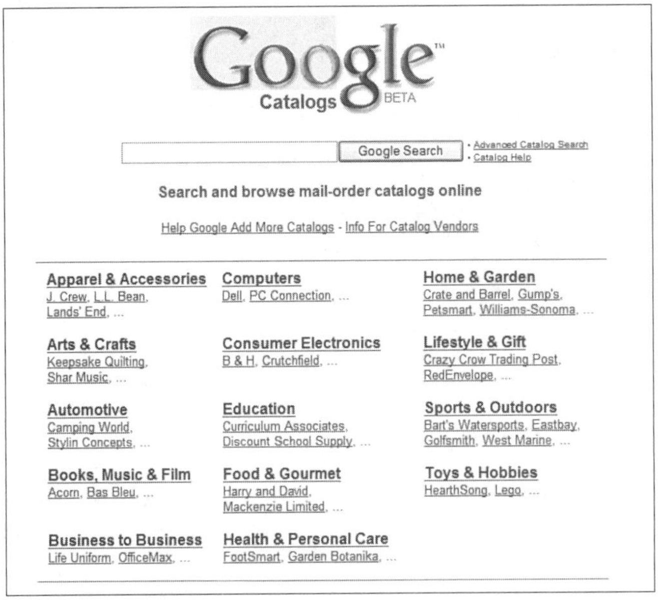

FIGURE 7.6
Searching for catalogs at Google Catalogs.

Unlike some online catalog sites, you can't order directly from Google Catalogs. Instead, look for the toll-free number on the printed catalog you're reading, and then call in your order.

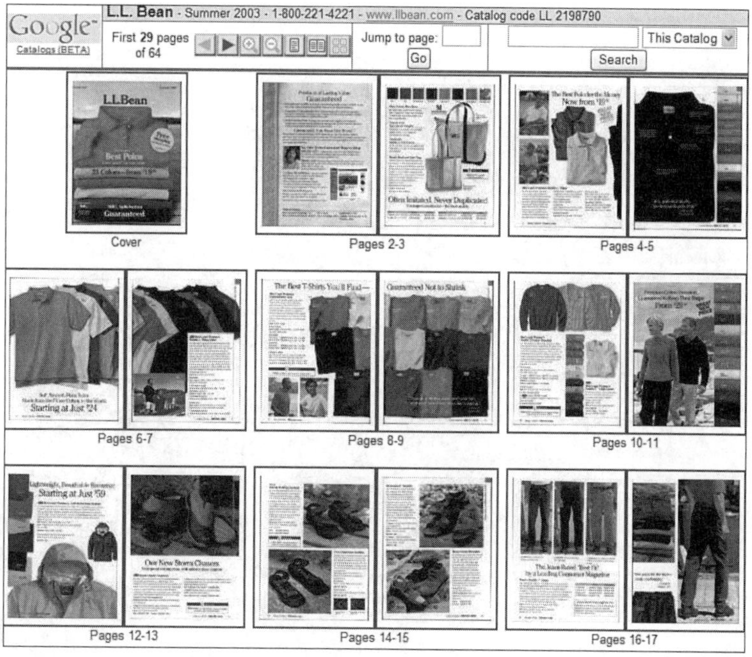

FIGURE 7.7
Browsing printed catalogs online.

Bargain Hunting at an Online Department Store

Another source of online bargains is the online department store. All the big mass merchants and department stores are on the Web, often with their entire stock of merchandise available for online ordering. Other stores, such as Nordstrom (shown in Figure 7.8), offer a slightly more limited selection—although still at Web-friendly prices.

The top online department stores are shown in Table 7.5.

Table 7.5 Online Department Stores

Department Store	URL
Bloomingdale's	bloomingdalesbymail.dailyshopper.com
Boscov's	www.boscovs.com
Dillard's	www.dillards.com
JCPenney	www.jcpenney.com
KMart	www.kmart.com
Kohl's	www.kohls.com
Macy's	www.macys.com
Neiman Marcus	www.neimanmarcus.com
Nordstrom	www.nordstrom.com

Part II

7

Table 7.5 Continued

Department Store	URL
Saks Fifth Avenue	`www.saksfifthavenue.com`
Sears	`www.sears.com`
Target	`www.target.com`
Wal-Mart	`www.walmart.com`

FIGURE 7.8
Nordstrom—a premier online department store.

When you're shopping at an online department store, look for links to clearance sales, closeouts, and the like. For example, the JCPenney site includes a link to its Online Outlet Store, shown in Figure 7.9, which offers a variety of closeout merchandise and specials. You can often find bargains here that aren't available in the traditional retail locations.

> **tip**
>
> And while we're on the topic of big retailers, let's not forget the wholesale clubs. These warehouse-like stores, such as Costco (`www.costco.com`) and Sam's Club (`www.samsclub.com`), also offer bargains to members at their Web sites.

FIGURE 7.9
Shopping for bargains at the JCPenney Online Outlet Store.

Bargain Hunting with Online Shopping Networks

The Internet is also home to that unique type of retailer known as the home shopping network. Yes, these are the same shopping networks you find on cable or satellite television, selling the same assortment of merchandise for the same prices. The big advantage to shopping these networks on the Web is that you have access to all their merchandise all the time—not just when it's featured on TV.

The most popular of these online shopping networks are shown in Table 7.6.

Table 7.6 Online Shopping Networks

Shopping Network	URL
Home Shopping Network	`www.hsn.com`
QVC	`www.qvc.com`
Shop At Home Network	`www.shopathometv.com`
ShopNBC	`www.shopnbc.com`

Bargain Hunter's Secret

On all these sites, the best bargains can be found among the clearance merchandise. On the Home Shopping Network site, look in the Clearance and Primetime Outlet sections. On the QVC site, look in the Clearance section, shown in Figure 7.10. On the Shop At Home Network site, check the Shopping Events and Clearance sections. And on the ShopNBC site, look for bargains on the Clearance tab.

FIGURE 7.10
Shopping for clearance merchandise at the QVC site.

What's Next: Hunting for Closeout Merchandise

All the sites in this chapter specialize in selling brand-new merchandise, although they sometimes offer closeout items as well. As you no doubt know, these closeouts are often some of the best bargains available. But did you know that there are entire Web sites devoted to nothing but closeout merchandise? Learn more in Chapter 8, "Hunting for Closeout, Overstock, and Wholesale Bargains."

8

HUNTING FOR CLOSEOUT, OVERSTOCK, AND WHOLESALE BARGAINS

Some of the biggest online bargains come from closeout and overstock items—new or refurbished goods that retailers and manufacturers price to move fast. There are all sorts of outlets for these bargain items on the Web, from bulk liquidators to online outlet stores. Although this type of bargain hunting isn't for everyone (you might not really want an older or refurbished item), it's a way to find some terrific deals.

Secrets of Online Liquidators

Some of the lowest prices online are offered by online liquidators. These are companies that purchase surplus items from other businesses in bulk. These items might be closeouts, factory seconds, customer returns, salvaged items, or overstocked merchandise—products the manufacturer made too many of and wants to get rid of. Liquidators help manufacturers and retailers dispose of this unwanted merchandise. And there are lots of liquidators now operating on the Web, selling these goods direct to consumers at bargain prices.

Bulk Liquidators

Just as liquidators purchase their inventory in bulk, you sometimes have to buy from them in bulk. Although some liquidators sell single quantities (we'll discuss them next), others only sell what are called *lots*. That means buying ten or twenty or a hundred units of a particular item or mix of items. You get a really good price for buying in quantity, of course, which is part of the appeal.

What kind of lots are we talking about? How about 280 pairs of athletic shoes, or 50 digital cameras, or 1,000 units of *The Addams Family* TV show on VHS tape—just for a start. From these kinds of numbers, it's easy to see that these liquidation sites cater to the resale market (and they're also good sources of merchandise to sell on eBay). That said, it's possible to find bulk deals that you as an individual can take advantage of.

The key to buying from a bulk liquidator is to pick and choose among the available deals. Try to find deals on merchandise that you can really use, packaged in manageable lots. Skip those "big lot" items that don't make a lot of sense for you. And if you don't want to deal with the commitment to a large quantity of a particular item, skip the bulk liquidators entirely and shop only at those sites that let you buy one item at a time.

tip

When it comes to buying from bulk liquidators, consider joining together with friends and neighbors to split some of these bulk orders. Even though you might not have 999 friends who are big *Addams Family* fans, you might be able to work with some of the smaller assortments of more common goods.

Finding a Bulk Liquidation Site

If you're curious about buying from a bulk liquidator, Table 8.1 lists some sites to check out.

Table 8.1 Bulk Liquidators

Bulk Liquidator	URL	Description
America's Best Closeouts	www.abcloseouts.com	Offers used and second-hand jeans and clothing
American Merchandise Liquidation	www.amlinc.com	Handles closeouts, overstocks, customer returns, and salvaged merchandise in a variety of categories
AmeriSurplus	www.amerisurplus.com	Sells salvaged merchandise by the pallet, including automotive supplies, groceries, small appliances and electronics, sporting goods, and toys
Liquidation.com	www.liquidation.com	Offers surplus, closeout, and returned merchandise in a variety of categories

Table 8.1 Continued

Bulk Liquidator	URL	Description
My Web Wholesaler	www.mywebwholesaler.com	Offers box lots, pallets, and truckloads of merchandise obtained from major department store returns, closeouts, overstocks, and liquidations
Salvage Closeouts	www.salvagecloseouts.com	Offers liquidated merchandise and department store closeouts in a wide variety of categories, as well as a variety of pallet and truckload specials
TDW Closeouts	www.tdwcloseouts.com	Distributes department store returns and closeout merchandise, including liquidated, salvage, overstock, and surplus items
USA Closeouts	www.usacloseouts.com	Offers brand-name department store closeouts

Bidding on Liquidated Merchandise

The biggest of these sites is Liquidation.com, shown in Figure 8.1. Liquidation.com actually serves as a middleman between the seller (the original manufacturer or retailer) and the buyer (you). Goods are sold in an online auction format, so you'll find yourself bidding on items just as you would in an eBay auction; all auctions start at $100. You can even pay for your merchandise with PayPal.

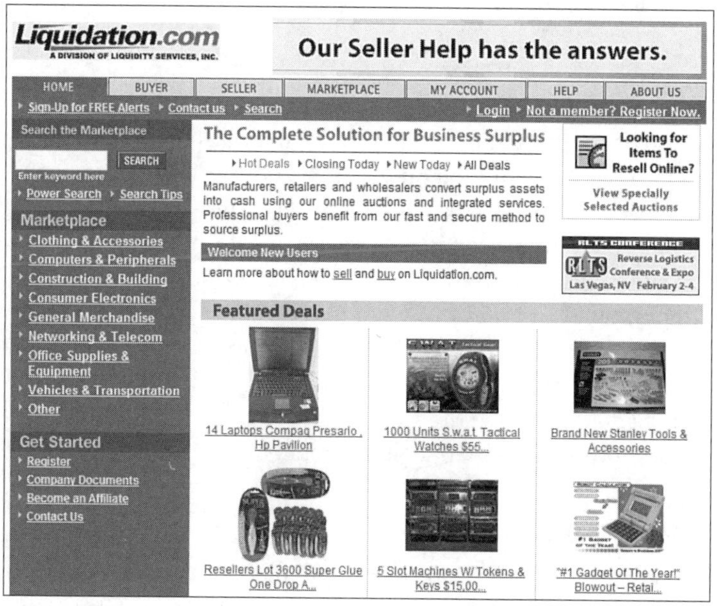

FIGURE 8.1
Bid on large lots of liquidated merchandise at Liquidation.com.

Let's take a quick look at how you purchase closeout merchandise from Liquidation.com. You start by registering at the site, just as you would at eBay or any online auction site. After you've registered, you can search or browse for merchandise from the Marketplace tab. Locate an item you're interested in, and the site displays the auction page shown in Figure 8.2. This page indicates what you're buying, how many items are in the lot, and the current bid price, on both a per-item and total lot basis.

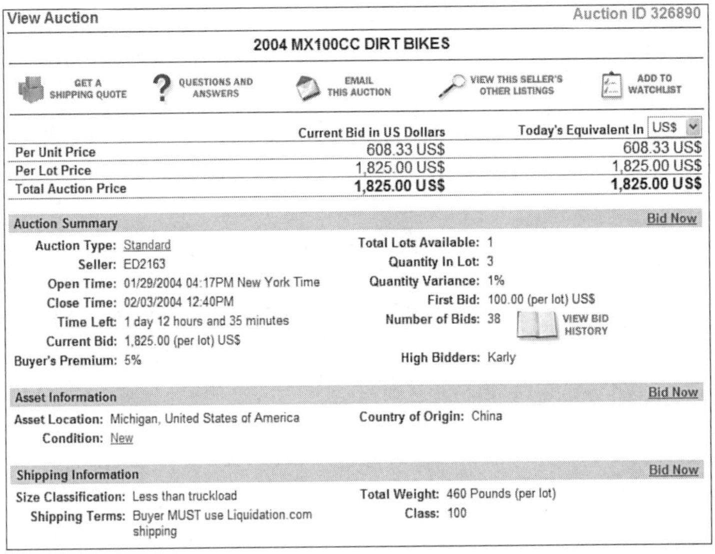

FIGURE 8.2
Placing a bid on liquidated merchandise.

You place your bid by scrolling to the bottom of the page and entering an amount in the Your Maximum Bid box. When you click the Submit Bid button, the auction works just like an eBay auction in that the site's proxy bidding software automatically handles the bidding process for you. If you win the auction, you pay the listing merchant and arrange shipment. Just make sure you really want those 3 dirt bikes—or 50 digital cameras!

> **caution**
>
> Many bulk liquidators offer no-name or lesser-quality merchandise. Make sure that you're comfortable with what you're buying—including the quantity—before you make a bulk purchase.

Single-Item Liquidators

If you'd rather skip the large lots and buy one item at a time, check out a single-item liquidator. Buying from one of these sites is like shopping at any other online retailer, with the caveat that you're buying closeout merchandise at very good prices. Unlike the new merchandise you purchase from traditional wholesalers, many liquidators sell their goods as-is; if it's bad, you're out of luck. Other liquidators offer a limited money-back guarantee of some sort, so you're not completely on the hook. Make sure you know what sort of guarantee (if any) the site offers before you place an order.

Shopping at a Single-Item Liquidator

Let's use the SmartBargains liquidation site as an example. As you can see in Figure 8.3, SmartBargains looks a lot like a normal retailing site. Browse through the categories or search for specific items, and you'll end up on an individual product page. The savings on these closeout items is often considerable. Place your order, and the item is promptly shipped from the SmartBargains warehouse.

FIGURE 8.3

Shopping for single closeout items at SmartBargains.

Bargain Hunter's Secret

Interestingly, many of these closeout sites have clearance sections of their own—closeout items that are *really* priced to move. For example, SmartBargains has a Bargain Bin page that features items discounted up to 80% off. The site also has a Last Chance page, shown in Figure 8.4, that lists items that are close to selling out—and when a closeout item is gone, it's really gone!

FIGURE 8.4
Last chance closeouts at SmartBargains.

Finding a Single-Item Liquidation Site

Table 8.2 presents some of the more popular single-item liquidation sites, and the types of merchandise they offer.

Table 8.2 Single-Item Liquidators

Liquidator	URL	Description
Bid4Assets	`www.bid4assets.com`	Offers merchandise obtained from bankruptcies, private companies, and the government, primarily high-ticket items in single quantity; sells both single items and large lots
Closeouts America	`www.closeoutsamerica.com`	Offers brand-name merchandise at closeout prices, in most major categories
Luxury Brands	`www.luxurybrandsllc.com`	Offers higher-end surplus merchandise than you find at other sites, including luxury branded European clothing, accessories, and gift items from Giorgio Armani, Ralph Lauren Polo, Givenchy, Gucci, and Burberry; sells both single items and large lots

Table 8.2 Continued

Liquidator	URL	Description
Overstock.com	`www.overstock.com`	Offers name-brand merchandise in most major categories
SmartBargains	`www.smartbargains.com`	Offers manufacturer closeouts and over-runs in most major product categories
Top Choice Closeouts	`www.topchoicecloseouts.com`	Offers closeout, discount, and overstock products in all major categories; sells both single items and large lots

Other Places to Find Clearance Merchandise

If an online liquidator isn't quite your cup of tea, the Web is still a great place to find clearance merchandise. Let's look at a few more options.

Retailer Clearance Sections

Bargain Hunter's Secret

First, look for the clearance sections at major online retailers. You might have to do a little hunting, but chances are there's a Clearance link *somewhere* on the retailer's home page.

For example, Sears does a good job of burying its Clearance link (it's hidden in the More Ways to Save section), but when you find it you're taken to Sears' Clearance Center, shown in Figure 8.5. Here you'll find closeout merchandise in most major product categories—Appliances, Automotive, Computers & Office, Electronics, Home, Kids, Lawn & Garden, Tools, and Toys & Games.

You'll often find more and different clearance merchandise online than you will in the merchant's retail stores. Just remember, this merchandise is limited in quantity—so if you see something you want, snatch it up while it lasts!

Factory Outlet Stores

Bargain Hunter's Secret

Along the same lines, many manufacturers sell clearance and refurbished merchandise at special online "outlet stores," typically accessible from the company's home page. A good example of this is Dell Outlet (`www.dell.com/outlet/`), shown in Figure 8.6. This outlet store sells refurbished Dell computer systems, repackaged to original factory specs. All merchandise on this site comes with a 30-day guarantee; savings are considerable.

FIGURE 8.5

Shopping for close-out merchandise at Sears' Clearance Center.

FIGURE 8.6

Browsing for reconditioned computers at Dell Outlet.

Secrets of Buying Wholesale

If you're a hardcore bargain hunter, you might want to bypass the retailer completely by buying wholesale. Wholesale distributors are those middlemen who buy from the manufacturer and sell to small retailers. Some wholesalers will also sell direct to consumers—although a minimum dollar order might be required.

How to Buy Merchandise from a Wholesaler

For example, CKBProducts.com (`www.ckbproducts.com`), shown in Figure 8.7, is a distributor of luggage, housewares, sporting goods, and other items. Consumers can order directly from the CKBProducts.com Web site; there's no minimum order, although you get free shipping with orders of $150 or more. You can even pay via credit card.

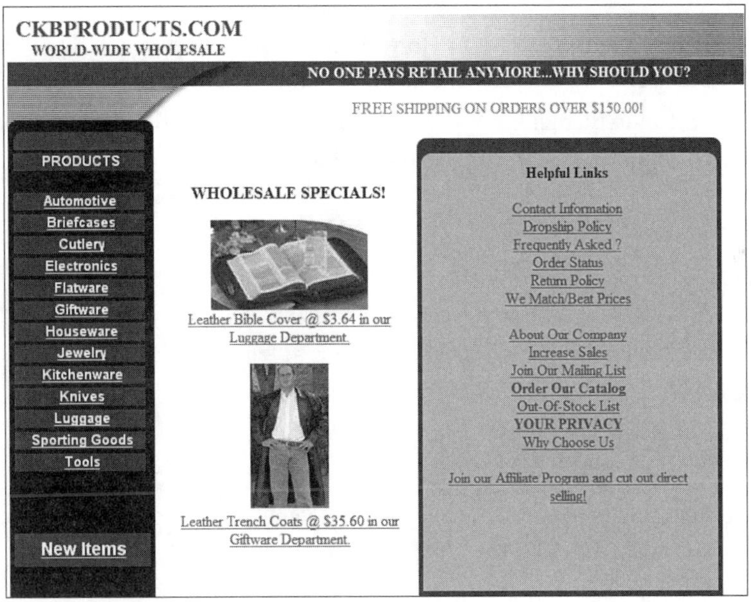

FIGURE 8.7
Buying at wholesale prices from CKBProducts.com.

Another example of a wholesaler that sells direct to the public is Shirt Distributor (`www.shirtdistributor.com`), shown in Figure 8.8. As you can probably tell from the name, this wholesaler sells shirts—t-shirts, polo shirts, denim shirts, and the like. You can order as little as a single item, at wholesale pricing, and pay via credit card.

FIGURE 8.8
Shirts wholesale to the public at Shirt Distributor.

Finding Wholesalers Online

If you like the idea of paying wholesale prices, there are many distributors willing to sell direct to consumers. But where can you find them?

Fortunately, there are several Web sites that offer directories of wholesale distributors. Some of these sites are listed in Table 8.3.

Table 8.3 Wholesaler Directories

Directory	URL
Buylink	`www.buylink.com`
Wholesale Central	`www.wholesalecentral.com`
Wholesale411	`www.wholesale411.com`
WholesalersCatalog.com	`www.wholesalerscatalog.com`

Remember, these sites aren't wholesalers themselves, and thus don't sell any merchandise. Instead, they help you find online wholesalers that you then deal with directly.

For example, you can use the Wholesale411 directory, shown in Figure 8.9, to find wholesalers in a number of product categories. Visit a wholesaler's Web site to see whether it sells directly to consumers. Some will, and some won't. It's your job to find out.

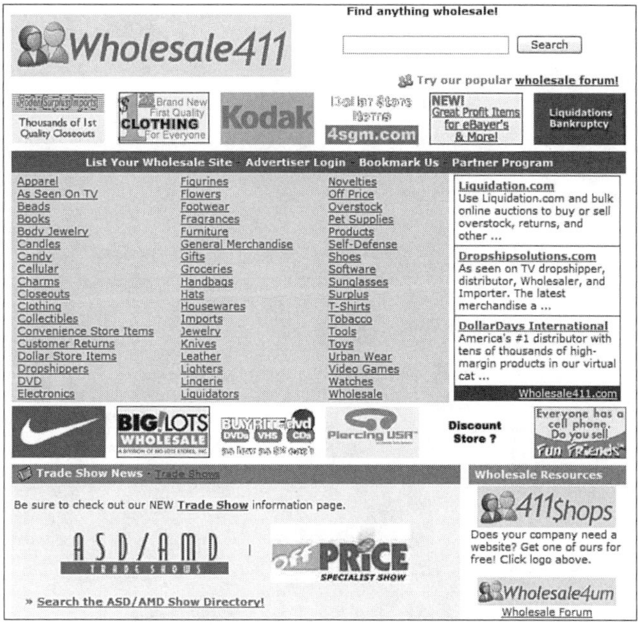

FIGURE 8.9
Search for wholesale bargains at Wholesale411.

What's Next: Finding Bargains on eBay

This leads us to the final place to look for closeouts and clearance items: online auctions. And when you're looking for online auctions, the biggest site is eBay (`www.ebay.com`).

Probably the best way to find these types of bargains on eBay is to use the site's search feature; make sure you include the words "case," "closeout," "lot," or "surplus" in your query. Another option is to go directly to eBay's Wholesale Lots category (`pages.ebay.com/catindex/catwholesale.html`), which lists auctions of surplus merchandise in almost all of eBay's major categories. Bid on those items that appeal to you.

Of course, surplus merchandise is just one type of bargain you can find on eBay. Learn more in Chapter 9, "Hunting for Bargains at eBay and Other Online Auctions."

9

HUNTING FOR BARGAINS AT EBAY AND OTHER ONLINE AUCTIONS

If you're a true bargain hunter, you'll look *anywhere* for a bargain—not just at traditional online retailer sites. Some of the best bargains on the Web come from other consumers, just like you, selling items via online auction. Learn how to bid on items for auction, and you'll move to a completely new level of online bargain hunting.

How Online Auctions Work

An online auction is lot like a traditional real-world auction—but without the auctioneer. Individuals and merchants put items up for auction and interested consumers place their bids. At the end of the auction, the customer with the highest bid gets to purchase the item. The buyer pays the seller, and the seller ships the item out. It's as simple as that.

Well, sort of.

The mechanics of an online auction are a bit more complex. To demonstrate, let's look at a typical auction on eBay (`www.ebay.com`), far and away the largest online auction site on the Web. On any given day, there are more than 24 million items listed for auction on eBay—which means there should be more than a few bargains to be had, if you know how to find them.

eBay Bidding, Step-by-Step

If you've never used eBay before, you may well be a little anxious about what might be involved. Never fear; participating in an online auction is a piece of cake, something close to 95 million other users have done before you. That means you don't have to reinvent any wheels; the procedures you have to follow are well established and well documented.

> **note**
>
> If you're a buyer, you don't pay any money to eBay. (Although you still have to pay the seller for your merchandise, of course.) eBay makes its money from insertion and final-value fees charged to sellers.

Here's how it works:

1. You begin by registering with eBay. Registration is free, and as a buyer all you have to provide is your name, address, and email. You can register directly from eBay's home page, shown in Figure 9.1; just click the Register link at the top of the page.

FIGURE 9.1

Start at eBay's home page.

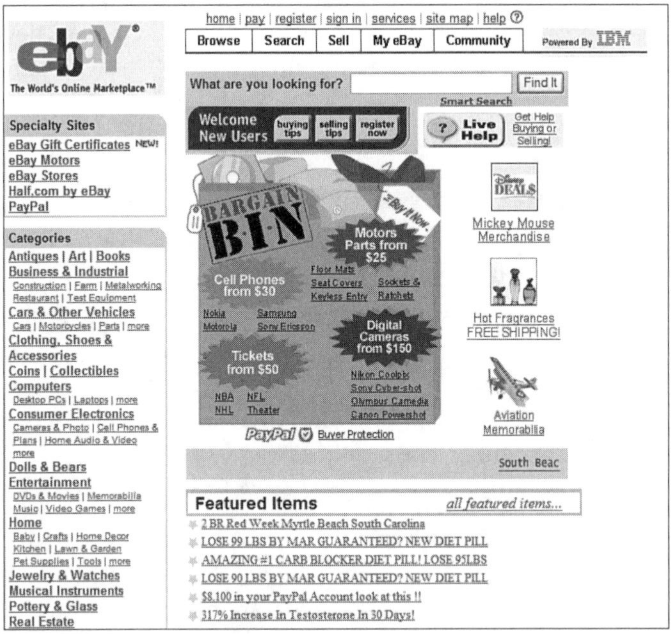

2. You look for items using eBay's search function or by browsing through the product categories. (More on searching for items later in this chapter.)
3. When you find an item you're interested in, take a moment to examine all the details. As you can see in Figure 9.2, a typical item listing includes a

photo of the item, a brief product description, the shipping and payment information, and the instructions on how to place a bid.

FIGURE 9.2

A typical eBay item listing.

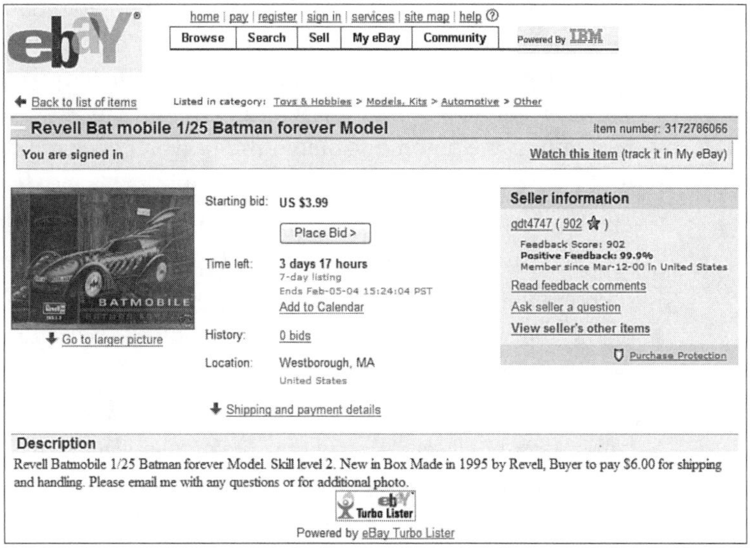

4. Now it's time to place your bid, which you do from the Ready to Bid? section near the bottom of the page, as shown in Figure 9.3. Remember, you're not buying the item at this point; you're just telling eBay how much you're willing to pay. Your bid must be at or above the current bid amount. My recommendation is to determine the maximum amount you'd be willing to pay for that item, and bid that amount—regardless of what the current bid level is.

FIGURE 9.3

Placing your bid.

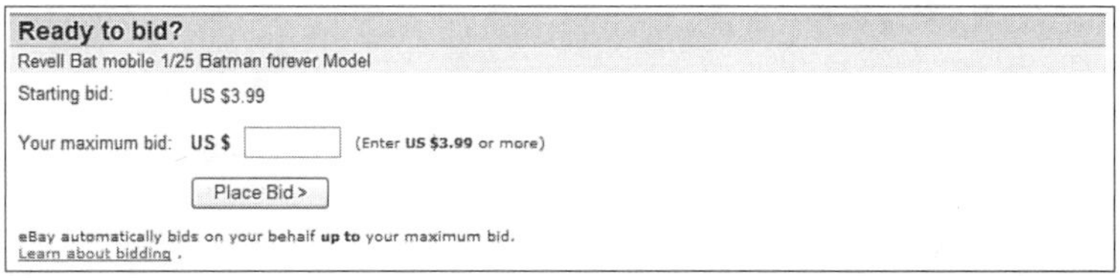

5. eBay has automatic proxy bidding software that automatically handles the bidding process from here. You bid the maximum amount you're willing to pay, and eBay's proxy software enters the minimum bid necessary—without revealing your maximum bid amount. For example, the current bid on an item might be $25. If you're willing to pay up to $40 for the item, you enter a maximum bid of $40. eBay's proxy software places a bid for you in the

amount of $26—more than the current bid, but less than your specified maximum bid. If there are no other bids by the end of the auction, you'll win the auction with a $26 bid. Other potential buyers, however, can place their own bids; unless their maximum bids are more than your $40 maximum, they're informed that they've been outbid—and your current bid is automatically raised to match the new bids (up to your specified maximum bid price). If someone else bids more than your maximum bid, eBay doesn't exceed your maximum; the automatic bidding stops when your maximum is reached, and you're notified that you've been outbid.

6. The auction proceeds. Most auctions run for 7 days, although sellers have the option of running 1-, 3-, 5-, 7-, and 10-day auctions.
7. If you're the high bidder at the end of the auction, eBay informs you (via email) that you're the winner. At this point, the seller should also contact you regarding payment.
8. You pay the seller, typically by check, money order, cashier's check, or credit card. (Most eBay sellers accept credit cards via the PayPal service.) Your payment includes both the cost of the item (the winning bid amount) and a reasonable shipping/handling charge, as determined by the seller.
9. The seller ships the item.
10. You receive the item; assuming that you're satisfied, you then leave positive feedback for the seller.

It's important to note that even though you've been using the services of the eBay site, the ultimate transaction is between you and the individual seller. You don't pay eBay; eBay is just the middleman.

Reserve Price Auctions

Every now and then you'll run into an auction that's a bit different, in that you can have the high bid but still not win the item. This type of auction is called a *reserve price* auction.

In a reserve price auction, the seller has reserved the option to set a second price (the *reserve price*) that's higher than the opening bid. At the end of an auction, if the high bid does not meet or exceed the seller's reserve price, the auction is unsuccessful and the seller does *not* sell the item to the high bidder. Sellers sometimes use a reserve price on high-end items if they want to make sure that the market does not undervalue what they're selling.

In other words, the reserve price is the lowest price at which a seller is willing to sell an item (unrelated to the opening bid price). The seller specifies the reserve price when the item is initially listed (naturally, the reserve price should be more than the minimum bid price). The reserve price is known only to the seller (and to eBay) and is never disclosed to bidders.

A reserve price auction begins, just like any other auction, at the minimum bid price. The only difference is the reserve price indication in the listing's auction details, as shown in Figure 9.4. You place your bid as you would in a normal auction, and the auction proceeds pretty much as normal.

If your maximum bid is equal to or greater than the reserve price, the item's current price is raised to the reserve price, and the reserve price has officially been met. If, through the course of the auction, the reserve price is *not* met, the auction ends with the item unsold.

FIGURE 9.4
A reserve price auction where the reserve price hasn't yet been met.

Buy It Now Auctions

Some sellers choose to list their items with eBay's Buy It Now option. With Buy It Now, the item is sold (and the auction ended) if the very first bidder places a bid for a specified price. (For this reason, some refer to Buy It Now auctions as *fixed-price* auctions.)

Buying an item with Buy It Now is really simple. If you see an item identified with a Buy It Now price (as shown in Figure 9.5), just enter a bid at that price. You'll immediately be notified that you've won the auction, and the auction will be officially closed.

FIGURE 9.5
A Buy It Now auction.

Bargain Hunter's Secret

Of course, you don't have to pay the Buy It Now price if you don't want to. You can bid at a lower price and hope that you win the auction, which proceeds normally. (The Buy It Now option disappears when the first bid is made—or, in a reserve price auction, when the reserve price is met.)

What to Do If You Get Outbid

You won't always be the high bidder in an auction. In fact, if you bid low (in an attempt to get a real steal), chances are someone else will come along and bid a higher amount. When this happens, eBay will send you an email informing you that you've been outbid.

When this happens, you have to decide whether you want to continue to play in this auction. If you decided up front that an item was only worth, let's say, $10, and the bidding has progressed to $15, you probably want to let this one go. In other words, if you think an item is worth a particular amount of money, don't let your bids exceed this amount; when the bidding gets too high, just walk away.

On the other hand, if you hedged your bet with the earlier bid, you might want to jump back into the fray with a new bid. If so, return to the item's listing page and make a new bid. If your new bid is higher than the current high bidder's maximum bid, you're back on top. If not, you can always bid again!

Hunting for Bargains on eBay

You can find lots of great bargains on eBay. Unfortunately, you can also find lots of stuff you don't want, and even more items that are way overpriced. With millions of users bidding every day, it's easy for uninformed buyers to bid some items up to unrealistic levels. How do you find the best bargains on the eBay site?

Using eBay's Search Function

The first thing you need to do is learn how to use eBay's search function. No big deal, it works pretty much like any site search. There's a search box right on the home page (labeled "What are you looking for?"); enter your query there, and then click the Find It button.

caution

Don't assume that just because an item is listed on eBay, it's an automatic bargain. eBay sellers list many brand-new, full-priced items for auction—and start bidding at or close to the normal retail price. In fact, it's not unusual to find items on eBay selling for *more* than retail, which happens when you have too many uninformed bidders chasing after a given item. Do your homework to determine what an item is really worth, and don't be fooled into thinking that the auction price is always a bargain.

eBay also includes a more powerful advanced search, which is accessed by clicking the Search link on the eBay navigation bar. This displays the Search page shown in Figure 9.6. Most of your searches can be done from the Basic Search tab; you can fine-tune your search by price range, category, and location, as well as show only those items that can be paid with via PayPal.

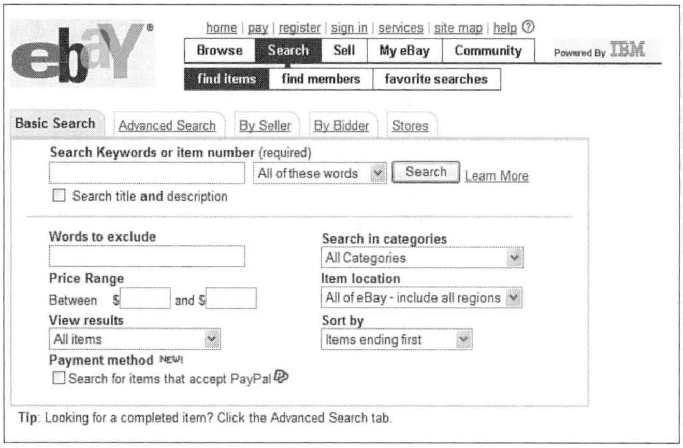

FIGURE 9.6
eBay's advanced search function.

Searching by Price

As a bargain hunter, you're interested in low-priced items. Fortunately, you can use eBay's advanced search function to search for those items that fall within a specific price range.

Start by going to the advanced search page, and then select the Basic Search tab. Enter the minimum and maximum price you're willing to pay into the Price Range boxes, along with your normal search keywords, and then click the Search button. eBay will now return a list of auctions where the current bid falls within the specified price range.

Know, however, that the current bid price won't always be the final bid price. If an auction is just starting, the current bid—even on high-value items—might be as low as a penny. Which means that an apparent low-priced item today might be a high-priced item tomorrow, after some more bids come in!

Searching for Good Deals on Used Goods

eBay sellers sell all manner of items. Some items are new in-box, some are closeout items, some are gently used, some are extremely used—the kind of stuff you find lying around the attic. If you like shopping at garage sales, you'll find a lot of garage sale–type merchandise for auction on eBay. And used goods are often just as good as new, for a fraction of the price.

If you're hunting for used goods on eBay, you'll have to sift through a lot of listings to find what you want. There's no easy way to filter your search results for used goods, so you're left with examining each item listing separately to see what's used and what's not. You can try including the word *used* in your search query, but doing so probably won't work that well; many eBay sellers don't put the word *used* in their item titles or descriptions. (For many items, used status is assumed.)

As is often the case when bargain hunting, the best deals take some work to find. Work your way through the listings, with your eye out for good used deals. They're there for the finding.

Searching for Closeout and Wholesale Merchandise

As I mentioned at the end of Chapter 8, "Hunting for Closeout, Overstock, and Wholesale Bargains," eBay is also a good source for clearance and closeout merchandise. That's because a lot of retailers, big and small, list closeout items for auction on eBay. You'll even find closeout and refurbished items from some big manufacturers; eBay has become *the* place to move unwanted goods.

There are a couple of ways to find closeout merchandise on eBay. The first is to use the standard search function, but include the words *closeout*, *clearance*, *surplus*, or *refurbished* in the query. This should return a list of auctions selling this type of merchandise.

The second option is to visit eBay's Wholesale Lots category (`pages.ebay.com/catindex/catwholesale.html`) by clicking the Wholesale link in the home page category list. As you can see in Figure 9.7, this is where you'll find "big lot" items in a variety of categories, at wholesale prices. Bid appropriately.

Searching for Off-Peak Auctions

One of the keys to winning an auction at a bargain price is to make sure that you're not competing with a ton of other bidders. One way to do this is to do your bidding during slow seasons, when there are likely to be fewer people shopping for that type of item. Although there is some category-specific seasonality, the best overall time of the year to pick up eBay bargains is during the summer months. Summer is the slowest period on eBay, which means fewer people bidding—and lower prices for you.

Another bidding secret is to look for auctions that end during off-peak times of the day—not during prime time, in other words. Believe it or not, some auctions are set to end in the wee hours of the morning, when there aren't a lot of bidders awake to make last-minute bids. Look for auctions ending between midnight and 5:00 a.m. Pacific time if you want some competition-free bidding.

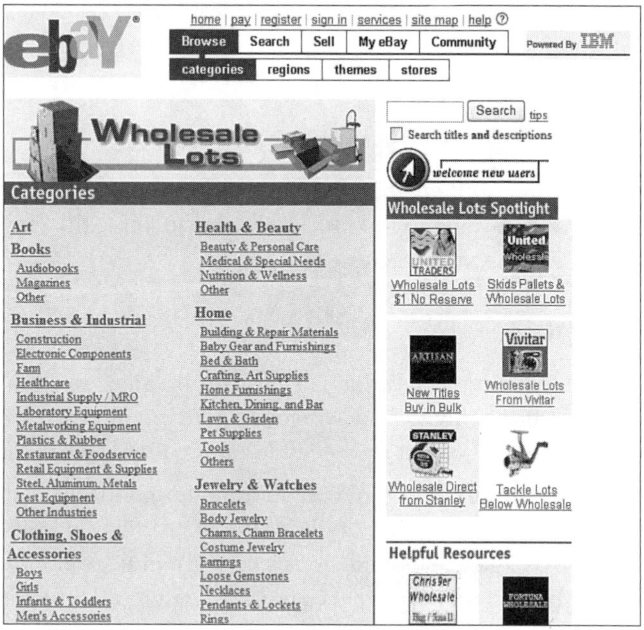

FIGURE 9.7

Bidding for wholesale lots.

Searching for Last-Minute Deals

Another way to find bargains is to look specifically for those items that have a low number of bids and are likely to remain that way. When you search the eBay listings, make sure that you display the results with auctions ending today listed first. Scan the list for soon-to-end items with no bids or few bids, and pick off some bargains that have slipped others' attention.

Searching for Misspellings

This one's a real trick. Some eBay sellers aren't great spellers—or are just prone to typing errors. This means you'll find some items listed for auction under misspelled titles. It's not hard to find the occasional Dell personal *commuter*, Apple *ipud*, or jewel *neklace*. The problem with this—and the opportunity for you—is that when you're searching for an item (correctly), listings with misspellings won't appear in the search results. If potential bidders can't find the listings, they can't bid on them, either—leaving these misspelled listings with few if any bidders. If you can locate these misspelled listings, you can often snap up a real deal without competition from other bidders.

The key, of course, is figuring out how an item might be misspelled. Let's assume that you're looking for a bargain on a toaster. Instead of searching for **toaster**, you might search for **toster**, **toastter**, **toastor**, and **toester**. Give it a try—you'll be surprised what you find!

Secrets of Successful Bidders

After you've found an item you want, how do you make sure that you place the winning bid without paying too much? It helps to know the most powerful eBay bidding secrets—which you'll learn next.

Snipe at the Last Minute

This is the one bidding secret that will win you the most auctions. Have you ever bid on an eBay auction, only to find someone swooping in at the last minute to beat your bid? This process of last-minute bidding is called *sniping*, and it works.

The idea behind sniping is to hold all your bidding until the last seconds of an auction. That's right, you don't bid at all for the first six and a half days or so; you place your bid as late as possible, hopefully with an insurmountable bid amount. The thinking behind this strategy is simple. By not disclosing your interest early on, you don't contribute to bidding up the price during the course of the auction. By bidding at the last minute, you don't leave enough time for other bidders to respond to your bid. The successful sniper makes only one bid—and makes it count.

Successful sniping requires large amounts of patience and split-second timing—but will reward you with a higher number of winning bids. Just follow these steps:

1. Identify the item you want to buy—and then don't bid! Resist the temptation to place a bid when you first notice an item. Make a note of the auction (and its closing time), or even put the item on your watch list, but don't let anyone else know your intentions.
2. Five minutes before the close of the auction, make sure that you're logged on to the Internet, and access the auction in question.
3. Open a second browser window to the auction in question.
4. In your first browser window, enter your maximum bid and click the Submit button to display the confirmation screen. Don't confirm the bid yet! Wait for the confirmation screen…
5. In your second browser window, click the Refresh or Reload button to update the official auction time. Keep doing this until the time remaining until close is 60 seconds.
6. Count down another 50 seconds, until there are only 10 seconds left in the auction.

7. When exactly 10 seconds are left in the auction, click the Confirm Bid button in your first browser window to send your bid.
8. Wait 10 seconds, and then click the Refresh or Reload button in your second browser window. The auction should now be closed, and (if your sniping was successful) you should be listed as the winning bidder.

Why bid 10 seconds before close? It takes about that long to transmit the bid from your computer to the online auction site and for the bid to be registered. If you bid any earlier than this, you leave time for the auction to send an outbid notice to the previous high bidder—and you don't want that person to know that until it's too late to do anything about it.

tip

If you can't personally be present to snipe at the end of an auction, check out an automated sniping program or Web-based sniping service to do your sniping for you. The most popular of these auto-snipe tools include Auction Sentry (www.auction-sentry.com), eSnipe (www.esnipe.com), and HammerSnipe (www.hammertap.com/HammerSnipe.html).

Bid in Odd Numbers

Bargain Hunter's Secret

Here's another small tip that will win lots of auctions for you. When you place your bid on an item, don't bid an even amount; instead, bid a few pennies more than an even buck. For example, if you want to bid $10, bid $10.03 instead. That way, your bid will beat any bids at the same approximate amount—$10.03 beats $10 even, any day—without you having to place a new bid at the next whole bid increment.

It's true—you can win an auction by bidding a penny more than the other guy!

Don't Bid Too Low

Bargain hunting aside, if you really, really, really want to win a particular auction, there's no point in being cheap. You think you can get by with a low-ball bid, so that's what you offer. The problem is, if the item is really worth a higher price, someone else will bid that amount—and you'll lose the auction.

It's especially tempting to bid low when the seller sets an unrealistically low starting price. Don't get suckered in by a low price early in the auction. If you think an item is really worth a particular price, bid that full amount. Remember, eBay's bidding software automatically sets the current bid level for you, so you'll never pay more than you have to—and if there's not much bidding, you might actually end up paying a lower amount. But if you want to win, you have to bid high enough to beat all other bidders. Don't be cheap!

Don't Bid Too High

On the other hand, you don't want to bid an unrealistically high amount for something that isn't worth that much. You're hunting for bargains, after all—and you don't do that by overpaying. You'd be shocked at how many items sell for *more* than their fair value on eBay; a lot of buyers simply pay too much for what they win. Do your homework ahead of time, and find out what that item is really worth. Then place an appropriate bid—and don't bid more than that. If you get outbid, tough; the item wasn't worth that much, anyway!

Don't Get Caught Up in a Bidding Frenzy

One reason that many items sell for too high a price is that it's easy to get caught up in a bidding frenzy. If an item is popular and several bidders are interested, you'll see the current bid price keep going up and up and up as each bidder tries to stay in the game. I know the feeling; when bidding starts to heat up, you don't want to lose. So, you keep placing higher bids, trying to stay a few dollars ahead of the other bidders—and end up bidding up the price way too high.

The solution to this problem is simple: Don't lose your head in the heat of the moment! Set a maximum amount you'll pay for the item, and do not—repeat, *do not*—bid any higher than that amount, no matter how hot and heavy the bidding. It's okay to lose one every now and then!

Don't Overpay for Shipping and Handling

Some auction sellers are sneaky. They'll try to jack up their total profit by adding a higher-than-expected shipping/handling charge. As a buyer, you have to pay the shipping costs, of course. But you shouldn't have to *overpay*—which is why you want to examine these details before you bid.

Bargain Hunter's Secret

Make sure that you know what the shipping and handling fee is before you place your bid. If the seller doesn't include this fee in the item listing, email him and ask him to estimate the fees to your location up-front. And always be on the lookout for higher-than-normal shipping/handling fees or other unexpected charges. Although it's common for sellers to include a handling charge on top of actual shipping charges (to pay for boxes, packing material, and so on), you don't want to pay *too much* over the actual costs.

Bargain Hunting at Other Online Auction Sites

eBay is a great place to find some terrific bargains—but it's not the only online auction site on the Web. There are two other big online auction sites that you might want to check out: Yahoo! Auctions and Amazon.com auctions.

Here's the thing about using an online auction other than eBay. Both of these sites have far fewer items for auction, and much less traffic. That means that you'll find fewer items for sale, but also have less competition when it comes to bidding. The bad news is it will be harder to find something you want to buy; the good news is you'll probably be able to get it for a lower price than you would on eBay.

Those points in mind, let's take a quick look at eBay's competitors in the online auction market.

Yahoo! Auctions

In addition to being a popular search site, Yahoo! is one of the largest portals on the Internet—which means you can find a little bit of everything somewhere in the Yahoo! family of sites. Back in Chapter 5, "Hunting for the Lowest Price," you learned all about the Yahoo! Shopping site. Well, that isn't the only part of Yahoo! where you can shop for bargains; even more savings can be found at Yahoo! Auctions.

Yahoo! Auctions (`auctions.yahoo.com`), shown in Figure 9.8, is very much like eBay in that it's a person-to-person auction site that also features some goods for sale from small merchants. It isn't near as big as eBay, of course, but as I explained previously, if you can find something you want on Yahoo! Auctions, you'll probably pay less for it than you would on eBay.

FIGURE 9.8
Browsing for bargains at Yahoo! Auctions.

Searching or browsing for items works pretty much the same as with eBay; a typical auction item page is shown in Figure 9.9. From here, you place your maximum bid, and let Yahoo!'s Automatic Bidding proxy software handle the rest of the bidding process for you.

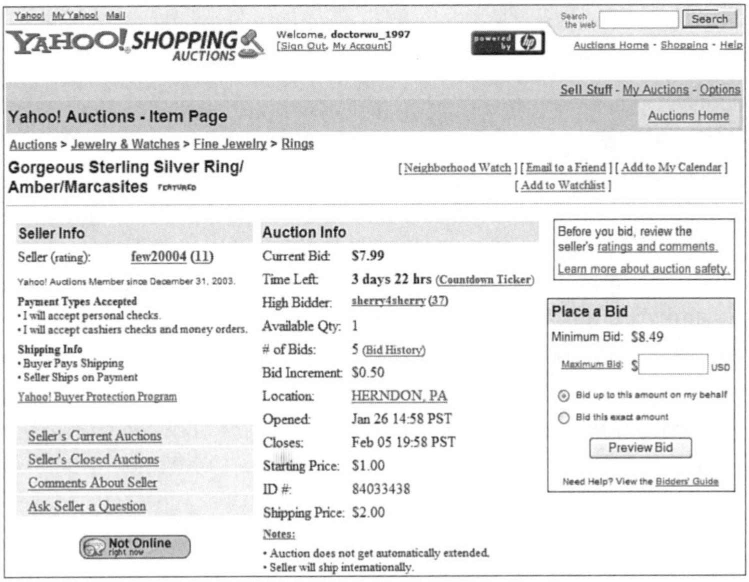

FIGURE 9.9

Placing a bid at Yahoo! Auctions.

I've found that Yahoo! Auctions has a greater percentage of merchant auctions than eBay does, often by *Yahoo! Merchants*—small retailers who sign up for Yahoo!'s merchant-management services. This means you'll find more "buy it now" auctions (what Yahoo! calls the Buy Now! option), where you can purchase an item at a fixed price without waiting for the normal auction process to play out. Watch out for these Buy Now! items; the fixed price often isn't much of a bargain.

> **tip**
>
> Yahoo! Auctions is unique in that it also lets you bypass the proxy bidding software and bid manually. Just select the Bid This Exact Amount option when you place a bid.

Amazon.com Auctions

Amazon.com Auctions (`auctions.amazon.com`), shown in Figure 9.10, is the other big online auction site—about the same size as Yahoo! Auctions (which means it's still much smaller than eBay, with far fewer items to choose from). The bidding process here is about the same as with eBay or Yahoo! Auctions; you search or browse for an item, and then review the information on the item listing page, shown in Figure

9.11. When you place your maximum bid, Amazon.com's Bid-Click proxy bidding software handles the bidding process from there.

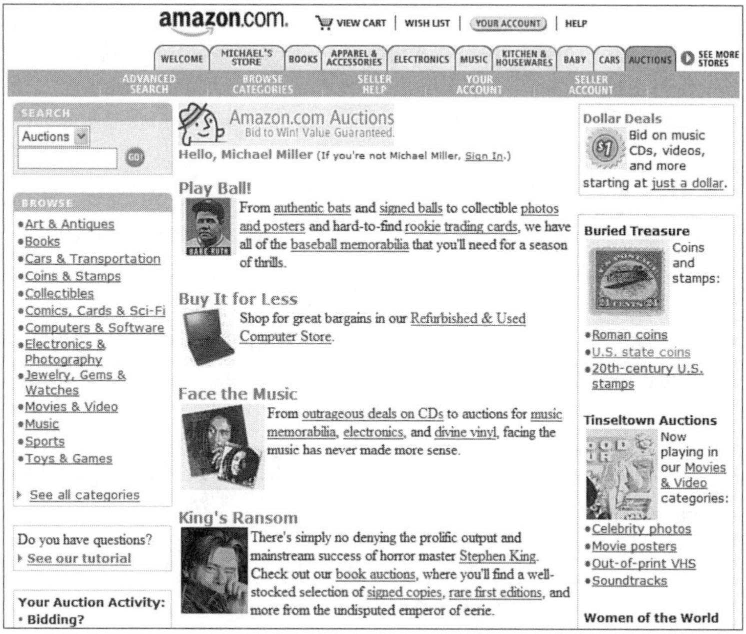

FIGURE 9.10

The familiar interface at Amazon.com Auctions.

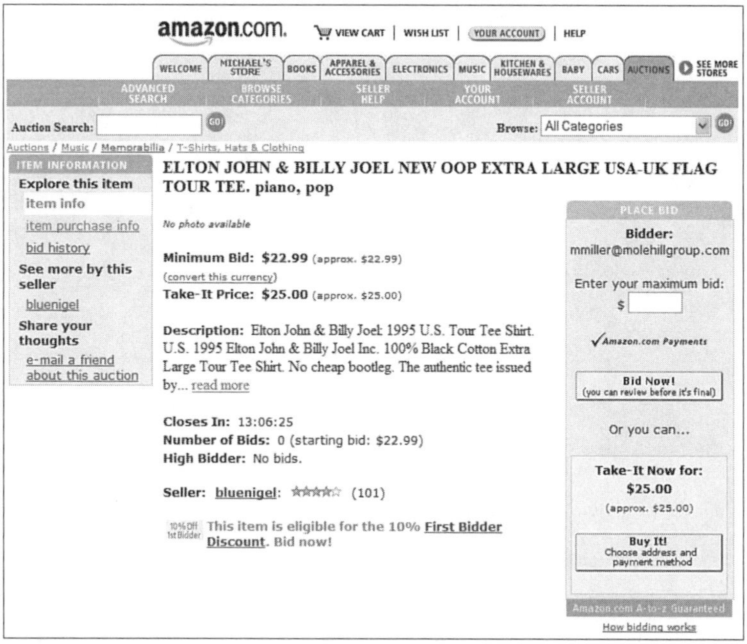

FIGURE 9.11

Placing a bid at Amazon.com Auctions.

Like Yahoo! Auctions, Amazon.com auctions have a high percentage of merchant sellers—in this case, from Amazon's Marketplace and zShop merchants. This results in a lot of fixed "buy it now" prices, or what Amazon calls the *Take-It Now* option.

One advantage to using Amazon.com Auctions is that most sellers accept payment in the form of Amazon Payments, which integrate into the normal Amazon.com checkout system. This means you can pay for your auction purchases the same way you pay for your regular Amazon purchases; it's fast, it's easy, and it's something you're probably already familiar with.

That said, Amazon.com Auctions isn't always a source of substantial bargains. Yes, you can sometimes find merchandise lower-priced here than on eBay, but the starting bid prices are often higher here than what you'll find at Yahoo! Auctions. That's because many Amazon Merchants dual-list their items both for auction and as used merchandise on the normal Amazon.com site, and can afford to wait out the auction process to get a higher price.

What's Next: Finding Nonauction Bargains on Amazon.com

Amazon.com is about more than just auctions, of course. Amazon is the largest retailer on the Web, period, and worth checking out when you're searching for bargains online. Learn more in Chapter 10, "Hunting for Bargains at Amazon.com."

HUNTING FOR BARGAINS AT AMAZON.COM

This book wouldn't be complete without a detailed look at the world's largest online retailer, Amazon.com. Not only can you find just about any product you want on the Amazon.com site, you can also find some pretty good bargains—if you know where to look. There are some definite secrets to bargain hunting on Amazon.com, so let's get started with the savings!

Navigating the Amazon.com Site

Amazon.com started out as an online bookstore, and still garners a large part of its revenues from book sales. But over the years, the folks at Amazon have added one new product category after another, to the point where the site now sells almost every type of product imaginable. (Their current slogan is "Earth's Biggest Selection"—a far cry from the original "World's Largest Bookstore.")

Navigating the Amazon.com site is relatively easy, considering the number of items it has for sale. After your first visit to the site, Amazon even presents a customized version of its home page (like the one in Figure 10.1) that features products it thinks you'll be interested in, based on your past browsing and purchasing.

FIGURE 10.1

Your own personalized Amazon.com home page.

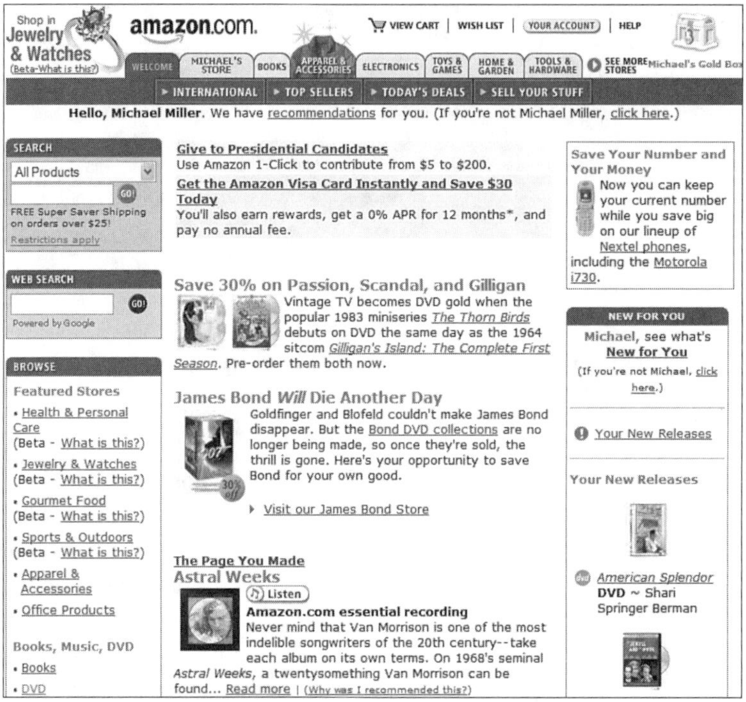
Shop in Jewelry & Watches
(Beta-What is this?)
amazon.com.
VIEW CART | WISH LIST | YOUR ACCOUNT | HELP
WELCOME
MICHAEL'S STORE
BOOKS
APPAREL & ACCESSORIES
ELECTRONICS
TOYS & GAMES
HOME & GARDEN
TOOLS & HARDWARE
SEE MORE STORES
Michael's Gold Box
INTERNATIONAL
TOP SELLERS
TODAY'S DEALS
SELL YOUR STUFF
Hello, Michael Miller. We have recommendations for you. (If you're not Michael Miller, click here.)
SEARCH
All Products
GO!
FREE Super Saver Shipping on orders over $25!
Restrictions apply
WEB SEARCH
Powered by Google
BROWSE
Featured Stores
• Health & Personal Care
(Beta - What is this?)
• Jewelry & Watches
(Beta - What is this?)
• Gourmet Food
(Beta - What is this?)
• Sports & Outdoors
(Beta - What is this?)
• Apparel & Accessories
• Office Products
Books, Music, DVD
• Books
• DVD
Give to Presidential Candidates
Use Amazon 1-Click to contribute from $5 to $200.
Get the Amazon Visa Card Instantly and Save $30 Today
You'll also earn rewards, get a 0% APR for 12 months*, and pay no annual fee.
Save 30% on Passion, Scandal, and Gilligan
Vintage TV becomes DVD gold when the popular 1983 miniseries The Thorn Birds debuts on DVD the same day as the 1964 sitcom Gilligan's Island: The Complete First Season. Pre-order them both now.
James Bond Will Die Another Day
Goldfinger and Blofeld couldn't make James Bond disappear. But the Bond DVD collections are no longer being made, so once they're sold, the thrill is gone. Here's your opportunity to save Bond for your own good.
Visit our James Bond Store
The Page You Made
Astral Weeks
Listen
Amazon.com essential recording
Never mind that Van Morrison is one of the most indelible songwriters of the 20th century--take each album on its own terms. On 1968's seminal Astral Weeks, a twentysomething Van Morrison can be found... Read more | (Why was I recommended this?)
Save Your Number and Your Money
Now you can keep your current number while you save big on our lineup of Nextel phones, including the Motorola i730.
NEW FOR YOU
Michael, see what's New for You
(If you're not Michael, click here.)
Your New Releases
Your New Releases
American Splendor
DVD ~ Shari Springer Berman

The left side of the home page is where you'll find Amazon's search box, which you can use to search for specific products. Also on the left are links to Amazon's individual "stores" for specific product categories; you can browse through these stores to find the products you want.

Site navigation remains constant from page to page, thanks to the navigation bar found at the top of every page. The navigation bar presents a series of tabs that take you directly to major categories and key sections of the site; click a tab, and subcategories are presented below the bar.

You should also become familiar with the See More Stores tab on the navigation bar, which displays a list of all available Amazon stores. This is often the quickest way to navigate from one store to another.

Where to Find the Best Bargains on Amazon.com

It's easy enough to search or browse through the Amazon site to find specific products. And when you find a product, like the one shown in Figure 10.2, you'll often find that Amazon has already discounted the price. But where do you go on the site to find even bigger savings? Read on to learn the true secrets of bargain hunting on Amazon.com.

FIGURE 10.2

A typical Amazon.com product listing—note the savings from list price.

Hunting for Today's Deals

The first place to find bargains on Amazon is the Today's Deals page, shown in Figure 10.3. This page lists all current promotions, discounts, sales, rebates, and the like across the entire Amazon.com site. Big deals are featured directly on this page; you can also browse through the deals offered in each of Amazon's main product categories.

You get to the Today's Deals page by clicking the Welcome tab and then clicking Today's Deals under the navigation bar. Or, if you want to look at current deals in a particular category, go to that store page and click Today's Deals under that page's navigation bar. (Not available with all stores.)

What kinds of deals are we talking about? Well, most of these deals are manufacturer-sponsored promotions, and many apply across multiple items. For example, Figure 10.4 shows a factory-sponsored rebate promotion for KitchenAid products; purchase a selected small appliance and get up to $20 back from the manufacturer. Other deals include extra discounts, free shipping, and that sort of thing.

tip

Remember back in Chapter 3, "Researching Your Purchases Before You Buy," when you learned about product research and review sites? Well, Amazon features customer reviews on almost every product page—just scroll down the page, past the Editorial Reviews (which are provided by the manufacturer) to the Customer Reviews section. Any customer can write a review, as well as provide a 1-to-5 star rating of the product. It's a great way to learn what others think about a particular item!

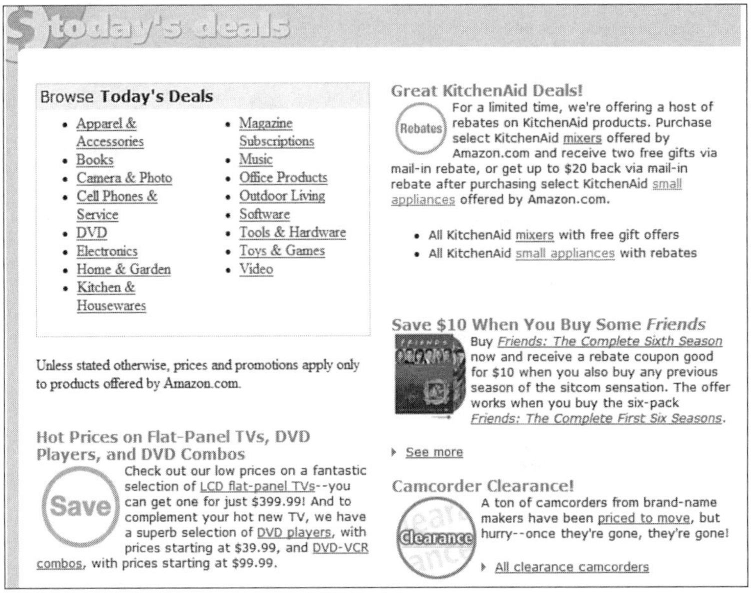
today's deals
Browse Today's Deals
Apparel & Accessories
Books
Camera & Photo
Cell Phones & Service
DVD
Electronics
Home & Garden
Kitchen & Housewares
Magazine Subscriptions
Music
Office Products
Outdoor Living
Software
Tools & Hardware
Toys & Games
Video
Unless stated otherwise, prices and promotions apply only to products offered by Amazon.com.
Hot Prices on Flat-Panel TVs, DVD Players, and DVD Combos
Save
Check out our low prices on a fantastic selection of LCD flat-panel TVs--you can get one for just $399.99! And to complement your hot new TV, we have a superb selection of DVD players, with prices starting at $39.99, and DVD-VCR combos, with prices starting at $99.99.
Great KitchenAid Deals!
Rebates
For a limited time, we're offering a host of rebates on KitchenAid products. Purchase select KitchenAid mixers offered by Amazon.com and receive two free gifts via mail-in rebate, or get up to $20 back via mail-in rebate after purchasing select KitchenAid small appliances offered by Amazon.com.
All KitchenAid mixers with free gift offers
All KitchenAid small appliances with rebates
Save $10 When You Buy Some Friends
Buy Friends: The Complete Sixth Season now and receive a rebate coupon good for $10 when you also buy any previous season of the sitcom sensation. The offer works when you buy the six-pack Friends: The Complete First Six Seasons.
See more
Camcorder Clearance!
Clearance
A ton of camcorders from brand-name makers have been priced to move, but hurry--once they're gone, they're gone!
All clearance camcorders

FIGURE 10.3
Hunting for bargains among Today's Deals.

Great Rebates from KitchenAid
For a limited time, you'll get up to $20 back via mail-in rebate on the following KitchenAid small appliances offered by Amazon.com.
KitchenAid KFP600 11-Cup Ultra Power Food Processor, White
KitchenAid KFP600 11-Cup Ultra Power Food Processor, Onyx Black
KitchenAid KFP600 11-Cup Ultra Power Food Processor, Majestic Yellow
KitchenAid KFP600 11-Cup Ultra Power Food Processor, Empire Red
KitchenAid
List Price: $249.99
Price: $198.99
You Save: $51.00 (20%)
Mail-In Rebates: $30.00
Price After Rebates: $168.99
Availability: Usually ships within 24 hours Colors: Black, Almond Cream, Cobalt Blue, Empire Red, Empire Green, Majestic Yellow

FIGURE 10.4
Details of a manufacturer-sponsored promotion on Amazon.

The deals found on the Today's Deals page are the equivalent of the in-store promotions you might find at a traditional "bricks and mortar" retailer. Placement on the Today's Deals page is the online version of an in-store display or endcap. Featured placement on this page is almost always paid for by the manufacturer.

Hunting for Bargains at the Bottom of the Page

Even more bargains can be found by scrolling to the bottom of any Amazon.com page. Here Amazon lists limited-time *Bottom of the Page deals*—savings updated every day at noon and good only for 24 hours. Figure 10.5 shows typical Bottom of the Page bargains.

FIGURE 10.5

Scroll all the way down for Bottom of the Page bargains.

Bottom of the Page™ Deals for February 01

Amazon.com = low prices. Save up to **50%** on these **24-hour** deals, updated every day at noon (central time).

	Our Price	You Save	
Sabatier Grand Chef 10-Piece Knife Set in Wood Block High-carbon, stainless-steel, hand-sharpened knives for a price you can't resist.	$129.99	$370.01 (74%)	☐
Oral-B 7850DLX Professional Care Deluxe Power Toothbrush Eat birthday cake and movie popcorn until you're 90--thanks to Oral-B.	$74.99	$25.00 (25%)	☐
Epson T032120 Twin Pack Black Ink Cartridge (2 Pack) Epson's superior-quality water-resistant inks won't smudge or fade.	$53.95	$6.04 (10%)	☐
Calphalon Commercial Nonstick 4-Quart Chef's Casserole with Lid A gift every home chef will love--a sturdy, nonstick Calphalon casserole.	$39.99	$83.01 (67%)	☐
SOLD OUT FOR TODAY ~~Revival Soy Protein Bar, Peanut Butter Chocolate Pal Bar 15 ea~~ The protein power of tofu in a delicious peanut-butter-chocolate bar.	$26.99		
Enfamil ProSobee Soy Infant Formula, Iron Fortified Powder 28.5 oz A milk-free, easy-to-digest soy formula from Enfamil.	$17.99	$2.00 (10%)	☐
SOLD OUT FOR TODAY ~~Nature Made SAM-e Mood Plus Double Strength 400mg, Tablets 10 ea~~ Improve your mood naturally with Nature Made SAM-e.	$16.99		
Schick Quattro Razor Cartridge Refill - 8 ea Stock up on cartridges for Schick's advanced four-blade disposable razor.	$14.99	$3.83 (20%)	☐
Ginsana All-Natural Enegizer, Bonus Pack 60+45, Softgels - 105 ea Perk up with Ginsana--the All-Natural Energizer.	$14.49	$1.54 (10%)	☐

FREE Super Saver Shipping on orders over $25. See details.

Add selected items to cart

Buy selected items with 1-Click®

These Bottom of the Page deals aren't always the best bargains on the Amazon site, but rather those deals that Amazon is pushing particularly hard today. The savings might be worth your while, but you might not be interested in what's being sold.

Hunting for Savings at the Friday Sale

Savvy Amazon shoppers know that Friday is the day to find the site's best bargains. That's because every Friday Amazon conducts a one-day sale, called the Friday Sale. Selected merchandise is put on sale for 24 hours only; prices return to normal at midnight (Pacific time) and quantities are limited.

You find the Friday Sale by going to the Outlet store (either from the Outlet tab or the Outlet link on the See More Stores page) and clicking The Friday Store under the navigation bar. The Friday Store page, shown in Figure 10.6, typically lists more than a hundred different sale items, from cordless shavers to computer games. Savings range from a few bucks to hundreds of dollars. Shop early (just after midnight is good) for the best selection.

FIGURE 10.6

Limited-time savings at Amazon's Friday Sale.

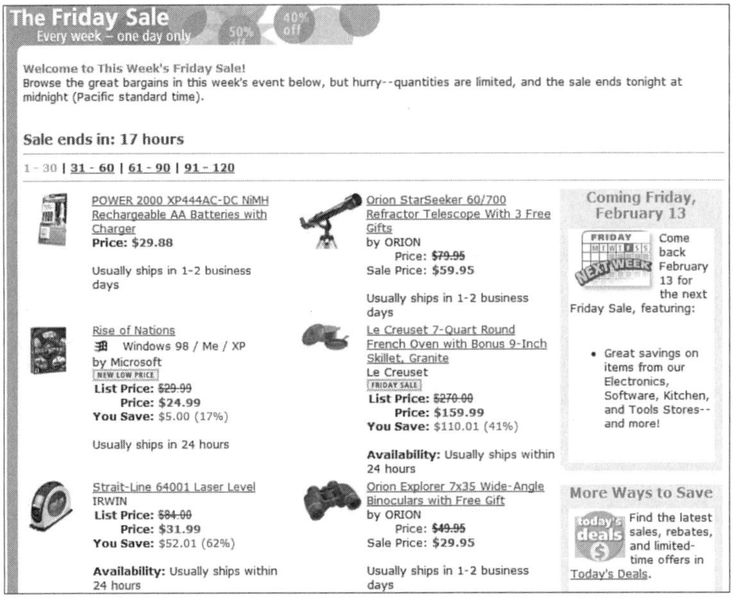

I find the Friday Sale to offer some of the best bargains on the Amazon site. I'm always surprised to discover how few people know about Amazon's Friday Sale—which leaves more bargains for the rest of us, I suppose.

Hunting for Clearance Merchandise from the Amazon.com Outlet

To get to the Friday Sale, you had to pass by the Amazon.com Outlet page. You access the Amazon.com Outlet by clicking the Outlet tab on the navigation bar, or the Outlet link on the See More Stores page.

The Amazon.com Outlet, shown in Figure 10.7, is where you can find all manner of clearance merchandise from Amazon and its retail partners. This section of the Amazon site is the equivalent of an outlet mall, with closeout products presented in all major product categories.

> **note**
>
> Amazon.com partners with Babies 'R' Us, Toys 'R' Us, Target, and other major retailers to offer their merchandise online.

To view category-specific outlet stores, click a category link (on the left side of the page). For example, Figure 10.8 shows the Kitchen & Housewares Outlet, where you can find clearance prices on cookware, cutlery, small appliances, and more.

The products presented in the Amazon.com Outlet are typical clearance items—merchandise that the manufacturer has too many of and has priced to move. These are often prior-year or discontinued items, but can also be regular-line merchandise that the manufacturer is overstocked on. In any case, the Amazon.com Outlet is a prime destination for serious bargain hunters; the selection here is constantly changing.

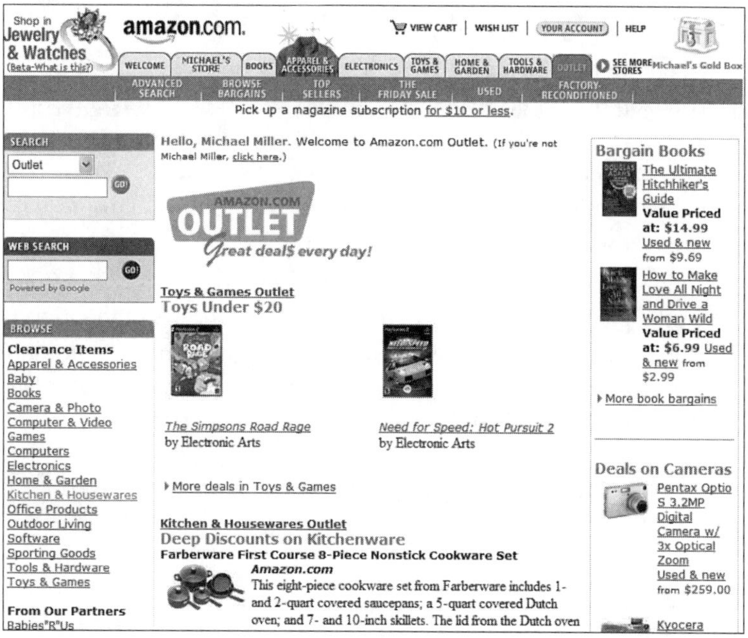

FIGURE 10.7

Find clearance items on sale at the Amazon.com Outlet.

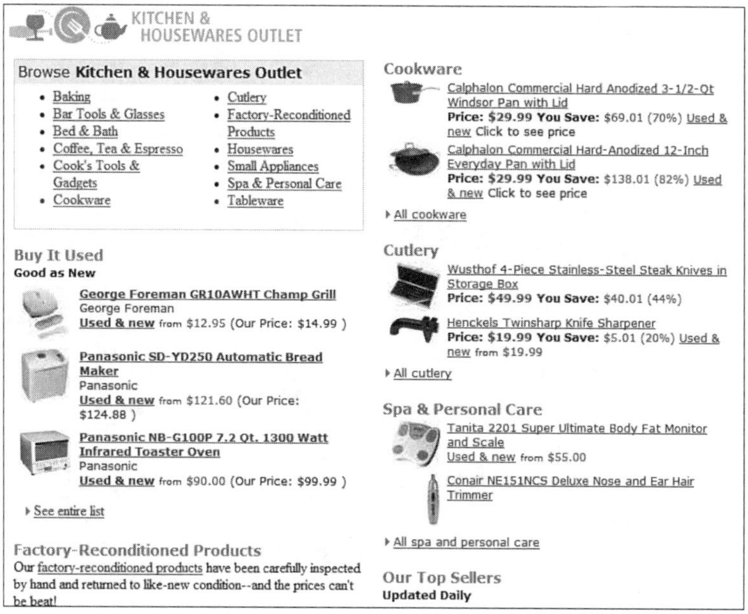

FIGURE 10.8

One of Amazon's product-specific outlet stores—the Kitchen & Housewares Outlet.

Part II 10

Hunting for Factory-Reconditioned Merchandise

In addition to the new items offered at clearance prices in the Amazon.com Outlet, Amazon also offers factory-reconditioned products direct from the manufacturers. These are items that have been returned to the manufacturer for whatever reason, and then cleaned and returned to like-new condition. These refurbished items are offered at substantial savings over equivalent new items, and come with full manufacturer warranties.

Amazon's Factory-Reconditioned Products page is accessed from the Amazon.com Outlet page; click Factory Reconditioned under the navigation bar. As you can see in Figure 10.9, Amazon offers refurbished items in the Kitchen & Housewares and Tools & Hardware categories. Products are available from Black & Decker, Cuisinart, KitchenAid, Singer, and other major brands.

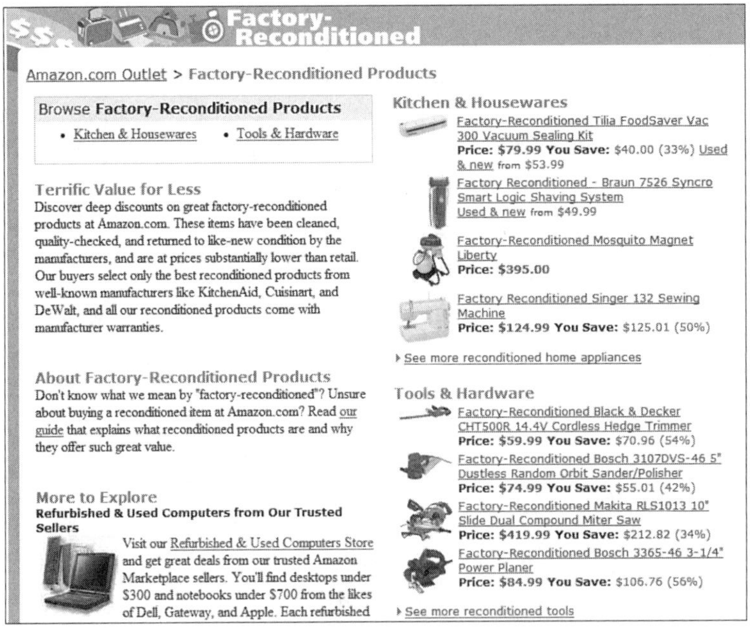

FIGURE 10.9
Hunting for bargains on factory-reconditioned merchandise.

Amazon also offers reconditioned computers from Apple, Compaq, Dell, Gateway, Sony, and other manufacturers in its Outlet, Used & Refurbished Computer Products store, shown in Figure 10.10. You get here by clicking the Computers tab on the navigation bar (or the Computers link on the See More Stores page), and then clicking Outlet, Used & Refurbished below the navigation bar. This is a great place to find bargains on both desktop and notebook PCs, as well as selected peripherals.

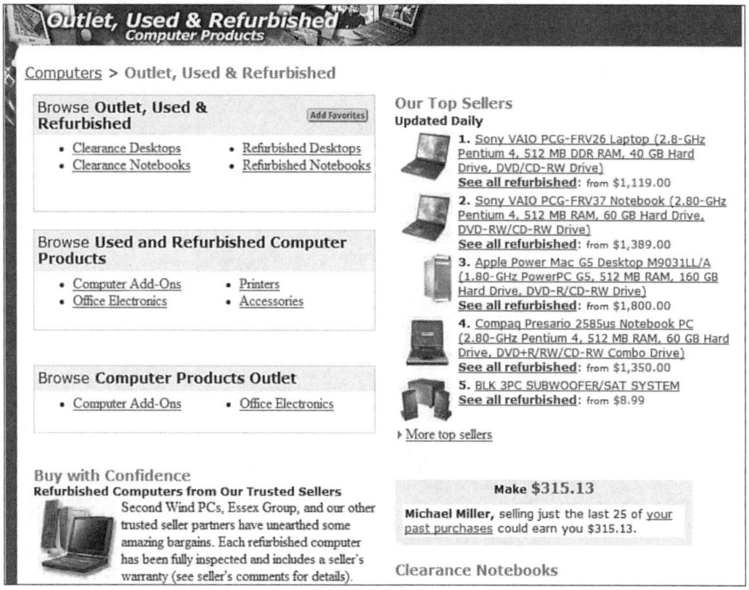

FIGURE 10.10

Shopping for factory-reconditioned PCs at Amazon's Outlet, Used & Refurbished Computer Products store.

Hunting for Used Merchandise

If refurbished prices aren't low enough for you, it's time to go directly to the used merchandise. In Amazon's case, it offers a variety of used products from Amazon Marketplace sellers. These are individuals and small merchants who offer their goods through the Amazon site. You place your order with and pay Amazon, but the merchandise is shipped by the individual Marketplace seller.

Where do you find this used merchandise? There are two places, actually.

> **note**
>
> Both new and used merchandise purchased from Amazon Marketplace and zShop merchants are protected by Amazon's A-to-Z Guarantee. If the merchandise you received isn't as described, you can file with Amazon to receive a full refund.

Bargain Hunter's Secret

To view all of Amazon's used merchandise in one place, try the Used page shown in Figure 10.11. You get here by going to the Amazon.com Outlet page, and then clicking Used under the navigation bar. As you can see, used merchandise is available in several different product categories: Books, Camera & Photo, DVD, Electronics, Music, Video, and Video Games. Click the category link to see the used merchandise available.

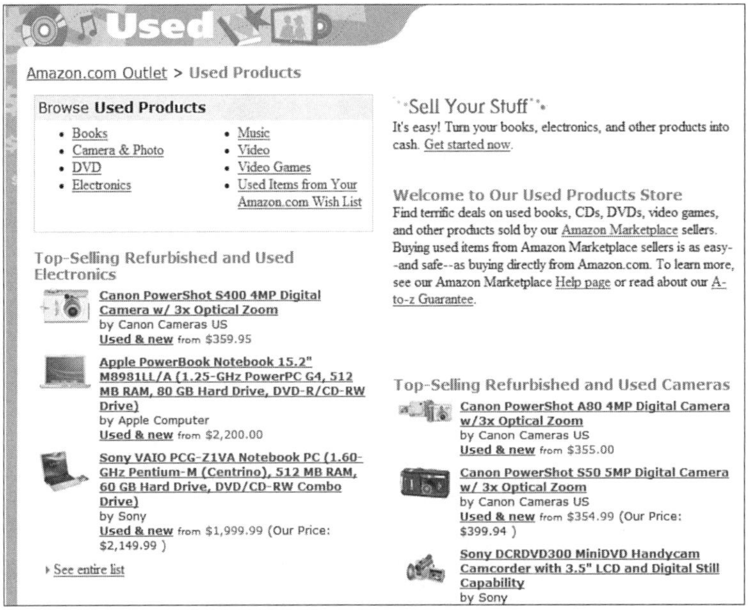

Used
Amazon.com Outlet > Used Products
Browse Used Products
Books
Camera & Photo
DVD
Electronics
Music
Video
Video Games
Used Items from Your Amazon.com Wish List
Sell Your Stuff
It's easy! Turn your books, electronics, and other products into cash. Get started now.
Welcome to Our Used Products Store
Find terrific deals on used books, CDs, DVDs, video games, and other products sold by our Amazon Marketplace sellers. Buying used items from Amazon Marketplace sellers is as easy--and safe--as buying directly from Amazon.com. To learn more, see our Amazon Marketplace Help page or read about our A-to-z Guarantee.
Top-Selling Refurbished and Used Electronics
Canon PowerShot S400 4MP Digital Camera w/ 3x Optical Zoom
by Canon Cameras US
Used & new from $359.95
Apple PowerBook Notebook 15.2" M8981LL/A (1.25-GHz PowerPC G4, 512 MB RAM, 80 GB Hard Drive, DVD-R/CD-RW Drive)
by Apple Computer
Used & new from $2,200.00
Sony VAIO PCG-Z1VA Notebook PC (1.60-GHz Pentium-M (Centrino), 512 MB RAM, 60 GB Hard Drive, DVD/CD-RW Combo Drive)
by Sony
Used & new from $1,999.99 (Our Price: $2,149.99)
See entire list
Top-Selling Refurbished and Used Cameras
Canon PowerShot A80 4MP Digital Camera w/3x Optical Zoom
by Canon Cameras US
Used & new from $355.00
Canon PowerShot S50 5MP Digital Camera w/ 3x Optical Zoom
by Canon Cameras US
Used & new from $354.99 (Our Price: $399.94)
Sony DCRDVD300 MiniDVD Handycam Camcorder with 3.5" LCD and Digital Still Capability
by Sony

FIGURE 10.11
Shopping for used merchandise from Amazon Marketplace merchants.

Another way to find a used item is to search for that item new. When you open a product listing page, if a used version is available, you'll see a "buy used" link in the More Buying Choices box, like the one shown in Figure 10.12. Click the link and you'll see a list of Amazon Marketplace sellers with used copies for sale; you can place your order from here. All used items you order are added to your standard Amazon Shopping Cart, and you check out and pay for that item as you would normally.

MORE BUYING CHOICES
7 used & new from $14.99
Have one to sell? Sell yours here

FIGURE 10.12
Check the More Buying Choices box to see whether used copies are available.

Hunting for Deals from zShop Merchants

Amazon also facilitates sales from larger merchants, through what it calls its *zShops*. zShops merchants offer both new and used merchandise, often goods that Amazon itself doesn't normally stock. Pricing is often quite good, although that's not a given. I've sometimes found zShops merchants underselling Amazon itself—which is why it's definitely worth your while to check out this purchasing option.

You can shop zShops merchants by selecting the zShops tab on the navigation bar, or clicking the zShops link on the See More Store page. As you can see in Figure 10.13, you can search zShops for specific items or browse the merchants by category.

FIGURE 10.13
Browsing Amazon's zShops.

There's a wide variety when it comes to zShops merchants. You'll find everything from really small guys to big national names, such as Wherehouse Music. In terms of purchasing, zShops merchants are integrated into the Amazon.com system—sort of. When you click the Buy Now from Seller button on a zShops item listing page (like the one shown in Figure 10.14), you choose a payment method, and Amazon arranges for payment to be sent to the zShops merchant. The merchant then ships the item directly to you.

FIGURE 10.14
Purchasing from a zShops merchant.

Remember, when you purchase from a zShops merchant, you're not purchasing from Amazon.com—which means you can't always expect stellar Amazon-like service and shipping. You can learn more about a specific zShops merchant by clicking the merchant name on the item listing page. This displays the merchant's zShops page, like the one shown in Figure 10.15, which lists the manufacturers and merchandise sold by this seller and displays the average customer feedback rating. Click the Learn More About link on this page to display even more information, including the store's service/returns policy and accepted payment and shipment methods, or click the Recent Feedback link to read feedback comments left by customers.

Hunting for Deals at Amazon.com Auctions

Bargain Hunter's Secret

There's one other place to find bargains on Amazon: Amazon.com Auctions. You learned about Amazon.com Auctions in Chapter 9, "Hunting for Bargains at eBay and Other Online Auctions"; turn there to learn more. Just remember that when you shop at Amazon.com Auctions, you're not actually buying an item, you're placing a bid on it. You get to buy the item only if you have the high bid at the end of the auction process.

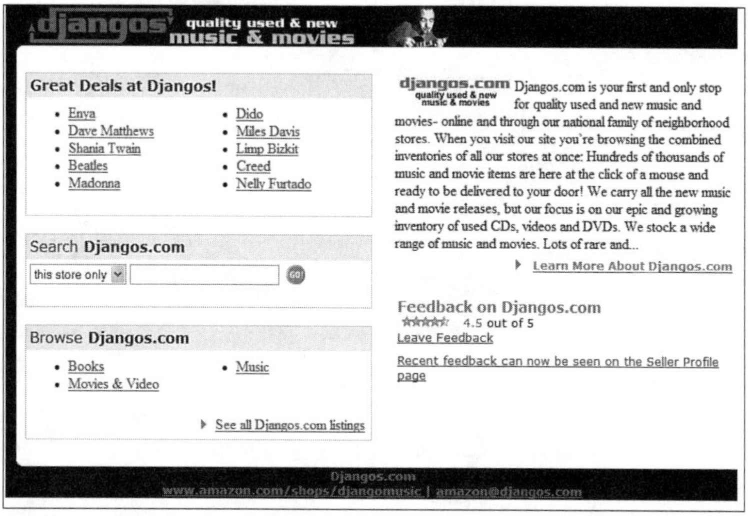
djangos quality used & new music & movies
Great Deals at Djangos!
Enya
Dave Matthews
Shania Twain
Beatles
Madonna
Dido
Miles Davis
Limp Bizkit
Creed
Nelly Furtado
Search Djangos.com
this store only
Browse Djangos.com
Books
Movies & Video
Music
See all Djangos.com listings
djangos.com quality used & new music & movies Djangos.com is your first and only stop for quality used and new music and movies- online and through our national family of neighborhood stores. When you visit our site you're browsing the combined inventories of all our stores at once: Hundreds of thousands of music and movie items are here at the click of a mouse and ready to be delivered to your door! We carry all the new music and movie releases, but our focus is on our epic and growing inventory of used CDs, videos and DVDs. We stock a wide range of music and movies. Lots of rare and...
Learn More About Djangos.com
Feedback on Djangos.com
4.5 out of 5
Leave Feedback
Recent feedback can now be seen on the Seller Profile page
Djangos.com
www.amazon.com/shops/djangomusic | amazon@djangos.com

FIGURE 10.15

Learn more about any zShops merchant.

Secrets of Saving Even More Money at Amazon

Okay, now you've learned where to find the best bargains on the Amazon.com site. But there's even more money to be saved, even if you purchase an item at little or no discount.

Place a Bigger Order for Free Shipping

Bargain Hunter's Secret

The first way to save money on your order is to cut out the shipping charge. Amazon offers free Super Saver Shipping if your order totals $25 or more, with some qualifications. The big qualification is that selected merchandise is excluded from the offer, specifically apparel, baby products, toys, video games, certain oversize items, products from Circuit City, J&R Music and Computer World, Marshall Field's, Office Depot, and Target, products from Marketplace and zShops sellers, and products that don't include the Super Saver Shipping icon shown in Figure 10.16. In other words, don't assume that what you order qualifies; look for the icon to be sure.

FIGURE 10.16

Look for the Super Saver Shipping icon.

Also know that Super Saver Shipping isn't automatically applied to your order; you have to select this option manually during the checkout process. You'll also have to select Group My Items Into As Few Shipments As Possible as your shipping preference. (More on that next.) You do this from the Place Your Order page, shown in Figure 10.17.

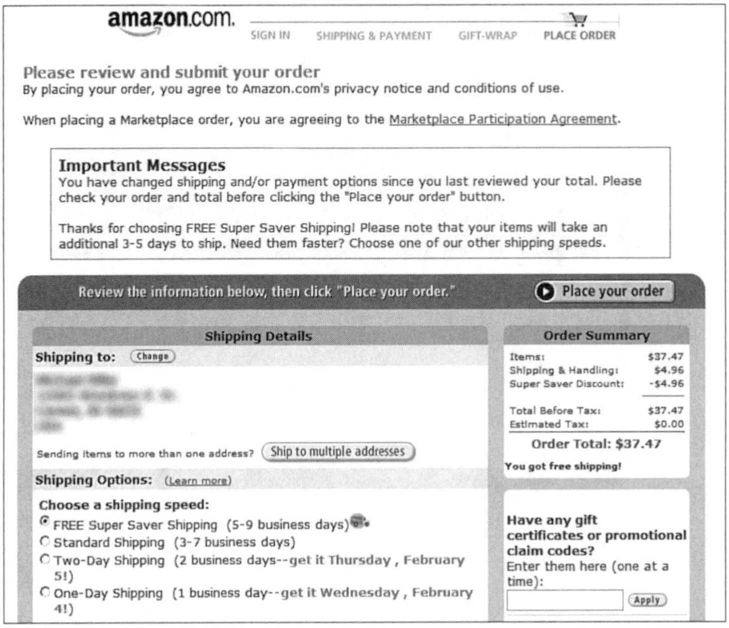
amazon.com.
SIGN IN
SHIPPING & PAYMENT
GIFT-WRAP
PLACE ORDER
Please review and submit your order
By placing your order, you agree to Amazon.com's privacy notice and conditions of use.
When placing a Marketplace order, you are agreeing to the Marketplace Participation Agreement.
Important Messages
You have changed shipping and/or payment options since you last reviewed your total. Please check your order and total before clicking the "Place your order" button.
Thanks for choosing FREE Super Saver Shipping! Please note that your items will take an additional 3-5 days to ship. Need them faster? Choose one of our other shipping speeds.
Review the information below, then click "Place your order."
Place your order
Shipping Details
Shipping to: Change
Sending items to more than one address? Ship to multiple addresses
Shipping Options: (Learn more)
Choose a shipping speed:
FREE Super Saver Shipping (5-9 business days)
Standard Shipping (3-7 business days)
Two-Day Shipping (2 business days--get it Thursday, February 5!)
One-Day Shipping (1 business day--get it Wednesday, February 4!)
Order Summary
Items: $37.47
Shipping & Handling: $4.96
Super Saver Discount: -$4.96
Total Before Tax: $37.47
Estimated Tax: $0.00
Order Total: $37.47
You got free shipping!
Have any gift certificates or promotional claim codes?
Enter them here (one at a time):
Apply

FIGURE 10.17
Select free shipping on the Place Your Order page.

One more thing—selecting Super Saver Shipping will add three-to-five days to your order. So, this isn't a good option if you need your merchandise quickly. On the other hand, if you don't mind waiting a few extra days, it can represent significant savings.

Ship Together—Not Separately

Bargain Hunter's Secret

While we're on the topic of shipping, you don't have to choose Super Saver Shipping to save on shipping charges. When you order more than one item, you can choose to group all the items into a single shipment, which will reduce your shipping charges no matter which shipping method you choose. This is opposed to splitting your order into multiple shipments, which might get you your items faster, but will cost more.

You make your choice during the checkout process, on the Place Your Order page (shown in Figure 10.17). Select the Group My Items Into as Few Shipments as Possible option to combine your order into a single shipment and save a few bucks—or select the I Want My Items Faster option to ungroup your order, with correspon-ding higher shipping charges.

Ship It Slower

Whichever type of order grouping you select, you also have a choice of shipping speed. You can choose from Standard Shipping (3–7 business days), Two-Day Shipping (2 business days), or One-Day Shipping (1 business day). Obviously, Standard Shipping costs less than One- or Two-Day Shipping. Save money by choosing the Standard Shipping option.

Pick It Up Yourself

If you order certain items, you can save money by picking them up yourself. That's right, even though Amazon.com is an online retailer, it partners with Borders, Circuit City, and Office Depot to make selected items available for pickup at their retail stores. In particular, you should be able to order books, CDs, DVDs, electronics, office products, and computer software for in-store pickup. And when you pick up your order in the store, you don't pay any shipping charges.

If an item is available for in-store pickup, you'll see a Need It Today? section under the product picture, as shown in Figure 10.18. Enter your ZIP code to see whether a store near you has the item in stock.

Panasonic DVD-F85S 5-Disc Progressive Scan DVD Player (Silver)
Other products by Panasonic
List Price: $149.99
Price: $129.84
You Save: $20.15 (13%)
Availability: Usually ships within 24 hours
This item ships for FREE with Super Saver Shipping. See details.
Need it today?Available for in-store pickup from $149.87 . Price may vary based on availability. To check availability in your area, enter your ZIP Code
Choose a store

FIGURE 10.18

Need it today? Enter your ZIP to see whether an item is available for in-store pickup.

After you've placed your order, you should receive an email from the retailer to let you know that the item is ready for pickup. When you go to pick up your order, you'll need to take with you a printout of the confirmation email, your driver's license or other photo ID, and the credit card you used to make the purchase.

tip

You can also browse through all the items Amazon offers for pickup on the In-Store Pickup page. Get there by clicking the In-Store Pickup link on the See More Stores page.

Share the Love

Here's another way to save some money on your next Amazon order. After you've completed the checkout process and finalized your purchase, Amazon displays an Amazon.com Thanks You page like the one shown in Figure 10.19. On the bottom side of the page is a section that encourages you to Share the Love, which actually translates to "we'll pay you if you get a friend to buy something."

Thanks, Michael!
Your order is being processed, and you'll receive an e-mail confirmation shortly.
Review or edit your order:
• View a summary of your order
• Track your order status
• Edit shipping and gift options
Make any other changes in your account:
View your account
New to Amazon.com?
Click below to watch one of our short animated demos:
• The basics of shopping at Amazon.com
• Discover 1-Click ordering
• Learn how to track your order status
Share the Love!™ Send Your Friends a 10% Discount on items you just ordered.
If they buy any of them within one week, you'll also earn credit toward future purchases. Learn more
Enter friends e-mail addresses*:
Separate addresses with a comma.
Select items to give discount on:
God Save the Mark : A Novel of Crime and Confusion (Hardcover)
Money for Nothing (Hardcover)
Send Discount
*NOTE: These people will be added to your Amazon Friends list. No additional Amazon.com or third-party promotional e-mail will be sent to these addresses as a result of your entering them above.

FIGURE 10.19
Get a discount if a friend purchases the same item you purchased.

It works like this. After you've purchased an item, you tell Amazon which of your friends might also be interested in that item, by supplying their email addresses. Amazon sends your friends an email message about the product, and if a friend actually buys that item within the next week, you'll get a credit worth 10% of that item's price that you can use on your next order. (Your friend also gets a 10% discount on the item.)

Now, if you know for sure that a friend is actually interested in this item, this is a pretty good deal. Otherwise, you stand the risk of annoying friends and family every time you make a purchase. Use this option sparingly!

Become an Amazon Associate and Purchase from Yourself

Here's one last secret you can use if you have your own Web site. You can sign up to be an Amazon Associate and direct users to purchase Amazon items from your site. For every purchase placed, you earn a sales commission—between 2.5% to 10%, according to sales volume and other variables.

The Amazon Associates program is free to join. All you have to do is sign up for the program, put a few links to Amazon on your Web site, and let Amazon do the rest. When someone clicks through your Associate link to the Amazon site, a 24-hour shopping window is opened. Anything that user adds to his or her shopping cart for the next 24 hours is eligible for Associate referral fees—even if the actual purchase happens at a later time. The money you earn is paid quarterly, either via check, direct deposit to your checking account, or Amazon gift certificate.

Adding an Associates link requires some rudimentary knowledge of HTML, of course, although Amazon makes the process as easy as cutting and pasting a line or two of code. You can get more detailed instructions—as well as sign up for the Associates program—at the Amazon Associates page (`associates.amazon.com`), shown in Figure 10.20.

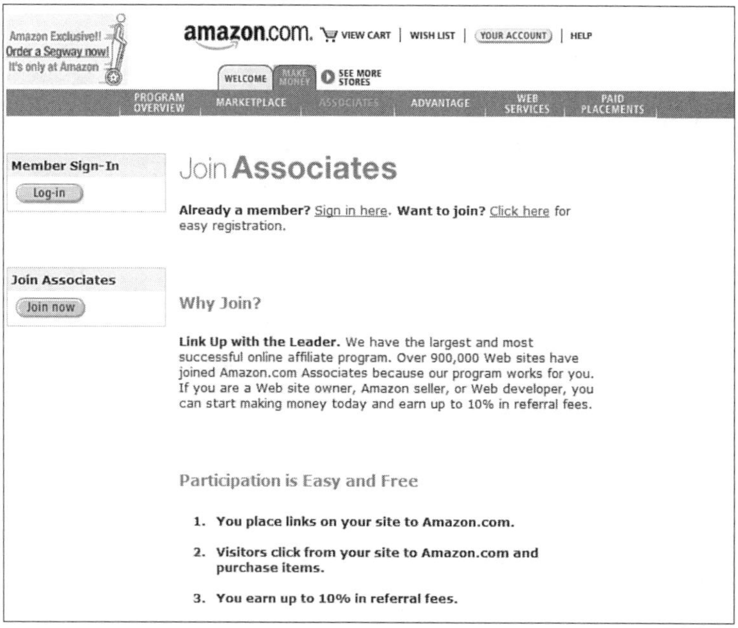
Amazon Exclusive!!
Order a Segway now!
It's only at Amazon
amazon.com.
VIEW CART
WISH LIST
YOUR ACCOUNT
HELP
WELCOME
MAKE MONEY
SEE MORE STORES
PROGRAM OVERVIEW
MARKETPLACE
ASSOCIATES
ADVANTAGE
WEB SERVICES
PAID PLACEMENTS
Member Sign-In
Log-in
Join Associates
Join now
Join Associates
Already a member? Sign in here. Want to join? Click here for easy registration.
Why Join?
Link Up with the Leader. We have the largest and most successful online affiliate program. Over 900,000 Web sites have joined Amazon.com Associates because our program works for you. If you are a Web site owner, Amazon seller, or Web developer, you can start making money today and earn up to 10% in referral fees.
Participation is Easy and Free
1. You place links on your site to Amazon.com.
2. Visitors click from your site to Amazon.com and purchase items.
3. You earn up to 10% in referral fees.

FIGURE 10.20
Earn money as an Amazon Associate.

Bargain Hunter's Secret

Now here's the real secret that Amazon doesn't want you to know. You can purchase from your own Associate links—and earn commissions on every item you buy from Amazon! That's right, you become your own referral, and earn a commission on every purchase you make. Those Amazon Associate referral fees are now like cash rebates on your own purchases. It's a cool deal, but only workable as long as you run your own Web site or pages. And don't forget to ask all your friends and family to route their Amazon purchases through your site as well!

What's Next: Hunting for Bargains at Other Online Retailers

Well, that covers all the different ways you can save money with Amazon.com. But, even though Amazon is a great place to shop, it isn't the only online retailer out there. There are thousands of other online retailers, all ripe for bargain hunting. To find the best stores for online bargain hunting, turn to the listings in Bargain Hunter's Online Shopping Directory—coming up next!

III

THE BARGAIN HUNTER'S ONLINE SHOPPING DIRECTORY

III

THE BARGAIN HUNTER'S ONLINE SHOPPING DIRECTORY

Although you could use a price-comparison site as the home base for all your online shopping (as discussed in Chapter 5, "Hunting for the Lowest Price"), shopping is even faster if you know directly where to go for precisely what you want. To that end, I present the Bargain Hunter's Online Shopping Directory, a listing of over 1,000 online merchants in 35 different product categories. These sites offer the best online bargains and are definitely worth your shopping attention.

Each listing consists of the merchant name, followed by the Web site address and phone number. (Although not all online merchants offer telephone service.) There's typically a brief description of the merchandise offered by that merchant, along with a section I call *Bargain Hunter's Secrets*. This section (when present) tells you where on the site to go for the best bargains—including sales, discounted items, closeouts, and other big savings. Note that some merchants don't have separate bargain areas on their sites; when all items are discounted, the best bargains are everywhere!

To help you with your online shopping, I've singled out notable merchants in two distinct areas:

- **Best Bargains**—Stores that consistently offer the lowest prices in a given category are designated with the Best Bargains icon. Look here first for the biggest savings.
- **Best Selection**—Stores that consistently offer the largest variety of merchandise in a given category are designated with the Best Selection icon. Look here first when you want the most choices in your shopping.

Know, however, that prices and selection vary from week to week and from store to store. Which means, of course, that it pays to shop at more than one store and compare both prices and products. Don't take the information presented here as gospel; things change fast on the Internet, so today's top-rated site could easily turn into tomorrow's clunker!

Note that all information in this chapter is as presented on individual merchant Web sites as of Spring 2003. Because things change quickly on the Internet, all information presented here is subject to change.

APPAREL

Apparel is one hot online shopping category. More and more consumers are buying clothes online, hence the proliferation of online clothing stores—and the growing number of online bargains.

That said, buying clothes online is often a difficult experience, especially if you're an odd size or otherwise hard to fit. If a medium always fits you well, no matter where you shop, you'll find buying clothes online a breeze. But if a medium from one store fits you like a small from another, prepare yourself for some online shopping challenges.

Here are some tips for buying clothes online:

- If you're comfortable with a particular brand of clothing from traditional retailers, look for that brand online. Levi's with a 34-inch waist will fit the same from an online merchant as they do from a "bricks and mortar" store.
- After you've found an online merchant that offers clothing that fits, stick with that merchant. There's no sense experimenting when you find something that works.
- Before you buy, look for detailed size and fit information. Many online merchants offer more specific sizes than traditional merchants, which can provide a more exact fit.
- For that matter, some online merchants offer custom-tailored merchandise. There's no better fit than clothing cut to your precise proportions.
- Most important, make sure that the merchant has a lenient returns policy. You're more likely to return clothing items than you are any other type of merchandise, so make sure that the merchant makes it easy to send back those items that don't fit as advertised.

Note, however, that most swimwear, lingerie, and men's underwear is, quite naturally, nonreturnable. Buy these items at your own risk.

Despite the sizing issues, the Internet is especially useful when shopping for hard-to-find sizes. If you know where to look online, you'll find a much wider selection of petite and plus-size women's clothing, and big and tall men's apparel, than you will in traditional retail stores. Whenever possible, I've noted those merchants that offer a wide selection of these sizes.

In addition to the clothing merchants listed in this section, you can also find wide selections of men's and women's apparel at most department store and mass merchant sites. Look in those sections for additional selection and bargains.

3 Wishes Lingerie

www.3wisheslingerie.com (800.438.6605)

Women's intimate apparel: lingerie, fantasy outfits, and shoes.

BARGAIN HUNTER'S SECRETS: Free shipping, no minimum purchase.

AB Lambdin

www.ablambdin.com (800.831.3330)

Women's casual clothing: swimwear, resortwear, lingerie, shoes, and accessories.

BARGAIN HUNTER'S SECRETS: Click the Sale link on the Shop Now page for clearance merchandise.

Abercrombie

www.abercrombiekids.com (888.856.4480)

Children's and **teens'** casual clothing.

BARGAIN HUNTER'S SECRETS: Click the Sale link in each category for sale merchandise.

Abercrombie & Fitch

www.abercrombie.com (888.856.4480)

Men's casual clothing: shirts, pants, underwear, outerwear, and accessories. **Women's** casual clothing: tops, pants, sleepwear, lingerie, outerwear, and accessories.

BARGAIN HUNTER'S SECRETS: Click the Sale links in the individual categories for sale merchandise.

AlexBlake.com

www.alexblake.com (818.501.4771)

Men's socks. **Women's** hosiery. Offers plus sizes.

BARGAIN HUNTER'S SECRETS: Join the AlexBlake Hosiery Club (free membership) and get a free pair of hosiery after you purchase a dozen pairs.

Alight.com

www.alight.com (516.367.1095)

Women's plus-size clothing: tops, skirts, pants, suits, activewear, swimwear, outerwear, lingerie, jewelry, and accessories.

BARGAIN HUNTER'S SECRETS: Click the Steals + Deals, 50% Off, and Sale Items Under $25 links for sale items. Also check out the Super Save Items and On Sale items on the home page.

AllJacketsAllTheTime.com

www.alljacketsallthetime.com (800.434.4729)

Men's jackets and sweaters. **Women's** jackets and sweaters.

BARGAIN HUNTER'S SECRETS: Look for savings on individual product pages.

Amazon.com

www.amazon.com (800.201.7575)

Men's casual clothing: shirts, sleepwear, outerwear, shoes, hats, and accessories. **Women's** casual clothing: sweaters, pants, sleepwear, maternity wear, shoes, and accessories. Offers plus and petite sizes. **Teens'** casual clothing. **Children's** casual clothing. (Select the Apparel & Accessories tab.) Many items offered by third-party partner retailers.

BARGAIN HUNTER'S SECRETS: Click the Sales & Deals tab for sale and promotional items. Look for clothing bargains during the sitewide Friday Sale. Also look for free shipping and other promotions on individual product pages.

American Eagle Outfitters

www.ae.com (888.232.4535)

Men's casual clothing: shirts, pants, underwear, shoes, and accessories. **Women's** casual clothing: tops, pants, skirts, dresses, lingerie, shoes, jewelry, and accessories.

BARGAIN HUNTER'S SECRETS: Click the Clearance link for closeout merchandise. Free shipping when you sign up for email promotions and spend $75. Also look for specials on main category pages.

Ann Taylor

www.anntaylor.com (800.342.5266)

Women's casual and career clothing: suits, tops, sweaters, pants, skirts, dresses, outerwear, shoes, and accessories.

BARGAIN HUNTER'S SECRETS: Click the Sale link for sale merchandise.

AnyKnockoff.com

www.anyknockoff.com (877.856.5199)

Women's handbags, watches, and accessories.

BARGAIN HUNTER'S SECRETS: No-name knock-offs of designer products offered at substantial savings. Click the Sale Items link for more bargains. Free Priority Mail shipping on orders of more than $100.

Athleta

www.athleta.com (888.322.5515)

Women's athletic apparel: swimwear, tops, shorts, pants, sports bras, and running shoes.

BARGAIN HUNTER'S SECRETS: Click the Sale Outlet link for clearance merchandise.

Avenue

www.avenue.com (800.441.1362)

Women's plus-size clothing: tops, pants, activewear, suits, dresses, shoes, and accessories.

BARGAIN HUNTER'S SECRETS: Click the Deals of the Week link for sale merchandise. Click the Clearance link for closeout merchandise.

Bachrach

www.bachrach.com (800.222.4722)

Men's casual, career, and fashion clothing: shirts, pants, suits, sweaters, formalwear, outerwear, shoes, and accessories.

BARGAIN HUNTER'S SECRETS: Click the Clearance link for closeout merchandise.

Banana Republic

www.bananarepublic.com (888.277.8953)

Men's casual clothing: shirts, pants, suits, outerwear, underwear, shoes, and accessories. **Women's** casual clothing: tops, pants, skirts, dresses, sleepwear, lingerie, swimwear, outerwear, shoes, jewelry, and accessories. Offers petite sizes.

BARGAIN HUNTER'S SECRETS: Click the Sales links in individual categories for sales merchandise. Free shipping on orders of $125 or more.

BareNecessities.com

www.barenecessities.com (877.728.9272)

Men's intimate apparel: underwear, sleepwear, and T-shirts. **Women's** intimate apparel: lingerie, sleepwear, and hosiery. Offers plus sizes.

BARGAIN HUNTER'S SECRETS: Click the Sales and Specials link for sale merchandise, clearance merchandise, and promotions.

BellaLingerie.com

www.bellalingerie.com (877.808.3322)

Men's intimate apparel: boxers and thongs. **Women's** intimate apparel: lingerie and stockings. Offers plus sizes.

BARGAIN HUNTER'S SECRETS: Click the On Sale! link for sale merchandise.

Beni Boutique Best Bargain

www.beniboutique.com (650.592.5787)

Women's designer clothing: tops, pants, dresses, shoes, and accessories. Offers petite sizes.

BARGAIN HUNTER'S SECRETS: All merchandise offered at discount prices; look for mark-downs on individual items. Click the Clearance Items link for closeout merchandise.

BestPromDresses.com

www.bestpromdresses.com (888.217.5655)

Women's formalwear: prom dresses, formal dresses.

BARGAIN HUNTER'S SECRETS: Free shipping.

BigTallDirect.com

www.bigtalldirect.com (800.214.9686)

Men's big and tall clothing: shirts, sweaters, pants, suits, athletic wear, swimwear, sleepwear, underwear, and accessories.

BARGAIN HUNTER'S SECRETS: Use the Clearance Sportswear selector to search for merchandise at 25%, 33%, and 50% off. Click the Clearance link to view all closeout merchandise.

Blair Best Bargain Best Selection

www.blair.com (800.821.5744)

Men's casual and career clothing: shirts, sweaters, pants, suits, sleepwear, swimwear, outerwear, underwear, shoes, and accessories. **Women's** casual and career clothing: tops, sweaters, pants, skirts, dresses, hosiery, lingerie, sleepwear, swimwear, outerwear, shoes, jewelry, and accessories.

BARGAIN HUNTER'S SECRETS: Most merchandise discounted; look for savings on individual product pages. Click the Clearance tab for closeout items. Click the Internet Specials link on individual category pages for sale merchandise. Sign up for email specials delivered to your inbox.

Bluefly.com Best Bargain

www.bluefly.com (877.258.3359)

Men's designer clothing: shirts, sweaters, pants, suits, outerwear, shoes, and accessories. **Women's** designer clothing: tops, pants, skirts, dresses, suits, swimwear, outerwear, shoes, jewelry, and accessories.

BARGAIN HUNTER'S SECRETS: Most merchandise discounted; look for savings on individual product pages. Click the Clearance link for closeout merchandise.

Bra Smyth

www.brasmyth.com (800.272.9466)

Women's intimate apparel: lingerie, sleepwear, and swimwear.

BARGAIN HUNTER'S SECRETS: Click the Sale Outlet link for clearance merchandise.

Brooks Brothers

www.brooksbrothers.com (800.274.1815)

Men's casual and career clothing: shirts, sweaters, pants, suits, formalwear, sleepwear, underwear, shoes, and accessories. **Women's** casual and career clothing: tops, sweaters, pants, skits, dresses, suits, outerwear, shoes, and accessories. **Boys'** casual clothing. Offers big and tall and petite sizes.

BARGAIN HUNTER'S SECRETS: Click the Brooks Buys link for sale merchandise. Click the Clearance links on category pages for closeout merchandise.

Buckle

www.buckle.com (800.522.8090)

Men's casual clothing: shirts, sweaters, pants, outerwear, shoes, and accessories. **Women's** casual clothing: tops, pants, swimwear, outerwear, shoes, and accessories.

BARGAIN HUNTER'S SECRETS: Click the Sale links on category pages for sale merchandise.

Burlington Coat Factory Direct

www.bcfdirect.com (800.444.2628)

Men's casual and career clothing: shirts, sweaters, pants, suits, outerwear, shoes, and accessories. **Women's** casual and career clothing: tops, sweaters, pants, skirts, dresses, suits, outerwear, maternity apparel, shoes, and accessories. **Children's** casual clothing. **Baby** clothing. Offers big and tall, plus, and petite sizes.

BARGAIN HUNTER'S SECRETS: Most merchandise discounted; look for savings on individual product pages.

Caché

www.cache.com (800.788.2224)

Women's fashion clothing: tops, pants, dresses, eveningwear, prom dresses, and accessories.

BARGAIN HUNTER'S SECRETS: Click the Sale Room link for sale merchandise.

Carabella Collection

www.carabella.com (800.227.2235)

Men's casual clothing: shirts, swimwear. **Women's** casual and fashion clothing: tops, pants, skirts, dresses, eveningwear, swimwear, lingerie, shoes, and accessories.

BARGAIN HUNTER'S SECRETS: Click the Sale & Clearance link for sale and closeout merchandise. Click the Weekly Specials link for limited-time specials. Sign up for clearance offers by email.

Casual Corner

www.casualcorner.com (800.662.8042)

Women's casual clothing: tops, sweaters, pants, skirts, dresses, outerwear, hosiery, lingerie, shoes, and accessories.

BARGAIN HUNTER'S SECRETS: Click the Sale link for sale merchandise. Additional sale items featured on the home page.

Casual Male Big & Tall

www.casualmale.com (800.767.0319)

Men's big and tall clothing: shirts, pants, outerwear, underwear, shoes, and accessories.

BARGAIN HUNTER'S SECRETS: Click the Sale Items link for sale merchandise. Click the Clearance link for closeout merchandise. Sign up for the CM Rewards card to receive 10% off all purchases.

Catherines

www.catherines.com

Women's plus size clothing: tops, sweaters, pants, skirts, dresses, suits, outerwear, swimwear, sleepwear, lingerie, jewelry, and accessories.

BARGAIN HUNTER'S SECRETS: Click the On Sale Now link for sale merchandise.

The Children's Place

www.childrensplace.com (877.752.2387)

Children's clothing. **Baby** clothing.

BARGAIN HUNTER'S SECRETS: Click the Shop Outlet link for clearance items. Free shipping on orders of $75 or more.

CWD Kids

www.cwdkids.com (800.242.5437)

Children's casual clothing.

BARGAIN HUNTER'S SECRETS: Click the Outlet link for clearance merchandise.

CyberSwim.com

www.cyberswim.com (800.291.2943)

Women's swimwear.

BARGAIN HUNTER'S SECRETS: Click the On Sale Today link for sale merchandise.

Danier Leather

www.danier.com (877.932.6437)

Men's leather clothing: shirts, pants, jackets, outerwear, and accessories. **Women's** leather clothing: tops, pants, skirts, jackets, outerwear, and accessories.

BARGAIN HUNTER'S SECRETS: Click the On Sale link for sale merchandise.

dELiAs.com

www.delias.com (888.533.5427)

Girls' and **teens'** casual and fashion clothing.

BARGAIN HUNTER'S SECRETS: Click the dELiAs on Sale link for sale and clearance merchandise.

Denim Express

www.denimexpress.com (800.824.9622)

Men's, **women's**, and **children's** jeans and accessories. Shop by brand; all major brands offered. Offers hard-to-find sizes. Also offers other merchandise (shirts, shoes, and so on) by brand.

BARGAIN HUNTER'S SECRETS: Free shipping on orders of more than $50.

DesignerOutlet.com

www.designeroutlet.com (800.923.9915)

Men's casual and designer clothing: shirts, sweaters, pants, underwear, and accessories. **Women's** casual and designer clothing: tops, sweaters, pants, skirts, dresses, suites, lingerie, and accessories. **Children's** casual and designer clothing. Offers plus sizes.

BARGAIN HUNTER'S SECRETS: Most items discounted; look for savings on individual product pages.

Discount Designer Men's Wear

www.menswear-discounts.com (866.761.1500)

Men's career clothing: shirts, pants, suits, formalwear, and outerwear. Offers big and tall sizes.

BARGAIN HUNTER'S SECRETS: Most items discounted; look for savings on individual product pages.

eBoxers

www.eboxersonline.com (866.326.9377)

Men's designer underwear, sleepwear, and swimwear.

BARGAIN HUNTER'S SECRETS: Free shipping on all orders.

Eddie Bauer

www.eddiebauer.com (800.625.7935)

Men's casual clothing: shirts, sweaters, pants, underwear, outerwear, shoes, and accessories. **Women's** casual clothing: tops, sweaters, pants, skirts, dresses, sleepwear, swimwear, outerwear, shoes, and accessories.

BARGAIN HUNTER'S SECRETS: Click the Sale link on each category page for sale items. Go to **www.eddiebaueroutlet.com** for clearance merchandise.

Elisabeth

www.elisabeth.com (800.683.7330)

Women's casual clothing: tops, pants, skirts, sleepwear, swimwear, and accessories. Offers petite sizes.

BARGAIN HUNTER'S SECRETS: Click the Sale link for sale items.

eLuxury

www.eluxury.com (877.890.7171)

Men's fashion clothing: shirts, pants, sleepwear, shoes, and accessories. **Women's** fashion clothing: tops, pants, skirts, lingerie, swimwear, outerwear, and accessories.

BARGAIN HUNTER'S SECRETS: Click the Shop Our Sale link for sale merchandise.

Frank Bee School Uniforms

www.schoolunif.com (800.372.6523)

Children's school uniforms and accessories.

BARGAIN HUNTER'S SECRETS: Look for savings on individual items.

Frederick's of Hollywood

www.fredericks.com (602.760.2111)

Women's intimate apparel: lingerie, hosiery, shoes, and accessories. Offers plus sizes.

BARGAIN HUNTER'S SECRETS: Click the Sale link for sale and closeout merchandise.

French Toast School Uniforms

www.frenchtoast.com (800.373.6248)

Children's school clothing and uniforms.

BARGAIN HUNTER'S SECRETS: Look for sale items on home page. Look for savings on individual items.

Freshpair.com Best Selection

www.freshpair.com (866.223.2216)

Men's intimate apparel: underwear, sleepwear, T-shirts, and socks. **Women's** intimate apparel: lingerie, sleepwear, and hosiery. Offers big and tall sizes.

BARGAIN HUNTER'S SECRETS: Most items discounted; see individual product pages for savings. Click the Sales links for sale merchandise by gender. Free shipping on orders of more than $95.

Gap Kids

www.gapkids.com (888.906.1104)

Children's casual clothing. **Baby** clothing.

BARGAIN HUNTER'S SECRETS: Free shipping on orders of $100 or more. Click Sale links on main category pages for sale merchandise.

Gap Online

www.gap.com (888.906.1104)

Men's casual clothing: shirts, pants, underwear, outerwear, shoes, and accessories. **Women's** casual clothing: tops, pants, skirts, sleepwear, lingerie, outerwear, shoes, and accessories.

BARGAIN HUNTER'S SECRETS: Free shipping on orders of more than $100. Click Sale links on category pages for sale merchandise.

GirlShop Best Selection

www.girlshop.com (888.450.7467)

Women's fashion clothing: tops, sweaters, pants, skirts, dresses, eveningwear, sleepwear, lingerie, swimwear, outerwear, maternity wear, shoes, jewelry, and accessories. Merchandise offered by a collection of individual small boutiques. (Men's clothing offered via partner site GuyShop.)

BARGAIN HUNTER'S SECRETS: Click the Sales! link for sale merchandise. Look for links to clearance merchandise at the bottom of the home page. Look for store sales at individual boutiques.

GoJane.com

www.gojane.com (800.846.5263)

Women's casual clothing: tops, pants, skirts, dresses, sleepwear, lingerie, and shoes.

BARGAIN HUNTER'S SECRETS: Click the Sale tab for sale merchandise.

Guess

www.guess.com (877.444.8377)

Men's casual clothing: jeans, shirts, outerwear, and accessories. **Women's** casual clothing: jeans, tops, dresses, swimwear, outerwear, shoes, jewelry, and accessories. **Children's** casual clothing. **Baby** clothing.

BARGAIN HUNTER'S SECRETS: Click the Sale links on main category pages for sale merchandise.

GuyShop Best Selection

www.guyshop.com (888.450.7467)

Men's fashion clothing: shirts, sweaters, pants, underwear, outerwear, shoes, and accessories. Merchandise offered by a collection of individual small boutiques. (GirlShop is GuyShop's sister site.)

BARGAIN HUNTER'S SECRETS: Click the Sales! link for sale merchandise. Look for links to clearance merchandise at the bottom of the home page. Look for store sales at individual boutiques.

Gymboree

www.gymboree.com (877.449.6932)

Children's casual clothing. **Baby** clothing, gifts, and toys.

BARGAIN HUNTER'S SECRETS: Look for sale items on home page. Look for Sale links on main category pages.

Henry and June Lingerie

www.henryandjune.com

Women's intimate apparel: lingerie, sleepwear, hosiery, and fantasy apparel. **Men's** intimate apparel: underwear and sleepwear. Offers plus sizes.

BARGAIN HUNTER'S SECRETS: Low price guarantee; will match pricing at other stores. Look for On Sale items on major category pages. Free shipping on orders of $75 or more.

HerRoom.com

www.herroom.com (800.558.6779)

Women's intimate apparel: lingerie, sleepwear, and accessories. Sister site to HisRoom.com.

BARGAIN HUNTER'S SECRETS: Click the Sale Items link for sale merchandise. Click the Coupons & Promotions link for clearance and promotional merchandise. Free shipping on orders $100 and higher.

HisRoom.com

www.hisroom.com (800.558.6779)

Men's intimate apparel: underwear, sleepwear, T-shirts, socks, and accessories. Companion site to HerRoom.com.

BARGAIN HUNTER'S SECRETS: Click the Sale Items link for sale merchandise. Click the Coupons & Promotions link for clearance and promotional merchandise. Free shipping on orders $100 and higher.

InFashion Kids

www.infashionkids.com (908.371.1733)

Children's clothing and Halloween costumes. **Baby** clothing.

BARGAIN HUNTER'S SECRETS: Look for savings on individual products.

International Male

www.internationalmale.com (800.293.9333)

Men's casual clothing: shirts, pants, suits, outerwear, underwear, sleepwear, swimwear, shoes, and accessories.

BARGAIN HUNTER'S SECRETS: Click the On Sale Now! link for sale and promotional merchandise.

Irvine Park

www.irvinepark.com (866.252.7400)

Men's casual and career clothing: shirts, sweaters, pants, suits, underwear, outerwear, formalwear, shoes, and accessories.

BARGAIN HUNTER'S SECRETS: Most items discounted; see individual product pages for savings. Sign up for specials via email.

J. Crew

www.jcrew.com (800.932.0043)

Men's casual clothing: shirts, sweaters, pants, sportcoats, underwear, outerwear, swimwear, shoes, and accessories. **Women's** casual clothing: tops, sweaters, pants, skirts, dresses, suits, swimwear, sleepwear, outerwear, shoes, and accessories. Offers extended sizes.

BARGAIN HUNTER'S SECRETS: Look for sale links on main category pages.

J. Jill

www.jjill.com (800.498.9960)

Women's casual clothing: tops, sweaters, pants, skirts, dresses, outerwear, shoes, and accessories. Offers tall and petite sizes.

BARGAIN HUNTER'S SECRETS: Click the Sale link for sale merchandise. Open a J. Jill credit card and receive 5% off every purchase.

Jemznjewels Best Bargain

www.jemznjewels.com (800.488.8265)

Women's designer bags, jewelry, and accessories.

BARGAIN HUNTER'S SECRETS: All merchandise offered at steep discounts. Click the On Sale link for best bargains. Click the Auctions tab for items offered for auction at eBay.

Jos A. Bank

www.josbank.com (800.285.2265)

Men's casual and career clothing: shirts, pants, sportcoats, suits, underwear, outerwear, formalwear, shoes, and accessories.

BARGAIN HUNTER'S SECRETS: Look for sales and promotions on the home page. Click the Clearance Center link for closeout merchandise.

Journeys

www.journeys.com (888.324.6356)

Teens' fashion clothing.

BARGAIN HUNTER'S SECRETS: Click the Sale Stuff link on main category pages for sale merchandise.

Just My Size

www.justmysize.com (800.261.5902)

Women's plus-size clothing: tops, sweaters, pants, skirts, dresses, lingerie, sleepwear, swimwear, active wear, hosiery, and accessories.

BARGAIN HUNTER'S SECRETS: Look for sales and promotions on the home page. Click the Clearance & Extras tab for closeout and promotional items.

Karmaloop

www.karmaloop.com (866.658.1902)

Men's urban clothing: shirts, sweaters, pants, hats, shoes, and accessories. **Women's** urban clothing: tops, sweaters, pants, skirts, dresses, hats, jewelry, shoes, and accessories.

BARGAIN HUNTER'S SECRETS: Click the On Sale! tab for sale merchandise.

Kaufman's Tall and Big Men's Shop

www.kaufmans.com (888.761.8255)

Men's big and tall clothing: shirts, sweaters, pants, sportcoats, underwear, outerwear, shoes, and accessories.

BARGAIN HUNTER'S SECRETS: Click the Hot Deals link for sale merchandise and promotions.

KingSize Direct

www.kingsizedirect.com (800.677.0249)

Men's big and tall clothing: shirts, pants, sportcoats, underwear, sleepwear, outerwear, shoes, and accessories.

BARGAIN HUNTER'S SECRETS: Look for sales and promotions on the home page. Click the Clearance tab for closeout items.

L.L. Bean

www.llbean.com (800.441.5713)

Men's casual clothing: shirts, sweaters, pants, underwear, sleepwear, outerwear, shoes, and accessories. **Women's** casual clothing: tops, sweaters, pants, skirts, dresses, sleepwear, swimwear, outerwear, shoes, and accessories. **Children's** casual clothing.

BARGAIN HUNTER'S SECRETS: Look for savings on individual product pages. Click the Sale link for sale merchandise and promotions.

Lands' End

www.landsend.com (800.963.4816)

Men's casual clothing: shirts, sweaters, pants, underwear, sleepwear, outerwear, shoes, and accessories. **Women's** casual clothing: tops, sweaters, pants, skirts, dresses, sleepwear, swimwear, outerwear, shoes, and accessories. **Children's** casual clothing. Offers plus sizes.

BARGAIN HUNTER'S SECRETS: Look for savings on individual product pages. Click the Overstocks tab for clearance merchandise, updated every Wednesday and Saturday.

LegWearDirect.com

www.legweardirect.com (877.534.3472)

Women's hosiery. **Men's** socks.

BARGAIN HUNTER'S SECRETS: Private-label versions of name-brand merchandise at discount prices; considerable savings on individual items. Look for special promotions on the home page. Click the Internet Specials icon for online-only promotions.

LingerieAtLarge

www.lingerieatlarge.com (866.285.2743)

Women's plus-size lingerie.

BARGAIN HUNTER'S SECRETS: Click the Specials link for sale merchandise and promotions.

Maidenform

www.maidenform.com (888.888.0328)

Women's lingerie.

BARGAIN HUNTER'S SECRETS: Free shipping on orders of more than $100.

Mark Shale

www.markshale.com (888.333.6964)

Men's casual clothing: shirts, sweaters, pants, sleepwear, shoes, and accessories. **Women's** casual clothing: tops, pants, skirts, and accessories.

BARGAIN HUNTER'S SECRETS: Click the Clearance link for closeout and sale merchandise.

MaxStudio.com

www.maxstudio.com (888.334.4629)

Women's fashion clothing: tops, pants, skirts, dresses, outerwear, and accessories.

BARGAIN HUNTER'S SECRETS: Free shipping on orders of more than $100.

Men's Wearhouse

www.menswearhouse.com (877.986.9669)

Men's career clothing: dress shirts, pants, sportcoats, suits, outerwear, formalwear, shoes, and accessories. Click the Website Exclusives link for casual clothing.

BARGAIN HUNTER'S SECRETS: Look for savings on individual items. Look for sales and promotions on main category pages. Click the Sale! link for sale merchandise.

Newport News

www.newport-news.com (800.759.3950)

Women's fashion clothing: tops, sweaters, pants, skirts, dresses, suits, swimwear, outerwear, lingerie, hosiery, and accessories. Offers petite and tall sizes.

BARGAIN HUNTER'S SECRETS: Click the Clearance link for closeout items. Click the Special Offers link for sale items and promotions.

Old Navy

www.oldnavy.com (800.653.6289)

Men's casual clothing: jeans, shirts, sweaters, pants, underwear, outerwear, and accessories. **Women's** casual clothing: jeans, tops, sweaters, pants, sleepwear, outerwear, and accessories. **Children's** casual clothing. **Baby** clothing. Offers larger sizes.

BARGAIN HUNTER'S SECRETS: Look for sales and promotions on home page. Click the Bargains links on main category pages for sale merchandise. Click the Item of the Week links on main category pages for weekly specials. Free shipping on orders of $85 or more.

One Hanes Place

www.onehanesplace.com (800.671.1674)

Women's intimate apparel: lingerie, sleepwear, and hosiery. **Men's** underwear and socks. **Children's** underwear.

BARGAIN HUNTER'S SECRETS: Click the Sale tab for sale merchandise. Click the Closeouts & Extras tab for clearance merchandise. Free shipping on orders of $75 or more.

OshKosh B'Gosh

www.oshkoshbgosh.com (800.692.4674)

Men's casual clothing: jeans, shirts, pants, jackets, and accessories. **Women's** casual clothing: jeans, pants, sweaters, shirts, and outerwear. **Children's** clothing and jeans.

BARGAIN HUNTER'S SECRETS: Click the Clearance link on main category pages for closeout merchandise. Free shipping on orders of $75 or more.

Pacific Sunwear

www.pacsun.com (877.372.2786)

Men's casual clothing: shirts, sweaters, shorts, jeans, and pants. **Women's** casual clothing: tops, sweaters, shorts, jeans, pants, and swimwear. Offers extended sizes.

BARGAIN HUNTER'S SECRETS: See the Special Offers section of the home page for sale merchandise and promotions.

Paul Frederick

www.paulfrederick.com (800.247.8162)

Men's career clothing: dress shirts, sweaters, pants, suits, outerwear, formalwear, and accessories.

BARGAIN HUNTER'S SECRETS: Click the Clearance link for closeout merchandise. Click the Deals of the Week link for weekly specials.

PecksOnline.com

www.pecksonline.com (877.467.3257)

Women's career clothing: sweaters, suits, outerwear, and accessories.

BARGAIN HUNTER'S SECRETS: Look for sales and promotions on the home page.

Pink Slip

www.thepinkslip.com (866.816.7465)

Women's intimate apparel: lingerie, sleepwear, and hosiery.

BARGAIN HUNTER'S SECRETS: Click the Specials link for sale and clearance merchandise.

PlusSize.com

www.plussize.com

Women's plus-size shopping mall with merchandise from a variety of merchants.

BARGAIN HUNTER'S SECRETS: Click the Specials link for sale merchandise. Click the eBay Store link for merchandise offered on eBay. Look for sale items at individual stores.

Polo.com

www.polo.com (888.475.7674)

Men's casual clothing: shirts, sweaters, pants, underwear, outerwear, swimwear, shoes, and accessories. **Women's** casual clothing: tops, sweaters, pants, skirts, dresses, sleepwear, swimwear, outerwear, shoes, and accessories. **Children's** casual clothing. Offers big and tall sizes.

BARGAIN HUNTER'S SECRETS: Click the Sale link for sale and clearance merchandise.

ShopBop.com

www.shopbop.com (877.746.7267)

Women's fashion clothing: jeans, tops, pants, skirts, dresses, swimwear, lingerie, jewelry, shoes, and accessories.

BARGAIN HUNTER'S SECRETS: Look for sales and promotions on the home page.

Silhouettes

www.silhouettes.com (888.651.8337)

Women's plus-size clothing: tops, sweaters, pants, skirts, dresses, lingerie, outerwear, shoes, and accessories.

BARGAIN HUNTER'S SECRETS: Click the Outlet Store link for clearance merchandise. Join the Buyer's Club to receive 10% off each order.

Sova Leather

www.sovaleather.com (415.626.8899)

Women's handbags and accessories.

BARGAIN HUNTER'S SECRETS: All items heavily discounted; look for savings on individual items. Click the Bonus link to receive free items with qualified purchases.

StockingShopping.com

www.stockingshopping.com (321.674.9377)

Women's hosiery and lingerie. Offers plus sizes.

BARGAIN HUNTER'S SECRETS: Free shipping on orders of more than $25. See Specials section on home page for sale items.

Trashy Lingerie

www.trashy.com (310.659.4550)

Women's intimate apparel: lingerie, costumes, hosiery, shoes, and accessories.

BARGAIN HUNTER'S SECRETS: Click the Bargains link for sale and clearance merchandise.

T-Shirts.com

www.t-shirts.com (800.588.1857)

Men's, women's, and **children's** blank and printed T-shirts.

BARGAIN HUNTER'S SECRETS: See Sales section on home page for sale and clearance merchandise.

Urban Outfitters

www.urbanoutfitters.com (800.959.8794)

Men's casual clothing: shirts, sweaters, pants, underwear, outerwear, shoes, and accessories. **Women's** casual clothing: tops, sweaters, pants, skirts, dresses, lingerie, outerwear, swimwear, shoes, and accessories.

BARGAIN HUNTER'S SECRETS: Look for sale items on the home page. Click the Sale links on main category pages for sale and clearance merchandise.

Victoria's Secret

www.victoriassecret.com (800.970.1109)

Women's intimate apparel: lingerie, sleepwear, swimwear, and shoes.

BARGAIN HUNTER'S SECRETS: Look for sale items on the home page. Click the Sale link for sale and clearance merchandise.

The Village Hat Shop (Best Selection)

www.villagehatshop.com (888.847.4287)

Men's and **women's** hats.

BARGAIN HUNTER'S SECRETS: Most items discounted; look for savings on individual product pages. Click the Sales Specials link for sale merchandise.

Wilson Leather

www.wilsonleather.com (800.236.9976)

Men's leather jackets and accessories. **Women's** leather jackets, skirts, and accessories. Offers big and tall and extended sizes.

BARGAIN HUNTER'S SECRETS: Look for sale items on home page. Click Hot Deals links on main category pages for sale items. Click Final Clearance links on main category pages for closeout merchandise.

YOOX

www.yoox.com (866.900.9266)

Men's designer clothing: shirts, pants, sportcoats, suits, outerwear, and accessories. **Women's** designer clothing: tops, sweaters, pants, skirts, dresses, suits, outerwear, and accessories.

BARGAIN HUNTER'S SECRETS: Most items discounted. Look for sales items on home page.

ART AND ANTIQUES

Buying art and antiques online is a double-edged sword. On one hand, the Internet is a great place to find rare or limited-quantity items that previously were available only in big-city galleries. On the other hand, this type of rare item is seldom discounted. So, you'll find many art and antique sites on the Web, but few that truly offer bargain prices.

Let's face it; merchandise in these categories is often overpriced. It's also difficult to compare prices because you can't find two identical copies of a one-of-a-kind item. The best you can do is shop around until you find what you want, and then make sure that the price you pay is reasonable.

When you're shopping for paintings and posters, pay close attention to the framing options. Some merchants might lure you in with a low price on the artwork, only to sock it to you with overpriced framing. Look at the *total* price to see whether you're getting a good bargain.

And that total price needs to include the shipping and handling costs. Big, heavy artwork can cost a lot to ship, so don't let yourself get surprised by a hefty shipping charge. Factor this in ahead of time—along with the shipping insurance necessary for high-priced items.

You also need to verify the authenticity of any antique or piece of art you purchase on line. Look for sites that offer certificates of authenticity, or some other form of official certification to make sure you're getting exactly what you think.

Finally, if you're looking for antiques off-line, check out the Directiques Web site (www.directiques.com). This site offers a searchable database of real-world antiques dealers, in a variety of different categories. Nothing like using the Web to find an antiques dealer near you!

AllPosters.com

www.allposters.com (888.654.0143)

Art prints and posters.

BARGAIN HUNTER'S SECRETS: Look for sale items on the home page. For low-priced items, click the Art Prints Under $12.99 link.

AntiqueArts.com

www.antiquearts.com

Antique mall with hundreds of individual dealers. Browse by shop or by category, including antiquities, art, books, china, clocks, coins, dolls, figurines, furniture, glass, jewelry, lamps, memorabilia, metalware, photography, porcelain, pottery, silver, textiles, and toys.

BARGAIN HUNTER'S SECRETS: Look for bargains in individual stores.

Art.com

www.art.com (800.952.5592)

Art prints and posters.

BARGAIN HUNTER'S SECRETS: Click the Clearance link for closeout merchandise.

Art4Sale.com

www.art4sale.com (561.392.7220)

Original artwork and limited edition prints.

BARGAIN HUNTER'S SECRETS: Click the Liquidations link for clearance merchandise. Click the Classified Ads tab for art being sold by private parties; you'll often find good bargains here.

Artful Style

www.artfulstyle.com (877.939.7270)

Original artwork, crafts, and jewelry.

BARGAIN HUNTER'S SECRETS: Click the Works Under $250 link for low-priced items.

ArtInAClick.com

www.artinaclick.com (888.799.7888)

Art prints and posters.

BARGAIN HUNTER'S SECRETS: Click the Outlet Center link for clearance and sale merchandise.

artrepublic

www.artrepublic.com (011.44.127.372.4829)

Art prints and posters. U.K. retailer.

BARGAIN HUNTER'S SECRETS: Free shipping worldwide. Click the Special Offers link for sale and clearance merchandise.

ArtSelect Best Bargain

www.artselect.com (888.686.4254)

Art prints and posters.

BARGAIN HUNTER'S SECRETS: Most items discounted. Click the Outlet tab for clearance and overstock merchandise. Free shipping.

barewalls.com

www.barewalls.com (800.455.3955)

Art prints and posters.

BARGAIN HUNTER'S SECRETS: Click the Specials tab for special offers and promotions.

Basil Street Gallery

www.basilstreet.com (800.525.9661)

Original artwork, tapestries, wall art, statues, and jewelry.

BARGAIN HUNTER'S SECRETS: Click the Gallery Sale link for specially priced items.

Eziba

www.eziba.com (888.404.5108)

Glass art, masks, wall art, and sculptures. (Click the Art & Artifacts tab; also offers jewelry and home décor items.)

BARGAIN HUNTER'S SECRETS: Click the Outlet link on the Art & Artifacts tab for sale and clearance merchandise.

GoAntiques Best Selection

www.goantiques.com

Antiques, clocks, coins, glass, jewelry, photography, porcelain, pottery, prints, silverware, textiles, and watches. An online antique mall that offers merchandise from more than 1000 collectors in 24 countries.

BARGAIN HUNTER'S SECRETS: Go to the Estate Items section for previously owned merchandise. Look for bargains offered by individual merchants.

Guild.com Best Selection

www.guild.com (877.344.8453)

Paintings, photography, sculpture, glass art, ceramics, fiber art, metal art, wood art, and wall art. Original art from individual artists.

BARGAIN HUNTER'S SECRETS: Click the Online Specials link for discounted items.

Heirloom European Tapestries

www.tapestries-inc.com (800.699.6836)

Tapestries and carpets.

BARGAIN HUNTER'S SECRETS: Click the Specials link for clearance and discounted merchandise.

Magellan Traders

www.magellantraders.com (520.622.4968)

Authentic handmade art from around the globe, including African masks, Mexican glassware, Egyptian treasures, Chinese baskets, New Guinea totems, and so on. Great source for world art.

BARGAIN HUNTER'S SECRETS: Join the Magellan Explorers Club (no charge) for email notification of new merchandise and periodic discounts.

Masters' Collection

www.masterscollection.com (800.222.6827)

Art prints and reproductions.

BARGAIN HUNTER'S SECRETS: Free shipping on all online orders. See home page for other sales and promotions.

NextMonet

www.nextmonet.com (888.914.5050)

Original artwork and prints.

BARGAIN HUNTER'S SECRETS: Click the Price link to browse for lower-priced items; merchandise is organized by price point (Under $150, $150–$300, $300–$500, and so on).

Streamlined Poster Gallery

www.streamlined-prints.com (877.771.6848)

Art prints and posters.

BARGAIN HUNTER'S SECRETS: Free shipping on all orders.

TIAS.com Antiques and Collectibles Mall

www.tias.com (888.653.7883)

Antique mall with merchandise from hundreds of individual shops; offers antiques, art, clocks, coins, dolls, figurines, furniture, glass, memorabilia, metalware, photographs, stamps, textiles, tools, toys, vintage clothing, and other collectibles.

BARGAIN HUNTER'S SECRETS: Look for bargains at individual stores.

Yoko Trading

www.yokodana.com (800.987.2926)

Japanese antiques and collectibles.

BARGAIN HUNTER'S SECRETS: Look for sale items on the main Web Catalog page.

AUTOMOBILES AND ACCESSORIES

Shopping online isn't limited to items that can be shipped in a box or envelope. It's possible to buy something as large as an automobile over the Internet, and buying something this expensive online can save you some really big bucks.

Buying a new car online isn't quite the same as buying a shirt or a DVD player online, however. For one thing, don't expect to open your mailbox and find a car inside. No, when you use a Web site to shop for a new car, you actually end up purchasing the vehicle from a local auto dealer. The online sites simply facilitate your purchase by letting you request price quotes from local dealers; these quotes, which incorporate volume discounts arranged by the online auto site, typically are much lower than what you can negotiate on your own.

You start the process by visiting one of the many automotive portal sites. The site offers a variety of pre-purchase information, including reports and reviews of individual models. Most sites will even show you the dealer's invoice cost so that you can judge for yourself what constitutes a good deal.

After you've decided on a specific model, you use the automotive portal to request price quotes. The portal sends your request to participating dealers in your area, who then contact you separately. If you like the price a dealer offers, you make the purchase.

To be honest, most of the automotive portal sites end up delivering similar deals on new cars. Most auto dealers have fixed pricing they offer their online customers, no matter which Web site does the referring. So, although you can request offers through more than one automotive portal, you'll often end up getting the same prices from the same dealers. That said, it never hurts to experiment—especially because some car dealers sign exclusive deals with one online site or another.

Most of the large automotive portals also offer similar pre-purchase information and services. Of these sites, a few stand out slightly from the rest; my favorites are Cars.com, Edmunds, and MSN Autos.

These automotive portals also make it easy to buy (and to sell) used cars. Most tap into large databases of cars for sale; here you *will* find a difference between sites, in terms of cars available. So, when you're shopping for a used car, it definitely pays to search more than one site.

Also in the automotive category are sites that sell auto parts, tires, and accessories. If you know exactly what you want and don't necessarily need it today, buying car parts online is often quite a bit cheaper than purchasing at a traditional auto part store—especially if you're looking to customize your ride.

AutoAccessories.com

www.autoaccessories.com

Auto parts and accessories.

BARGAIN HUNTER'S SECRETS: Free shipping on orders of more than $100.

autobytel.com

www.autobytel.com (949.225.4500)

Full-service automotive portal. New car research and price quotes. Used car listings and vehicle history reports.

BARGAIN HUNTER'S SECRETS: Click the Get a Price Quote link to request new car quotes from local dealers.

AutoNation.com

www.autonation.com

Full-service automotive portal. New car research and price quotes. Used car listings and vehicle history reports.

BARGAIN HUNTER'S SECRETS: Browse for a specific vehicle to request new car quotes from local dealers.

AutoSite

www.autosite.com

Full-service automotive portal. New car research and price quotes. Used car listings and vehicle history reports.

BARGAIN HUNTER'S SECRETS: Click the Free Price Quote link to request new car quotes from local dealers via partner site autobytel.com.

AutoTrader.com

www.autotrader.com

Full-service automotive portal. New car research and price quotes. Used car listings and vehicle history reports.

BARGAIN HUNTER'S SECRETS: Use an auction-style format to submit bids on both new and used cars; click the Bid Now! link.

AutoVantage

www.autovantage.com (877.259.2696)

Full-service automotive portal. New car research and price quotes. Used car listings and vehicle history reports. Members-only auto club.

BARGAIN HUNTER'S SECRETS: Click the Special Offers link for coupons good at various automotive retailers. Join the AutoVantage Gold club ($1 for first three months) and receive discounts good at more than 25,000 car service centers nationwide, as well as Avis and Budget rental car agencies. (No need to join to request free new car quotes from local dealers.)

Autoweb

www.autoweb.com (877.381.7433)

Full-service automotive portal. New car research and price quotes. Used car listings and vehicle history reports.

BARGAIN HUNTER'S SECRETS: Click the Get a Price Quote link to request new car quotes from local dealers.

AutoZone.com

www.autozone.com (800.288.6966)

Auto parts and accessories. (Click the Shopping link.)

BARGAIN HUNTER'S SECRETS: Free shipping on orders of $100 or more.

CarPrices.com

www.carprices.com

Full-service automotive portal. New car research and price quotes. Used car listings and vehicle history reports.

BARGAIN HUNTER'S SECRETS: Use the Quick Price Quote section to request new car quotes from local dealers.

Cars.com

www.cars.com

Full-service automotive portal. New car research and price quotes. Used car listings and vehicle history reports.

BARGAIN HUNTER'S SECRETS: Search for a specific vehicle to request new car quotes from local dealers.

CarsDirect.com

www.carsdirect.com (800.431.2500)

Full-service automotive portal. New car research and price quotes. Used car listings and vehicle history reports.

BARGAIN HUNTER'S SECRETS: Search for specific new car models to see prices from dealers in your area. Offers a low-price guarantee for new vehicles purchased via its site.

DealerNet.com

www.dealernet.com

Full-service automotive portal. New car research and price quotes. Used car listings and vehicle history reports.

BARGAIN HUNTER'S SECRETS: Search for specific new car models to see availability at dealers in your area; click the Send Me a Price Quote link to request a price quote from that dealer.

Discount Tire Company

www.discounttiredirect.com (800.589.6789)

Tires and wheels.

BARGAIN HUNTER'S SECRETS: Most items discounted; see individual products for savings. Scroll to the bottom of the home page for specials available via eBay auction.

Edmunds.com

www.edmunds.com

Full-service automotive portal. New car research and price quotes. Used car listings and vehicle history reports.

BARGAIN HUNTER'S SECRETS: Search for a specific vehicle to request new car prices from local dealers.

eTires

www.etires.com (877.463.8473)

Tires.

BARGAIN HUNTER'S SECRETS: Look for savings on individual products.

ExpressAutoParts.com Best Bargain

www.expressautoparts.com

Auto parts and accessories.

BARGAIN HUNTER'S SECRETS: Free shipping on all orders of more than $50. Most items discounted; see individual items for savings.

JC Whitney Best Selection

www.jcwhitney.com (800.529.4486)

Auto parts and accessories.

BARGAIN HUNTER'S SECRETS: Click the Clearance link for closeout merchandise.

Kelley Blue Book

www.kbb.com

Full-service automotive portal. New car research and price quotes. Used car listings and vehicle history reports.

BARGAIN HUNTER'S SECRETS: Click the Free Price Quote link to request new car prices from local dealers.

MSN Autos

autos.msn.com

Full-service automotive portal. New car research and price quotes. Used car listings and vehicle history reports.

BARGAIN HUNTER'S SECRETS: Click the Need a Price Quote? link to receive new car quotes from local dealers.

NAPAonline.com

www.napaonline.com (877.805.6272)

Auto parts and accessories. (Click the Parts & Accessories tab, and then select Browse Catalog.)

BARGAIN HUNTER'S SECRETS: Look for savings on individual products.

PartsAmerica.com Best Selection

www.partsamerica.com (877.808.0698)

Auto parts and accessories.

BARGAIN HUNTER'S SECRETS: Click the Hot Deals link for sale and clearance merchandise.

BABIES AND MATERNITY

The Web is a great place to prepare for new arrivals. There are tons of online merchants that specialize in maternity clothing and baby supplies, all at discount prices.

When you're buying maternity clothing, know that maternity sizes correspond to your original size. That is, if you normally wear a size 6, you'll also wear a size 6 in maternity clothing. But as your body grows over your pregnancy, you might want to size up a tad—comfort matters.

You should also look for regular women's clothing in sizes larger than your normal size, especially for your first and second trimester. You don't have to spend extra for maternity clothes if regular clothes can fit the bill. And look at men's clothing while you're shopping; you'd be surprised what can actually fit!

In addition to the merchants listed here, many of the general clothing stores listed in the Apparel section also offer maternity clothing, as do stores in the Department Stores and Mass Merchants section. Baby gear can also be found at most department store merchants, and at some retailers in the Toys and Games section.

Another good resource for cost-conscious mothers is the Mommysavers.com Web site (www.mommysavers.com). This site offers tips and links that can help you save big on maternity, baby, and family-related items. Especially useful is the Shopping Tips/Bargain Board, where users share the most recent bargains they've found on the Web.

Amazon.com Best Selection

www.amazon.com (800.201.7575)

Select the Baby tab for merchandise from Babies 'R' Us: strollers and other gear, baby care items, nursery furniture, and toys. Select the Kids & Baby Clothing tab for infant and toddler clothing.

BARGAIN HUNTER'S SECRETS: In the Baby store, click the Baby Outlet tab for clearance and sale merchandise. In the Kids & Baby Clothing store, click the Sales & Deals tab for sale and promotional merchandise. Look for additional bargains during Amazon's sitewide Friday Sale. Also look for free shipping and other promotions on individual product pages.

Anna Cris

www.annacris.com (800.281.2662)

Maternity clothing.

BARGAIN HUNTER'S SECRETS: Look for sale and promotional items on the home page. Sign up for email notification of sales and promotions. Click the Free Offers button for coupons and offers from partner companies.

Baby Becoming

www.babybecoming.com (401.658.0688)

Plus-size maternity clothing.

BARGAIN HUNTER'S SECRETS: Click the Special Sales link for sale items. Click the Close Outs! link for clearance merchandise.

BabyAge.com Best Bargain

www.babyage.com (800.222.9243)

Baby gear, nursing accessories, bath accessories, healthcare, and furniture.

BARGAIN HUNTER'S SECRETS: Flat $3.95 shipping per order. All items deeply discounted; see individual product pages for savings. Click the Clearance Center link for closeout merchandise.

BabyBazaar

www.babybazaar.com (877.543.7186)

Baby clothing, gear, furniture, toys, and accessories.

BARGAIN HUNTER'S SECRETS: Free shipping. Look for sale merchandise on the home page.

BabyCenter Store

store.babycenter.com (866.241.2229)

Baby clothing, gear, furniture, healthcare, toys, and accessories.

BARGAIN HUNTER'S SECRETS: Click the On Sale Now link for sale and clearance merchandise. Join BabyCenter Plus ($24.95) to receive free shipping, twice-yearly members-only sales, and other services.

BabyStyle

www.babystyle.com (877.378.9537)

Maternity clothing. Baby clothing, gear, furniture, and toys.

BARGAIN HUNTER'S SECRETS: Click the Outlet link for clearance and overstock merchandise.

BabyUniverse.com Best Selection

www.babyuniverse.com (877.615.2229)

Maternity clothing. Baby clothing, gear, furniture, healthcare, toys, and accessories. Toddler clothing, gear, furniture, healthcare, toys, and accessories.

BARGAIN HUNTER'S SECRETS: Click the On Sale! links on main category pages for sale and clearance merchandise. Click the Free Shipping links to view items that qualify for free shipping.

Chic & Showing

www.chicandshowing.com (877.295.6103)

Maternity clothing.

BARGAIN HUNTER'S SECRETS: Click the Chic sale link for sale merchandise.

Fit Maternity & Beyond

www.fitmaternity.com (888.961.9100)

Maternity activewear.

BARGAIN HUNTER'S SECRETS: Click the Sale link for sale merchandise.

GeniusBabies.com

www.geniusbabies.com (704.573.4500)

Baby toys and gifts.

BARGAIN HUNTER'S SECRETS: Click the Sale! link for weekly specials.

iMaternity

www.imaternity.com (800.466.6223)

Maternity clothing. Offers plus sizes.

BARGAIN HUNTER'S SECRETS: Look for sale items on home page. Click the Sale links in main category listings for sale merchandise.

Jordan Marie

www.jordanmarie.com (888.949.7363)

Boutique baby clothing.

BARGAIN HUNTER'S SECRETS: 15% off your first order on orders of more than $75. Free shipping on orders of $50 or more. Click the Clearance link for closeout merchandise. Most items heavily discounted; see individual items for savings.

Just Babies

www.justbabies.com (888.900.2229)

Maternity clothing. Baby care, furniture, clothing, toys, nursing supplies, and accessories.

BARGAIN HUNTER'S SECRETS: Click the Clearance Items link for closeout merchandise.

Motherhood Maternity

www.motherhood.com (800.466.6223)

Maternity clothing.

BARGAIN HUNTER'S SECRETS: Everyday low prices; see individual items for savings. Click the Sale link for sale merchandise.

Mother's Best

www.mothersbest.com (877.226.2464)

Nursing bras and accessories. Baby gear and healthcare.

BARGAIN HUNTER'S SECRETS: Click the On Sale link for sale merchandise.

Motherwear

www.motherwear.com (800.950.2500)

Nursing bras, clothing, and accessories.

BARGAIN HUNTER'S SECRETS: Click the Weekly Web Specials link for weekly sale merchandise. Click the Clearance Rack link for closeout items.

Nursery Depot

www.nurserydepot.com (888.238.0987)

Baby furniture and bedding.

BARGAIN HUNTER'S SECRETS: Free shipping on bedding orders of more than $99. All items discounted; see individual product pages for savings.

One Step Ahead

www.onestepahead.com (800.274.8440)

Baby gear, clothing, healthcare, furniture, toys, and accessories.

BARGAIN HUNTER'S SECRETS: Look for sale items on the home page. Click the Outlet link for clearance and sale merchandise.

TheBabyOutlet.com (Best Bargain)

www.thebabyoutlet.com (877.693.2229)

Baby care, clothing, toys, and nursing accessories.

BARGAIN HUNTER'S SECRETS: Free shipping. All items discounted; see individual items for savings.

TotShop.com (Best Selection)

www.totshop.com (888.450.7467)

Baby clothing. Merchandise offered by a collection of individual small boutiques. (Partner site to GirlShop and GuyShop.)

BARGAIN HUNTER'S SECRETS: Click the Sales! link for sale merchandise. Look for links to clearance merchandise at the bottom of the home page. Look for store sales at individual boutiques.

Tummies Maternity

www.tummiesmaternity.com (410.358.0116)

Maternity clothing.

BARGAIN HUNTER'S SECRETS: Click the Clearance link on the Shop menu for closeout merchandise.

WebClothes.com (Best Bargain)

www.webclothes.com (888.575.9303)

Baby clothing.

BARGAIN HUNTER'S SECRETS: Most merchandise heavily discounted; see individual items for savings. Look for sale items on home page. Click the $10 or Less link for low-priced items. Click the Bargain Bin link for sale and clearance merchandise.

BOOKS

Books were one of the first products offered for sale on the Web. It's a particularly appropriate category for online shopping, as there's such a large number of titles—too large, really, for everything to be stocked at a traditional "bricks and mortar" store. An online bookstore can offer a much larger virtual inventory without actually have to stock each and every item. (It lets the publisher hold the stock, and then orders what it needs when a customer places an order.)

In fact, the largest online merchant, Amazon.com, started out as an online bookseller. Amazon remains the largest online bookstore, and also one with the lowest prices. And if Amazon doesn't have a title in stock, chances are one of its associate merchants has a used copy available, which you can purchase through the Amazon system. (Learn more about Amazon in Chapter 10, "Hunting for Bargains at Amazon.com.")

Amazon.com is so good it was recognized as the top online retailer in the 2003 American Customer Satisfaction Index, with a stunning 88% satisfaction rating. Competitor Barnes & Noble was a close second, with an 86% rating.

When you're shopping for the best price on a particular book, you might want to avail yourself of a book-specific price-comparison engine. The best sites to compare pricing on books include AAABookSearch.com (**www.aaabooksearch.com**), Best Web Buys (**www.bestwebbuys.com**), EveryBookstore.com (**www.everybookstore.com**), MetaPrices (**www.metaprices.com**), Price.com (**www.price.com**), ShoppingAisles.com (**www.shoppingaisles.com**), and ValueCompare (**www.valuecompare.com**).

And don't limit your shopping to new books. Some of the best bargains can be found at merchants (and individuals) selling all manner of used books. (Amazon, remember, offers links to used copies on most of their book product pages.)

A Common Reader

www.commonreader.com (800.832.7323)

Specializing in hard-to-find titles and uncommon books.

BARGAIN HUNTER'S SECRETS: Click the Warehouse Sale link for sale and clearance merchandise.

A1 Books Best Bargain

www.a1books.com

Specializing in nonfiction books.

BARGAIN HUNTER'S SECRETS: Most items heavily discounted; look for savings on individual items. See the Great Savings sections for books priced under $2. Low shipping charges.

Abebooks.com

www.abebooks.com (250.475.6013)

Specializing in used, rare, and out-of-print books.

BARGAIN HUNTER'S SECRETS: Look for savings on individual titles.

Alibris

www.alibris.com (877.254.2747)

Specializing in used, out-of-print, and hard-to-find books.

BARGAIN HUNTER'S SECRETS: Click the Bargain Books link for remainders and sale merchandise.

Amazon.com Best Selection Best Bargain

www.amazon.com (800.201.7575)

Huge selection of new books in all categories. (Click the Books tab.) Many titles also available used from third-party merchants.

BARGAIN HUNTER'S SECRETS: Most titles heavily discounted; see individual product pages for savings. Click the Bargain Books tab for remainders and sale titles. Click the Used Books tab for used titles in all categories. Look for savings on new and used copies from third parties in the More Buying Choices section on individual product pages. Free shipping on orders of $25 or more.

Barnes & Noble Best Selection

www.barnesandnoble.com (877.275.2626)

Huge selection of new books in all categories. (Click the Books tab.)

BARGAIN HUNTER'S SECRETS: Most titles discounted; see individual product pages for savings. Click the Used & Out of Print tab for used book bargains. Click the Sale Annex tab for remainders and sale merchandise. Free shipping on orders of $25 or more.

BookCloseouts.com

www.bookcloseouts.com (888.402.7323)

Bargain books.

BARGAIN HUNTER'S SECRETS: All titles heavily discounted. Click the Clearance tab for additional savings.

BookHutch.com

www.bookhutch.com (330.656.1510)

Bargain books.

BARGAIN HUNTER'S SECRETS: All titles heavily discounted.

BookPool.com

www.bookpool.com

Specializing in technical and computer books.

BARGAIN HUNTER'S SECRETS: Most titles discounted; look for savings on individual products. Look for the Special Offers section on the home page for current promotions.

Books-A-Million

www.booksamillion.com (800.201.3550)

Huge selection of new books in all categories.

BARGAIN HUNTER'S SECRETS: Look for savings on individual titles. Click the Bargain Books link for remainders and sale merchandise. Purchase a Millionaire's Club membership ($10/year) to save 10% on all orders.

Christianbook.com

www.christianbook.com (800.247.4784)

Religious books.

BARGAIN HUNTER'S SECRETS: Look for savings on individual titles.

Collector Bookstore

www.collector-bookstore.com (913.651.0600)

Antique, rare, and collectible books. (Click the Books tab.)

BARGAIN HUNTER'S SECRETS: Look for savings on individual titles.

eCampus.com

www.ecampus.com (888.388.9909)

New and used college textbooks.

BARGAIN HUNTER'S SECRETS: Click the Clearance link for sale and closeout merchandise. Look for savings on used copies.

eFollett.com

www.efollett.com (800.381.5151)

New and used college textbooks.

BARGAIN HUNTER'S SECRETS: Look for savings on used copies.

ElephantBooks.com

www.elephantbooks.com

Specializing in used, rare, and out-of-print books.

BARGAIN HUNTER'S SECRETS: Look for savings on individual titles.

HamiltonBook.com

www.hamiltonbook.com

Bargain books.

BARGAIN HUNTER'S SECRETS: Most titles heavily discounted. Click the Specials link for additional savings.

Impact Christian Books

www.impactchristianbooks.com (314.822.3309)

Religious books.

BARGAIN HUNTER'S SECRETS: Click the Discount Books link for sale merchandise.

Powell's Books

www.powells.com (800.291.9676)

Huge selection of new and used books.

BARGAIN HUNTER'S SECRETS: Click the Sale link for remainders and sale titles. Click the Used link for used book bargains.

VarsityBooks.com

www.varsitybooks.com (877.827.2665)

New and used college textbooks.

BARGAIN HUNTER'S SECRETS: Look for savings on used copies.

WordsWorth Books

www.wordsworth.com (800.899.2202)

New and used books.

BARGAIN HUNTER'S SECRETS: Look for savings on individual titles. Look for weekly specials on home page.

CAMERAS

Cameras have always been big mail-order items, going back to the glory days of 35mm photography. Photography magazines are full of ads for East Coast merchants offering heavily discounted prices on the latest gear, all available from a convenient toll-free phone call.

Well, most of these mail-order merchants have migrated to the Web and adapted to the age of digital photography. And many of the big online computer merchants have also expanded into digital cameras, which means that there's a huge number of online merchants offering both film and digital cameras—which should translate into really good bargains for you.

When you're buying cameras online, it's definitely worth your while to check out more than one merchant. Pricing fluctuates *daily*, and you'll find considerable price differences between stores. And don't assume that just because a particular merchant had the best price on one model that it'll be the cheapest on all models; pricing is much more complicated than that.

One thing that complicates camera pricing is the propensity of some stores to offer low-ball pricing on individual cameras, but try to make it back by upselling accessories. The worst offenders are stores that won't finalize your order online, but insist on calling you on the phone to "confirm" your credit card number. When they have you on the line, they apply the pressure for high-profit accessory packages. Resist these add-ons; you can often find better prices elsewhere, if you really need the accessories at all.

Another complicating factor are merchants trying to pass off refurbished items as new merchandise, and merchants offering "gray market" goods without full manufacturer warranty. Make sure that the product you're buying is brand-new, in the box (unless you specifically want a refurbished deal), and comes with a full manufacturer warranty. If not, pass on that merchant.

There are a lot of Web sites that can help you research different cameras before you make your purchase. The best of the bunch include CNET Reviews (**reviews.cnet.com**), DCViews (**www.dcviews.com**), Digital Camera Resource Page (**www.dcresource.com**), Digital Photography Review (**www.dpreview.com**), PCPhotoREVIEW (**www.pcphotoreview.com**), PhotographyREVIEW.com (**www.photographyreview.com**), ReviewFinder (**www.reviewfinder.com**), and Steve's DigiCams (**www.steves-digicams.com**).

In addition, there are several sites that offer camera-specific price comparison engines. These sites include Active Buyer's Guide (**www.activebuyersguide.com**), CNET Shopper.com (**shopper.cnet.com**), and Price.com (**www.price.com**). Most of the general price comparison sites also are good for finding digital camera bargains.

17th St. Photo Supply

www.17photo.com (800.664.1971)

Digital cameras, 35mm cameras, camcorders, and accessories.

BARGAIN HUNTER'S SECRETS: Most items heavily discounted; look for savings on individual product pages.

42nd St. Photo Best Bargain

www.42photo.com (888.810.4242)

Digital cameras, 35mm cameras, camcorders, and accessories.

BARGAIN HUNTER'S SECRETS: Most items heavily discounted; look for savings on individual product pages.

Abt Electronics

www.abtelectronics.com (888.228.5800)

Digital cameras, camcorders, and accessories.

BARGAIN HUNTER'S SECRETS: Most items discounted; look for savings on individual product pages. Click the Clearance Center link for closeout merchandise.

Adorama Best Selection

www.adorama.com (800.223.2500)

Digital cameras, 35mm cameras, camcorders, and accessories. New and used equipment.

BARGAIN HUNTER'S SECRETS: Most items heavily discounted; look for savings on individual product pages. Click the Used Equipment link for bargains on used and reconditioned items; click the We Buy Used link if you have equipment to sell. Click the Specials link for discounted items. Click the Closeouts link for clearance merchandise. Click the Overstocks link for discounts on overstocked items. Click the Rebate Center link for manufacturer rebates. Free shipping on selected items.

Advanced Photo Source

www.advancedphotosource.com (212.675.2309)

Digital cameras, 35mm cameras, and accessories.

BARGAIN HUNTER'S SECRETS: Most items heavily discounted; look for savings on individual product pages.

Amazon.com

www.amazon.com (800.201.7575)

Digital cameras, 35mm cameras, camcorders, and accessories. (Click the Camera & Photo tab.)

BARGAIN HUNTER'S SECRETS: Look for savings on individual product pages; also look for lower prices from third-party merchants in the More Buying Choices section of each product page. Click the Today's Deals tab for sale and promotional items. Click the Outlet, Used & Refurbished tab for clearance and refurbished merchandise. Free shipping on orders of $25 or more.

B&H Photo-Video

www.bhphotovideo.com (800.606.6969)

Digital cameras, 35mm cameras, camcorders, and accessories. New and used equipment.

BARGAIN HUNTER'S SECRETS: Most items heavily discounted; look for savings on individual product pages. Click the Used Equipment link for bargains on used merchandise. Click the Specials link for sale and promotional merchandise. Click the Open Box Specials link for deals on returned and refurbished items. Click the Rebates and Promotions link for information on manufacturer rebates and promotions.

Beach Camera

www.beachcamera.com (800.572.3224)

Digital cameras, 35mm cameras, camcorders, and accessories.

BARGAIN HUNTER'S SECRETS: Most items heavily discounted; look for savings on individual product pages. Click the Clearance link for closeout items. Click the Closeout Corner link for refurbished merchandise.

Best Buy

www.bestbuy.com (888.237.8289)

Digital cameras, 35mm cameras, camcorders, and accessories. (Click the Cameras & Camcorders tab.)

BARGAIN HUNTER'S SECRETS: See individual products for savings. Free shipping.

BestBuyPCs.com

www.bestbuypcs.com (877.692.3787)

Digital cameras, camcorders, and accessories.

BARGAIN HUNTER'S SECRETS: Most items heavily discounted; look for savings on individual product pages.

BestPriceAudioVideo.com

www.bestpriceaudiovideo.com

Digital cameras, 35mm cameras, camcorders, and accessories.

BARGAIN HUNTER'S SECRETS: Most items heavily discounted; look for savings on individual product pages. Click the On Clearance! links for closeout and sale merchandise. Click the Rebate Central tab to view manufacturer rebates.

Buy.com

www.buy.com (800.800.0900)

Digital cameras and accessories.

BARGAIN HUNTER'S SECRETS: Most items heavily discounted; look for savings on individual product pages. Click the Today's Deals link for specials and promotions. Click the Clearance Items link on the Digital Cameras page for closeout merchandise.

Buydig.com

www.buydig.com (800.617.4686)

Digital cameras, 35mm cameras, camcorders, and accessories.

BARGAIN HUNTER'S SECRETS: Most items heavily discounted; look for savings on individual product pages. Click the Clearance link for closeout merchandise. Click the Closeout Corner link for refurbished items.

Canoga Camera

www.canogacamera.com (800.201.4201)

Digital cameras, 35mm cameras, camcorders, and accessories. New and used equipment.

BARGAIN HUNTER'S SECRETS: Most items heavily discounted; look for savings on individual product pages. Click the Used link for bargains on used equipment.

ChiefValue

www.chiefvalue.com (800.230.4233)

Digital cameras, camcorders, and accessories.

BARGAIN HUNTER'S SECRETS: Most items heavily discounted; look for savings on individual product pages.

Circuit City

www.circuitcity.com (800.843.2489)

Digital cameras, 35mm cameras, camcorders, and accessories. (Click the Cameras and Camcorders link.)

BARGAIN HUNTER'S SECRETS: Look for savings on individual products. Look for Deals of the Week on the Cameras and Camcorders page.

Computers4SURE.com

www.computers4sure.com (800.266.7883)

Digital cameras, camcorders, and accessories.

BARGAIN HUNTER'S SECRETS: Look for savings on individual products. Click the Clearance Center tab for open-box and closeout items. Click the Manufacturer Reconditioned tab for refurbished items. Free shipping on orders more than $50 and items weighing less than 20 pounds.

Digital Foto Discount Club

www.digitalfotoclub.com (888.920.3332)

Digital cameras, 35mm cameras, camcorders, and accessories.

BARGAIN HUNTER'S SECRETS: Most items heavily discounted; look for savings on individual product pages. Click the Close-Outs link for clearance merchandise.

eCOST.com

www.ecost.com (877.888.2678)

Digital cameras, camcorders, and accessories.

BARGAIN HUNTER'S SECRETS: Most items heavily discounted; look for savings on individual product pages. Click the Auction tab for items available for bidding. Click the Clearance Countdown tab for closeout and overstock merchandise available for a limited time only. Click the Bargain Countdown tab for refurbished items.

ePhotoCraft Best Bargain

www.ephotocraft.com (877.374.6869)

Digital cameras, camcorders, and accessories.

BARGAIN HUNTER'S SECRETS: Most items heavily discounted; look for savings on individual product pages. Click the Hot Items link for bargains on top sellers. Click the Super Deals link for sale items.

etronics.com

www.etronics.com (800.323.7669)

Digital cameras, 35mm cameras, camcorders, and accessories.

BARGAIN HUNTER'S SECRETS: Most items heavily discounted; look for savings on individual product pages.

Inoax

www.inoax.com (800.842.1195)

Digital cameras, 35mm cameras, camcorders, and accessories.

BARGAIN HUNTER'S SECRETS: Most items heavily discounted; look for savings on individual product pages. Click the Rebate Center link for manufacturer rebates.

Marine Park Superstore

www.mpsuperstore.com (800.300.0615)

Digital cameras, 35mm cameras, camcorders, and accessories.

BARGAIN HUNTER'S SECRETS: Most items heavily discounted; look for savings on individual product pages. Click the Closeouts tab for clearance merchandise.

NewEgg.com

www.newegg.com (800.390.1119)

Digital cameras and accessories.

BARGAIN HUNTER'S SECRETS: Most items heavily discounted; look for savings on individual product pages. Click the Refurbished/Clearance tab for closeout and reconditioned merchandise.

Outpost.com

www.outpost.com (877.688.7678)

Digital cameras, 35mm cameras, camcorders, and accessories. (Owned by Fry's Electronics.)

BARGAIN HUNTER'S SECRETS: Most items heavily discounted; look for savings on individual product pages. Click the Advertised Specials link on the Cameras & Telescopes page for current sale items.

Radio Active Deals

www.radioactivedeals.com (866.526.8080)

Digital cameras, 35mm cameras, camcorders, and accessories.

BARGAIN HUNTER'S SECRETS: Most items heavily discounted; look for savings on individual product pages.

RitzCamera.com

www.ritzcamera.com (877.690.0177)

Digital cameras, 35mm cameras, camcorders, and accessories.

BARGAIN HUNTER'S SECRETS: Most items heavily discounted; look for savings on individual product pages. Click the Coupons & Rebates link for manufacturer rebates and promotions. Free shipping on orders of more than $100.

UniquePhoto.com

www.uniquephoto.com (800.631.0300)

Digital cameras, 35mm cameras, camcorders, and accessories.

BARGAIN HUNTER'S SECRETS: Most items heavily discounted; look for savings on individual product pages. Click the Rebates link for manufacturer rebates. Look for savings on refurbished items.

Zoommania Best Bargain

www.zoommania.com (800.966.6494)

Digital cameras, 35mm cameras, camcorders, and accessories.

BARGAIN HUNTER'S SECRETS: Most items heavily discounted; look for savings on individual product pages.

CATALOGS

It might seem odd to use the Internet to facilitate catalog shopping, but there you go. Even if you don't like shopping online, you can still use the Web to find printed catalogs to shop from. As you learned in Chapter 7, "Hunting for Bargains at Online Malls, Catalogs, and Department Stores," there are a handful of sites that enable you to order printed catalogs, or that present printed catalog pages online.

Of course, most of the major catalog merchants operate their own Web sites, in addition to their catalog operations. You'll find pretty much the same merchandise online as you will in the catalog, sometimes with an expanded or more up-to-date selection. You often have the option of ordering either online or by phone, whichever is more convenient to you. Shop by whichever method you prefer.

You can find the Web sites of these catalog merchants listed in several different areas of this directory. Look for listings under specific product categories; for example, catalogs such as L.L. Bean, who primarily sell clothing, are listed in the Apparel category.

CatalogCity.com

www.catalogcity.com

Online ordering from multiple catalog merchants.

CatalogDirect

www.catalogdirect.com

Request print catalogs online.

CatalogLink

www.cataloglink.com

Request print catalogs online (click the Catalogs tab). Online ordering from multiple catalog merchants (click the Shopping tab).

Catalogs.com

www.catalogs.com

Request print catalogs online.

Google Catalogs

catalogs.google.com

View print catalogs online.

CLOSEOUT, LIQUIDATED, AND WHOLESALE MERCHANDISE

Most online merchants offer brand-new merchandise. But if you really want deep discounts, consider buying closeout, distressed, refurbished, or otherwise liquidated merchandise—or, if you can handle bulk quantities, consider buying wholesale.

All types of nonretail shopping can now be done over the Internet. As you learned in Chapter 8, "Hunting for Closeout, Overstock, and Wholesale Bargains," there are numerous Web sites that enable you to purchase nonretail goods at extremely deep discounts.

Closeout merchandise can be found all over the Web, even in "outlet store" sections of normal retail sites. This type of merchandise includes overstocks, last year's models, discontinued items, and the like. Closeout goods typically come with full manufacturer warranties.

Liquidated merchandise is found most often at special liquidator sites, and includes merchandise offloaded by the manufacturer or retailer in large quantities. Some liquidation sites require you to purchase items in bulk; other sites let you buy individual items, at considerable savings.

Finally, wholesale merchandise is merchandise you purchase directly from the distributor, bypassing the traditional retail outlet. Not all distributors sell wholesale to the general public, but many do, which lets you pocket the money normally earned by the retailer. As with liquidation sites, some wholesale sites will require you to buy in bulk.

America's Best Closeouts

www.abcloseouts.com (305.477.0280)

Bulk liquidator; used and second-hand jeans and clothing.

American Merchandise Liquidation

www.amlinc.com (251.970.1100)

Bulk liquidator; closeouts, overstocks, customer returns, and salvaged merchandise in a variety of categories.

AmeriSurplus

www.amerisurplus.com (803.643.0606)

Bulk liquidator; salvage merchandise by the pallet, including automotive supplies, groceries, small appliances and electronics, sporting goods, and toys.

Bid4Assets

www.bid4assets.com (301.650.0003)

Single-item and bulk liquidator; merchandise obtained from bankruptcies, private companies, and the government, primarily high-ticket items in single quantity. Auction format.

Big Lots Wholesale

www.biglotswholesale.com

Bulk liquidator; case quantities of clothing, electronics, food, sporting goods, toys, and other home goods. Wholesale arm of the Big Lots chain.

Buylink

www.buylink.com (888.220.1300)

Wholesaler directory.

Closeouts America

www.closeoutsamerica.com (845.796.3046)

Single-item liquidator; brand-name merchandise at closeout prices, in hardware, houseware, and other home categories.

Liquidation.com

www.liquidation.com

Bulk liquidator; surplus, closeout, and returned merchandise in a variety of categories. Auction format.

Luxury Brands

www.luxurybrandsllc.com (888.739.8774)

Single-item and bulk liquidator; higher-end surplus merchandise, including luxury branded European clothing, accessories, and gift items from Giorgio Armani, Ralph Lauren Polo, Givenchy, Gucci, and Burberry.

My Web Wholesaler

www.mywebwholesaler.com (800.259.9053)

Bulk liquidator; box lots, pallets, and truckloads of merchandise obtained from major department store returns, closeouts, overstocks, and liquidations.

Overstock.com (Best Selection)

www.overstock.com (800.989.0135)

Single-item liquidator; name-brand merchandise in most major categories.

BARGAIN HUNTER'S SECRETS: Flat $2.95 shipping per order. Free shipping on selected items. Click Our Weekly Specials link for extra savings.

OverstockB2B.com

www.overstockb2b.com (800.273.6063)

Single-item liquidator; no minimum purchase on apparel, housewares, electronics, and other home items.

Salvage Closeouts

www.salvagecloseouts.com (800.567.9844)

Bulk liquidator; liquidated merchandise and department store closeouts in a wide variety of categories, as well as a variety of pallet and truckload specials.

BARGAIN HUNTER'S SECRETS: Click the Product Specials link for extra savings.

SmartBargains

www.smartbargains.com (866.692.2742)

Single-item liquidator; manufacturer closeouts and over-runs in apparel, housewares, and other home categories.

BARGAIN HUNTER'S SECRETS: Flat $4.95 shipping per order. Click the New Events link for special promotions. Click Last Chance link for items close to selling out. Click the Bargain Bin link for items with additional markdowns.

TDW Closeouts

www.tdwcloseouts.com (954.746.8000)

Bulk liquidator; department store returns and closeout merchandise, including liquidated, salvage, overstock, and surplus items.

BARGAIN HUNTER'S SECRETS: Click the Product Info & Daily Hot Specials link for first-come, first-serve truckload and pallet specials.

Top Choice Closeouts

www.topchoicecloseouts.com

Single-item and bulk liquidator; closeout, discount, and overstock products in all major categories.

USA Closeouts

www.usacloseouts.com (800.750.6152)

Bulk liquidator; brand-name department store closeouts.

Wholesale Central

www.wholesalecentral.com (800.999.8281)

Wholesaler directory.

Wholesale411

www.wholesale411.com (877.519.5784)

Wholesaler directory.

WholesalersCatalog.com

www.wholesalerscatalog.com (888.556.4441)

Wholesaler directory.

COMPARISON SHOPPING AND PRODUCT RESEARCH

If you're looking for the absolute lowest price on an item, you don't have to visit dozens of sites yourself. Instead, use a price comparison site to do the searching for you.

As you learned in Chapter 5, "Hunting for the Lowest Price," there are a number of these price comparison sites on the Web. Some look for all types of products, others shop within particular product categories, but all can help you find the best bargains with just a few clicks of the mouse.

And while you're looking, don't forget those sites that help you determine which products to buy in the first place. As discussed in Chapter 3, "Researching Your Purchases Before You Buy," there are lots of Web sites that offer product reviews and ratings, which can help you narrow down your choices. Turn to Chapters 3 and 4 to learn more about the sites listed here.

AAABookSearch.com
www.aaabooksearch.com

Price comparisons for books.

Active Buyer's Guide
www.activebuyersguide.com

Product comparisons for cameras, computers, electronics, and cell phones.

AimLower.com
www.aimlower.com

Price comparisons in most major categories.

Ars Technica
www.arstechnica.com

Product reviews and price comparisons for computers.

AudioREVIEW.com
www.audioreview.com

Product reviews for audio equipment.

AVguide.com
www.avguide.com

Product reviews for audio/video equipment.

Best Web Buys
www.bestwebbuys.com

Price comparisons for books, CDs, DVDs, electronics, and bikes.

BizRate
www.bizrate.com

Product comparisons and reviews in most major categories. Retailer reviews.

BuyPath
www.buypath.com

Price comparisons in most major categories.

CarREVIEW.com
www.carreview.com

Product reviews for cars and automotive accessories.

CheapestRate.com
www.cheapestrate.com

Price comparisons in most major categories.

CNET Reviews
reviews.cnet.com

Product reviews and comparisons for computers, cameras, and electronics.

CNET Shopper.com
shopper.cnet.com

Price comparisons for computers, cameras, and electronics.

CompareSite
www.comparesite.com

Price comparisons in most major categories.

ComputingREVIEW.com
www.computingreview.com

Product reviews for computers and accessories.

ConsumerReports.org
www.consumerreports.org

Product reviews in most major categories.

ConsumerREVIEW.com
www.consumerreview.com

Product reviews for cameras, electronics, computers, videogames, PC games, sports equipment, and automobiles.

ConsumerSearch
www.consumersearch.com

Product reviews in most major categories.

DCViews
www.dcviews.com

Product reviews for digital cameras.

Digital Camera Resource Page
www.dcresource.com

Product reviews for digital cameras.

Digital Photography Review
www.dpreview.com

Product reviews for digital cameras.

DVD Price Search
www.dvdpricesearch.com

Price comparisons for DVDs.

eCoustics.com

www.ecoustics.com

Product reviews and price comparisons for audio/video, cameras, and computers.

Epinions.com

www.epinions.com

Product reviews in all major categories.

ePublicEye

www.epubliceye.com

Retailer reviews.

EveryBookstore.com

www.everybookstore.com

Price comparisons for books.

ExtremeTech

www.extremetech.com

Product reviews for computers and accessories.

FindAll.com

www.findall.com

Price comparisons in all major categories.

Froogle

froogle.google.com

Price comparisons in all major categories.

The Gadgeteer

www.the-gadgeteer.com

Product reviews for electronics equipment.

Game Pricezone

www.gamepricezone.com

Price comparisons for videogames.

GolfREVIEW.com

www.golfreview.com

Product reviews for golfing equipment.

Maximum PC

www.maximumpc.com

Product reviews for computers and accessories.

MetaPrices

www.metaprices.com

Price comparisons for books, CDs, DVDs, and software.

MtbREVIEW.com

www.mtbreview.com

Product reviews for mountain bikes.

mySimon

www.mysimon.com

Price comparisons in all major categories.

NexTag

www.nextag.com

Price comparisons in all major categories.

OutdoorREVIEW.com

www.outdoorreview.com

Product reviews for outdoor sporting equipment.

PC Magazine

www.pcmag.com

Product reviews for computers and accessories.

PCGameREVIEW.com

www.pcgamereview.com

Product reviews for PC games.

PCPhotoREVIEW.com

www.pcphotoreview.com

Product reviews for digital cameras.

PhotographyREVIEW.com

www.photographyreview.com

Product reviews for 35mm cameras.

PlanetFeedback

www.planetfeedback.com/consumer/

Retailer reviews.

Plasma TV Buying Guide

www.plasmatvbuyingguide.com

Product reviews for large-screen plasma televisions.

Price RX

www.price-rx.com

Price comparisons for commonly prescribed drugs at major online pharmacies.

Price.com

www.price.com

Price comparisons for computers, cameras, electronics, books, CDs, DVDs, office supplies, cars, and travel services.

PriceGrabber.com
www.pricegrabber.com

Price comparisons in all major categories.

PriceMix
www.pricemix.com

Price comparisons for electronics, appliances, and office equipment.

PriceSCAN.com
www.pricescan.com

Price comparisons in all major categories.

Price Watch
www.pricewatch.com

Price comparisons for computers and accessories.

PricingCentral.com
www.pricingcentral.com

Price comparisons in all major categories.

RateItAll
www.rateitall.com

Product reviews in all major categories.

ResellerRatings.com
www.resellerratings.com

Price comparisons of computers and accessories. Retailer reviews.

Review Centre
www.reviewcentre.com

Product reviews and pricing comparisons in all major categories.

ReviewFinder
www.reviewfinder.com

Product reviews for computers, cameras, electronics, videogames, and related categories.

RoadbikeREVIEW.com
www.roadbikereview.com

Product reviews of bicycles.

RoboShopper.com
www.roboshopper.com

Price comparisons in all major categories.

Shopping.com
www.shopping.com

Price comparisons in all major categories.

ShoppingAisles.com
www.shoppingaisles.com

Pricing comparisons for books, CDs, DVDs, and videogames.

ShopSearchEngine.com
www.shopsearchengine.com

Price comparisons in all major categories.

SimplyQuick
www.simplyquick.com

Retailer reviews.

Steve's DigiCams
www.steves-digicams.com

Product reviews for digital cameras.

StreetPrices
www.streetprices.com

Price comparisons for computers and electronics.

Tom's Hardware Guide
www.tomshardware.com

Product reviews for computers and electronics.

ValueCompare
www.valuecompare.com

Price comparisons for books.

VideogameREVIEW.com
www.videogamereview.com

Product reviews for videogames.

Yahoo! Shopping
shopping.yahoo.com

Price comparisons in all major categories.

COMPUTER HARDWARE AND SOFTWARE

It should come as no surprise that the Internet is a great place to shop for computer equipment. After all, you need a PC to get online, so why not go online to purchase your PC?

There are a ton of online merchants that sell computer hardware and software, almost all at substantial discounts. As with all products, it pays to shop around before you make a PC purchase because pricing can vary considerably. And make sure that you're not comparing apples and oranges; there are many differences between products, and slight variations can result in large price discrepancies.

Before you make your purchase, you can look for product reviews and comparisons at the following sites: Active Buyer's Guide (**www.activebuyersguide.com**), Ars Technica (**www.arstechnica.com**), CNET Reviews (**reviews.cnet.com**), ComputingREVIEW (**www.computingreview.com**), ExtremeTech (**www.extremetech.com**), The Gadgeteer (**www.the-gadgeteer.com**), Maximum PC (**www.maximumpc.com**), PC Magazine (**www.pcmagazine.com**), ReviewFinder (**www.reviewfinder.com**), and Tom's Hardware Guide (**www.tomshardware.com**).

When you're looking for the lowest prices, it might pay to use a price comparison engine that specializes in computer equipment. The best of these include CNET Shopper.com (**shopper.cnet.com**), Price.com (**www.price.com**), Price Watch (**www.pricewatch.com**), and StreetPrices (**www.streetprices.com**). In addition, most general price comparison sites do a good job finding low prices on computer equipment.

Two merchants in this category received high ratings on the 2003 American Customer Satisfaction Index. Amazon.com was the #1 online retailer, with an 88% satisfaction rating. Buy.com ranked #3, with an 80% rating.

Many of the merchants in the Electronics category also sell personal computers and PDAs, as do several retailers in the Department Stores and Mass Merchants category. Look there for additional savings.

Ajump.com

www.ajump.com (877.692.5867)

Computer hardware and accessories. Specializes in "build your own" systems and hardware.

BARGAIN HUNTER'S SECRETS: Most items discounted; look for savings on individual products. Click the Bundle Deals link for multiple-item specials. Click the Outlet Center link for clearance and refurbished items. Click the Rebate Center link for manufacturer rebates. Get a 1% cash-back rebate for each $1 you spend. Free shipping on most products.

Amazon.com

www.amazon.com (800.201.7575)

Click the Computers tab for computer hardware and accessories. Click the Software tab for computer software.

BARGAIN HUNTER'S SECRETS: In the Computers store, click the Today's Deal tab for sale and promotional items; click the Outlet, Used & Refurbished tab for clearance and reconditioned items. In the Software stores, click the Today's Deal tab for sale and promotional items; click the Outlet tab for clearance merchandise. Look for additional bargains during the sitewide Friday Sale. Also look for lower prices on new and used merchandise from third-party merchants in the More Buying Choices section of each product page. Free shipping on orders of more than $25.

The Apple Store

store.apple.com (800.692.7753)

Computer hardware, software, and accessories. Manufacturer-direct.

BARGAIN HUNTER'S SECRETS: Click the Sale graphic for limited-time specials. Click the Rebates graphic for manufacturer rebates. See the Apple Promotions section of the Store page for sales and promotions. Free shipping on all orders of more than $25.

Best Buy

www.bestbuy.com (888.237.8289)

Computer hardware, software, and accessories. (Click the Computers tab.)

BARGAIN HUNTER'S SECRETS: See individual products for savings. Free shipping.

BestBuyPCs.com

www.bestbuypcs.com (877.692.3787)

Computer hardware and accessories.

BARGAIN HUNTER'S SECRETS: Most items heavily discounted; look for savings on individual product pages.

Buy.com

www.buy.com (800.800.0900)

Computer hardware, software, and accessories.

BARGAIN HUNTER'S SECRETS: See individual products for savings. Click the Rebates link for manufacturer rebates. Free shipping.

CableWholesale.com

www.cablewholesale.com (888.212.8295)

Computer and audio/video cables.

BARGAIN HUNTER'S SECRETS: See individual items for savings. Click the Hot Deals link for sale and overstocked items.

CDW Computer Centers

www.cdw.com (800.840.4239)

Computer hardware, software, and accessories.

BARGAIN HUNTER'S SECRETS: See individual products for savings. Click the CDW Outlet link for returned and reconditioned items. Click the Rebates link for manufacturer rebates.

Chumbo.com

www.chumbo.com (800.343.7530)

Computer hardware, software, and accessories.

BARGAIN HUNTER'S SECRETS: See individual products for savings. Click the Daily Price Reductions link for recently discounted items.

Circuit City

www.circuitcity.com (800.843.2489)

Computer hardware, software, and accessories.

BARGAIN HUNTER'S SECRETS: Look for savings on individual products. Look for Deals of the Week on main category pages. Click the Shop for Clearance Items link (very bottom of the page) for closeout merchandise.

Clearance Club Laptops

www.clearanceclub.com (877.855.0230)

Computer hardware and accessories. Specializes in notebook/laptop PCs.

BARGAIN HUNTER'S SECRETS: Look for savings on individual products. Click the Notebook Deals Under $999 button for low-priced systems.

CompUSA

www.compusa.com (800.266.7872)

Computer hardware, software, and accessories.

BARGAIN HUNTER'S SECRETS: Look for savings on individual products. Click the Store Ad link for advertised specials. Click the Clearance link for closeout and reconditioned merchandise. Click the Auctions link to bid on auction items at CompUSA Auctions (**www.compusaauctions.com**). Click the Rebate Center link for manufacturer rebates. One-cent shipping on orders of more than $150.

Computer Geeks Discount Outlet

www.compgeeks.com (760.726.7700)

Computer hardware, software, and accessories.

BARGAIN HUNTER'S SECRETS: Look for savings on individual products. Look for bargains on refurbished items.

Computers4SURE.com

www.computers4sure.com (800.266.7883)

Computer hardware, software, and accessories.

BARGAIN HUNTER'S SECRETS: Look for savings on individual products. Click the Clearance Center tab for open-box and closeout items. Click the Manufacturer Reconditioned tab for refurbished items. Free shipping on orders more than $50 and items weighing less than 20 pounds.

Dell

www.dell.com (800.999.3355)

Computer hardware and accessories. Manufacturer direct.

BARGAIN HUNTER'S SECRETS: Look for savings on individual products. Go to the Dell Outlet (**www.dell.com/outlet/**) for bargains on refurbished systems.

DownloadStore.com

www.downloadstore.com (800.656.5426)

Computer software for download only.

BARGAIN HUNTER'S SECRETS: Look for savings on individual products; save money by downloading rather than shipping boxed software.

eCost.com

www.ecost.com (877.888.2678)

Computer hardware, software, and accessories.

BARGAIN HUNTER'S SECRETS: Look for savings on individual products. Click the Auction tab for items available for bidding. Click the Clearance Countdown tab for closeout and overstock merchandise available for a limited time only. Click the Bargain Countdown tab for refurbished items.

Gateway

www.gateway.com (800.846.4208)

Computer hardware and accessories. Manufacturer direct.

BARGAIN HUNTER'S SECRETS: Look for savings on individual products. Look for sales and promotions on the home page. Click the Great Deals links for sale and promotional items.

HPshopping.com

shopping.hp.com (888.999.4747)

Computer hardware and accessories. Manufacturer direct for Compaq and Hewlett Packard equipment.

BARGAIN HUNTER'S SECRETS: Look for savings on individual products. See the Special Offers! section of the home page for current promotions. Click the Outlet Store link for returned and reconditioned merchandise. Free shipping on select items of more than $250.

J&R Music & Computer World

www.jandr.com (800.806.1115)

Computer hardware, software, and accessories.

BARGAIN HUNTER'S SECRETS: Look for savings on individual products. Click the New York Times Ad link for advertised specials. Click the Deal of the Week Specials link for limited-time bargains, updated each Tuesday. Click the Clearance link for closeout, discontinued, and refurbished merchandise. Click the Rebate Center for manufacturer rebates. Free shipping on selected items.

Laptop Travel

www.laptoptravel.com (888.527.8728)

Computer accessories. Specializing in accessories for laptop computers.

BARGAIN HUNTER'S SECRETS: Click the Current Specials link for sale and promotional items. Click the Under $30 link for low-priced items.

Marine Park Superstore

www.mpsuperstore.com (800.300.0615)

Computer hardware, software, and accessories.

BARGAIN HUNTER'S SECRETS: Look for savings on individual products. Click the Closeouts tab for clearance merchandise.

Market Warehouse

www.marketwarehouse.com (800.223.3724)

Computer software.

BARGAIN HUNTER'S SECRETS: Look for savings on individual products. Click the Specials, Closeouts & Irregulars link for sale and closeout merchandise. Free shipping on orders of more than $50.

The Monitor Outlet

www.monitoroutlet.com (888.478.6161)

Computer monitors.

BARGAIN HUNTER'S SECRETS: Look for savings on individual products. Free shipping.

MPC

www.buympc.com (888.224.4247)

Computer hardware and accessories. Manufacturer direct. (Formerly Micron PC.)

BARGAIN HUNTER'S SECRETS: Look for savings on individual products. Click the Factory Outlet links on main category pages for reconditioned units.

NewEgg.com

www.newegg.com (800.390.1119)

Computer hardware, software, and accessories.

BARGAIN HUNTER'S SECRETS: Look for savings on individual products. Click the Refurbished/Clearance tab for closeout and reconditioned merchandise.

Nothing But Software

www.nothingbutsoftware.com (800.755.4619)

Computer software.

BARGAIN HUNTER'S SECRETS: Look for savings on individual products. Click the Specials tab for sale items.

Office Depot

www.officedepot.com (800.463.3768)

Computer hardware, software, and accessories.

BARGAIN HUNTER'S SECRETS: Look for savings on individual products. Click the Super Values link for sale and clearance items. Click the Advertised Specials link for advertised items. Click the Rebate Center link for manufacturer rebates.

Office Max

www.officemax.com (800.283.7674)

Computer hardware, software, and accessories.

BARGAIN HUNTER'S SECRETS: Look for savings on individual products. Click the Weekly In-Store Specials link for limited-time offers. Click the Rebate Center link for manufacturer rebates. Free delivery on most orders of more than $50.

Outpost.com

www.outpost.com (877.688.7678)

Computer hardware, software, and accessories. (Owned by Fry's Electronics.)

BARGAIN HUNTER'S SECRETS: Look for savings on individual products.

PC Connection

www.pcconnection.com (888.213.0607)

Computer hardware and accessories.

BARGAIN HUNTER'S SECRETS: Look for savings on individual products.

PC Mall

www.pcmall.com (800.555.6255)

Computer hardware, software, and accessories.

BARGAIN HUNTER'S SECRETS: Look for savings on individual products. Click the Blowout Deals link for discounted items.

PC Sound

www.pcsound.com (800.727.6863)

Computer hardware, software, and accessories.

BARGAIN HUNTER'S SECRETS: Look for savings on individual products.

PCNation

www.pcnation.com (800.235.4050)

Computer hardware, software, and accessories.

BARGAIN HUNTER'S SECRETS: Look for savings on individual products. Click the Rebates link for manufacturer rebates. Free delivery.

SonyStyle

www.sonystyle.com (877.865.7669)

Computer hardware and accessories. Manufacturer direct.

BARGAIN HUNTER'S SECRETS: Look for savings on individual products. Click the Clearance link on the Computers and Peripherals page for closeout and reconditioned merchandise; click the Great Deals link for sales and promotions.

Staples.com

www.staples.com (800.378.2753)

Computer hardware, software, and accessories.

BARGAIN HUNTER'S SECRETS: Look for savings on individual products. Click the Weekly Specials link for limited-time offers. Click the Clearance Center link for closeout and reconditioned merchandise. Click the Rebate Center link for manufacturer rebates.

TigerDirect.com

www.tigerdirect.com (800.800.8300)

Computer Parts, Components, Laptop Computer parts, Desktop Computers, and notebooks.

BARGAIN HUNTER'S SECRETS: Look for savings on individual products. Click the Save On "Open Box" Deals! link for returned and reconditioned items. Click the Rebate Center link for manufacturer rebates. Register for offers via email.

Vio Software Store

www.viosoftware.com (888.617.9922)

Computer software.

BARGAIN HUNTER'S SECRETS: Look for savings on individual products. Free shipping.

ZipZoomFly.com

www.zipzoomfly.com (510.739.1890)

Computer hardware, software, and accessories.

BARGAIN HUNTER'S SECRETS: Look for savings on individual products. Click the Open Box link for returned and reconditioned merchandise. Click the Rebate Center link for manufacturer rebates.

Zones Best Bargain

www.zones.com (800.408.9663)

BARGAIN HUNTER'S SECRETS: Look for savings on individual products. Look for Specials of the Week on the home page. Click the Clearance link for closeout and reconditioned items. Click the Rebates link for manufacturer rebates.

CONSUMER COMPLAINTS

This section of the directory is a bit of an anomaly in that it's not about finding the best bargains—it's about avoiding and resolving problems. Use these resources (along with the information in Chapter 2, "Shopping Safely—and Securely") if you run into any problems when purchasing items online.

To head off any problems that might cause you to use these consumer resources, you should take the normal precautions before you make a purchase online. These precautions include:

- Researching the online merchant and reading customer reviews
- Making sure the merchant has a phone number to call if you have a problem
- Reading the merchant's returns and privacy policies
- Ordering only from sites that offer a secure server
- Paying by credit card
- Only entering the minimum amount of information you need to complete the order
- Not checking the option to receive promotional mailings (spam) from this or other merchants
- Keeping copies of your completed checkout page and any confirmation mailings sent to you

American Arbitration Association
www.adr.org (212.716.5800)
Dispute resolution.

Better Business Bureau
search.bbb.org
Retailer reports.

Better Business Bureau OnLine Complaint System
complaints.bbb.org
Retailer complaints.

Complaints.com
www.complaints.com (630.245.000)
Retailer complaints.

Federal Trade Commission
www.ftc.gov/ftc/consumer.htm (202-382-4357 or 877-FTC-HELP)
Retailer complaints.

National Association of Attorneys General
www.naag.org (202.326.6000)
Retailer complaints.

National Fraud Information Center
www.fraud.org (800.876.7060)
Retailer complaints.

Safeshopping.org
www.safeshopping.org
Consumer information.

Scam Busters
www.scambusters.org (828.262.5885)
Consumer information.

Squaretrade
www.squaretrade.com
Dispute resolution.

WebAssured
www.webassured.com (806.358.6103)
Dispute resolution.

COUPONS, PROMOTIONS, AND REBATES

Your bargain hunting isn't over when you find a merchant offering a low price on a particular product. Often you can save even more by applying online coupons or promotion codes or by taking advantage of manufacturer rebate programs. There are even some Web sites that offer cash-back purchase programs, where you can earn cash rebates on every dollar you spend online. Learn more about these coupon and promotion sites in Chapter 6, "Hunting for Rebates, Coupons, and Promotions."

Online coupons are typically applied via a coupon or promotion code that you enter on a retail site's checkout page. Online coupon sites offer lists of these codes for literally thousands of retailers, and can save you big bucks.

Online rebate sites provide lists of manufacturer rebates from a variety of manufacturers. You can use these manufacturer rebates to get money back no matter where you purchase a product; many of the rebate sites also let you track the status of your in-process rebates.

Finally, many sites offer money-back frequent customer plans. After you sign up, you earn money back on every purchase you make at participating retailers. It's a great way to save money every time you shop!

#1 Free Stuff
www.1freestuff.com
Free items and offers.

About.com Coupons/Bargains
couponing.about.com
Online coupons.

Ask Mr. Rebates
www.askmrrebates.com
Cash-back purchasing program.

Bargain Boardwalk
www.bargainboardwalk.com
Online coupons and promotions.

Bargain Shopping.org
www.bargainshopping.org
Online coupons and promotions.

Bargain-Central
www.bargain-central.com
Online coupons and promotions.

Best Free Stuff Online.com
www.bestfreestuffonline.com
Free items and offers.

CoolSavings.com
www.coolsavings.com
Print coupons.

CouponCart.com
www.couponcart.com
Print coupons.

CouponMountain
www.couponmountain.com
Online coupons and promotions.

CouponPages.com
www.couponpages.com
Print coupons.

CouponsandRefunds.com
www.couponsandrefunds.com
Consumer information.

Daily eDeals
www.dailyedeals.com
Online coupons and promotions.

dealcoupon
www.dealcoupon.com
Online coupons and promotions.

DealofDay.com
www.dealofday.com
Online coupons and promotions.

dealsdujour.com
www.dealsdujour.com
Online coupons and promotions.

Ebates
www.ebates.com
Cash-back purchasing program.

eCoupons
www.ecoupons.com
Online coupons and promotions.

eSmarts.com
www.esmarts.com
Online coupons and promotions.

Free-Stuff.com
www.free-stuff.com
Free items and offers.

FreeClutter.com
www.freeclutter.com
Free items and offers.

H.O.T! Coupons
www.hotcoupons.com
Print coupons.

KEYCODE
www.keycode.com
Online coupons and promotions.

KovalchikFarms.com
www.kovalchikfarms.com
Online coupons and promotions.

MoreRebates
www.morerebates.com
Cash-back purchasing program.

MyCoupons
www.mycoupons.com
Online coupons and promotions.

myRebates.com
www.myrebates.com
Manufacturer rebates.

PayDrop.com
www.paydrop.com
Cash-back purchasing program.

QDeals.com
www.qdeals.com
Cash-back purchasing program.

RebateCatcher.com
www.rebatecatcher.com
Manufacturer rebates.

RebatePlace.com
www.rebateplace.com
Manufacturer rebates.

RebateShare.com
www.rebateshare.com
Cash-back purchasing program.

rebatesHQ.com
www.rebateshq.com
Manufacturer rebates.

RefundSweepers
www.refundsweepers.com
Online coupons and promotions.

SalesHound
www.saleshound.com
In-store sales and promotions.

ShoppingList.com
www.shoppinglist.com
Print coupons.

Simple Rebates.com
www.simplerebates.com
Cash-back purchasing program.

SiteforSavings.com
www.siteforsavings.com
Print coupons.

SlickDeals
www.slickdeals.net
Online coupons and promotions.

Specialoffers.com
www.specialoffers.com
Online coupons and promotions.

TotalDeals.com
www.totaldeals.com
Online coupons and promotions.

Totally Free Stuff
www.totallyfreestuff.com
Free items and offers.

Valpack.com
www.valpack.com
Print coupons.

ValuPage
www.valupage.com
Print coupons.

DEPARTMENT STORES AND MASS MERCHANTS

Most traditional retailers have very strong Web presences—including the biggest department stores and mass merchants. In most instances, these merchants compete in most major product categories, and often offer significant bargains, especially on clearance merchandise.

Many of these sites offer bargains you can't find in their "bricks and mortar" stores. Look for links to sale, closeout, or outlet sections; this is where you'll find the best bargains.

You can also find department store sites listed in several major categories within this directory. In particular, look in the Apparel, Electronics, Home and Garden, and Shoes categories.

(Learn more about these big retailer Web sites in Chapter 7, "Hunting for Bargains at Online Malls, Catalogs, and Department Stores.")

Bloomingdale's

bloomingdalesbymail.dailyshopper.com (866.593.2540)

Women's clothing, bed and bath, housewares, furniture, and electronics.

BARGAIN HUNTER'S SECRETS: Click the Clearance tab for closeout items.

Boscov's

www.boscovs.com (800.284.8155)

Men's clothing, women's clothing, children's clothing, shoes, cosmetics, jewelry, bed and bath, housewares, home and garden, electronics, furniture, tools and hardware, and pictures and art.

BARGAIN HUNTER'S SECRETS: Click the This Week's Ads link for limited-time offers. Click the Outlet Center link for closeout merchandise.

brandsmall.com

www.brandsmall.com (877.568.3272)

Electronics, home and garden, health and beauty, home office, jewelry and watches, art, toys, and sporting goods.

BARGAIN HUNTER'S SECRETS: Click the Clearance & Closeouts graphic for clearance merchandise. Click the Blowouts! link for heavily discounted items.

Dillard's

www.dillards.com (800.345.5273)

Men's clothing, women's clothing, juniors' clothing, children's clothing, shoes, bed and bath, home and leisure, and cosmetics.

BARGAIN HUNTER'S SECRETS: Click the Sale links on the main category pages for sale and promotional items.

JCPenney

www.jcpenney.com (800.222.6161)

Men's clothing, women's clothing, children's clothing, shoes, toys, bed and bath, home furnishings, sporting goods, and electronics.

BARGAIN HUNTER'S SECRETS: Click the Online Outlet Store link for clearance and discontinued merchandise. Click Today's Store Ad link for limited-time offers. Click the Big Savings links on main category pages for sale and promotional merchandise.

KMart

www.kmart.com (866.562.7848)

Men's clothing, women's clothing, children's clothing, baby clothing, shoes, health and beauty, bed and bath, housewares, luggage, sporting goods, toys, electronics, computer software, videogames, and jewelry.

BARGAIN HUNTER'S SECRETS: Click the Deal Zone link for sale and promotional merchandise.

Kohl's

www.kohls.com (866.887.8884)

Men's clothing, women's clothing, juniors' clothing, children's clothing, shoes, bed and bath, housewares, and luggage.

BARGAIN HUNTER'S SECRETS: Click the Clearance link for closeout merchandise. Look for sale items on home page and category pages.

Macy's

www.macys.com (800.289.6229)

Men's clothing, women's clothing, baby clothing, housewares, bed and bath, cosmetics, and jewelry. Also functions as the online shopping site for Bon-Macy's, Burdines-Macy's, Goldsmith's-Macy's, Lazarus-Macy's, and Rich's-Macy's.

BARGAIN HUNTER'S SECRETS: Click the Sale tab for sale and promotional items. Click the Sale links on main category pages for sale items; click the Clearance links for closeout merchandise.

Neiman Marcus

www.neimanmarcus.com (888.888.4757)

Men's clothing, women's clothing, shoes, cosmetics, jewelry, electronics, bed and bath, housewares, and furniture.

BARGAIN HUNTER'S SECRETS: Click the Sale links on the home page and category pages for sale and promotional merchandise.

Nordstrom

www.nordstrom.com (888.282.6060)

Men's clothing, women's clothing, juniors' clothing, children's clothing, baby clothing, shoes, jewelry, and cosmetics.

BARGAIN HUNTER'S SECRETS: Click the Sale tab for sale and clearance items.

Saks Fifth Avenue

www.saksfifthavenue.com (877.551.7257)

Men's clothing, women's clothing, cosmetics, jewelry, and home décor.

BARGAIN HUNTER'S SECRETS: Click the Sale links on category pages for sale and clearance items.

Sears Best Selection

www.sears.com (800.349.4358)

Men's clothing, women's clothing, children's clothing, appliances, electronics, computers, automotive, sporting goods, housewares, bed and bath, lawn and garden, tools, toys, videogames, CDs, and DVDs. (Some merchandise offered by partner merchants, such as Lands' End.)

BARGAIN HUNTER'S SECRETS: Click the Clearance link for closeout and discontinued items. Click the Auctions on eBay link to bid on auction items. Look for sale items on main category pages.

Spiegel

www.spiegel.com (800.345. 4500)

Women's clothing, shoes, housewares, bed and bath, electronics, and furniture.

BARGAIN HUNTER'S SECRETS: Click the Clearance link for closeout and discontinued items. Click the Sale links on home page and main category pages for sale and promotional items.

Target

www.target.com (800.591. 3869)

Men's clothing, women's clothing, children's clothing, baby clothing, housewares, bed and bath, luggage, electronics, sporting goods, toys, DVDs, CDs, videogames, and jewelry. Also links to partner sites for Marshall Field's (**www.fields.com**) and Mervyn's (**www.mervyns.com**).

BARGAIN HUNTER'S SECRETS: Click the Clearance link for closeout merchandise. Click the Weekly Ad link for limited-time offers. Look for sale items on home page and category pages.

Wal-Mart Best Bargain

www.walmart.com

Baby goods, electronics, CDs, DVDs, videogames, books, bed and bath, housewares, home and garden, sporting goods, tires, and jewelry.

BARGAIN HUNTER'S SECRETS: Look for savings on individual items.

ELECTRONICS

The consumer electronics category is a broad one. Here you'll find merchants selling everything from portable MP3 players to high-end home theater systems, and lots of other items in-between—including CD players, DVD players, televisions, plasma and big-screen TVs, audio equipment, telephones, cell phones, and all manner of gadgets and gizmos.

There are lots of consumer electronics bargains to be had online. Pricing is often considerably lower online than it is in traditional retail stores, although you need to factor in shipping charges when you're comparing your total cost. Also, many electronics manufacturers offer rebates on selected models, so examine the rebate programs before you purchase.

The Internet is also a great place to research electronics products before you buy. For product reviews and comparisons, check out Active Buyer's Guide (**www.activebuyersguide.com**), AudioREVIEW.com (**www.audioreview.com**), AVguide.com (**www.avguide.com**), CNET Reviews (**reviews.cnet.com**), eCoustics.com (**www.ecoustics.com**), The Gadgeteer (**www.the-gadgeteer.com**), Plasma TV Buying Guide (**www.plasmatvbuyingguide.com**), and ReviewFinder (**www.reviewfinder.com**).

There are considerable price differences between merchants in this category, so shopping around is recommended. You might want to use a price comparison engine that specializes in electronics products, such as Best Web Buys (**www.bestwebbuys.com**), CNET Shopper.com (**shopper.cnet.com**), Price.com (**www.price.com**), PriceMix (**www.pricemix.com**), and StreetPrices (**www.streetprices.com**). Most general price comparison sites also do a good job finding the lowest prices on electronic equipment.

Two merchants in this category received high ratings on the 2003 American Customer Satisfaction Index. Amazon.com was the #1 online retailer, with an 88% satisfaction rating. Buy.com ranked #3, with an 80% rating.

Many of the merchants in this category, such as Best Buy and Radio Shack, are probably familiar to you from their "bricks and mortar" outlets. You'll find a similar, if not expanded, selection in their online stores. Many of the merchants in the Computer Hardware and Software category also sell consumer electronics items, as do several retailers in the Department Stores and Mass Merchants category. Look there for additional savings.

Amazon.com

www.amazon.com (800.201.7575)

Home audio and video, portable audio, videogame systems, telephones, cell phones, GPS receivers, and accessories. (Click the Electronics tab.)

BARGAIN HUNTER'S SECRETS: In the Electronics store, click the Today's Deals tab for sale and promotional items; click the Outlet, Used & Refurbished tab for clearance and reconditioned items. Look for additional bargains during the sitewide Friday Sale. Also look for lower prices on new and used merchandise from third-party merchants in the More Buying Choices section of each product page. Free shipping on orders of more than $25.

Batteries.com

www.batteries.com (888.288.6500)

Batteries for laptop PCs, camcorders, digital cameras, and cell phones.

BARGAIN HUNTER'S SECRETS: Look for savings on individual items.

Best Buy

www.bestbuy.com (888.237.8289)

Home audio and video, portable audio, videogame systems, satellite systems, car audio, telephones, cell phones, and accessories.

BARGAIN HUNTER'S SECRETS: See individual products for savings. Free shipping.

Best Buy Plasma

www.bestbuyplasma.com (866.660.6602)

Plasma, LCD, and projection TVs. (Not associated with the Best Buy chain.)

BARGAIN HUNTER'S SECRETS: Look for savings on individual products. Look for This Week's Picks at the bottom of the home page.

BetterCables.com

www.bettercables.com (877.433.7039)

Audio/video cables.

BARGAIN HUNTER'S SECRETS: Free shipping.

Buy.com

www.buy.com (800.800.0900)

Home audio and video, portable audio, videogame systems, car audio, cell phones, GPS systems, and accessories.

BARGAIN HUNTER'S SECRETS: See individual products for savings. Click the Today's Deals link for sale items. Click the Rebates link for manufacturer rebates. Free shipping.

CableWholesale.com

www.cablewholesale.com (888.212.8295)

Computer and audio/video cables.

BARGAIN HUNTER'S SECRETS: See individual items for savings. Click the Hot Deals link for sale and overstocked items.

Cambridge Soundworks

www.hifi.com (800.945.4434)

Home audio and video, portable audio, and accessories.

BARGAIN HUNTER'S SECRETS: Click the Specials link for clearance and open box items. Free shipping.

Circuit City

www.circuitcity.com (800.843.2489)

Home audio and video, portable audio, videogame systems, satellite systems, car audio, telephones, cell phones, and accessories.

BARGAIN HUNTER'S SECRETS: Look for savings on individual products. Look for Deals of the Week on main category pages. Click the Shop for Clearance Items link (very bottom of the page) for closeout merchandise.

Crutchfield Best Selection

www.crutchfield.com (888.955.6000)

Home audio and video, portable audio, car audio, telephones, and accessories.

BARGAIN HUNTER'S SECRETS: Look for savings on individual products. Click the Specials link for sale and promotional items. Click the Outlet link for returned and refurbished merchandise. Click the Scratch & Dent link for like-new damaged items.

Dish Direct

www.dishonline.com (888.834.1999)

DirecTV and Dish Network satellite systems.

BARGAIN HUNTER'S SECRETS: Click the Promotions link for manufacturer promotions.

DTV Express

www.dtvexpress.com (800.806.4757)

Plasma, LCD, and projection TVs.

BARGAIN HUNTER'S SECRETS: Look for savings on individual models.

DynaDirect.com

www.dynadirect.com (877.438.3962)

Home audio and video, portable audio, car audio, telephones, and accessories.

BARGAIN HUNTER'S SECRETS: Click the Special Offers link for sale and promotion items. Click the Current Rebates link for manufacturer rebates. Click the Free Shipping link for items that qualify for free shipping.

eBatts.com

www.ebatts.com (800.300.1540)

Batteries for laptop PCs, camcorders, digital cameras, and phones.

BARGAIN HUNTER'S SECRETS: See This Week's Specials section of the home page. Look for savings on individual items.

eCost.com

www.ecost.com (877.888.2678)

Home audio and video, portable audio, GPS receivers, and accessories.

BARGAIN HUNTER'S SECRETS: Look for savings on individual products. Click the Auction tab for items available for bidding. Click the Clearance Countdown tab for closeout and overstock merchandise available for a limited time only. Click the Bargain Countdown tab for refurbished items. Free shipping on orders of more than $25.

etronics.com Best Bargain

www.etronics.com (800.323.7669)

Home audio and video, portable audio, car audio, videogame systems, and accessories.

BARGAIN HUNTER'S SECRETS: Most items heavily discounted; look for savings on individual products. Click the Rebate Center link for manufacturer rebates.

Gadget Universe

www.gadgetuniverse.com (800.872.6250)

Small electronics, small appliances, and gadgets.

BARGAIN HUNTER'S SECRETS: Look for savings on individual products.

Get Connected

www.getconnected.com (800.775.2506)

Cell phones and service plans; satellite systems.

BARGAIN HUNTER'S SECRETS: Search for best bargains.

Good Guys

www.goodguys.com (888.937.7004)

Home audio and video, portable audio, car audio, and accessories.

BARGAIN HUNTER'S SECRETS: Look for savings on individual products. Click the Clearance Sale link for closeout merchandise.

GPSNOW.com

www.gpsnow.com (308.381.4410)

GPS receivers.

BARGAIN HUNTER'S SECRETS: Look for savings on individual products.

Hammacher Schlemmer

www.hammacherschlemmer.com (800.321.1484)

Small electronics and gadgets.

BARGAIN HUNTER'S SECRETS: Click the Sale link for closeout and sale merchandise.

Hello Direct.com

www.hellodirect.com (800.435.5634

Telephones, cell phones, and accessories. Specializes in small business systems, multi-line phones, hands-free headsets, and so on.

BARGAIN HUNTER'S SECRETS: Click the Special Offers link for sale and promotional items.

HookedOnTronics.com

www.hookedontronics.com (800.265.1030)

Home audio and video, portable audio, car audio, and accessories.

BARGAIN HUNTER'S SECRETS: Look for savings on individual products. Click the Outlet Superstore link for refurbished items.

HTmarket.com Best Selection

www.htmarket.com (888.764.9273)

Home audio and video, home theater furniture, popcorn machines, posters, and accessories.

BARGAIN HUNTER'S SECRETS: Click the Reduced Items link for sale merchandise.

HypAudio.com Best Bargain

www.hypaudio.com (888.766.4442)

Home audio and video, portable audio, car audio, telephones, cell phones, satellite systems, GPS devices, small electronics, gadgets, and accessories.

BARGAIN HUNTER'S SECRETS: Factory outlet pricing; look for bargains on discontinued and reconditioned merchandise.

iGadgets.com

www.igadgets.com (877.287.1358)

Small electronics, small appliances, and gadgets.

BARGAIN HUNTER'S SECRETS: Look for savings on individual items. Click the Buy 1 Get 1 Free link for quantity bargains. Click the Free Shipping link for items with free shipping. Look for Sale links for additional savings.

iGo

www.igo.com (888.205.0064)

Accessories for cell phones, laptop PCs, PDAs, and other portable devices.

BARGAIN HUNTER'S SECRETS: Look for iGo Outpost links for open-box bargains.

J&R Music & Computer World Best Bargain Best Selection

www.jandr.com (800.806.1115)

Home audio and video, portable audio, car audio, videogame systems, satellite systems, and accessories.

BARGAIN HUNTER'S SECRETS: Most items heavily discounted; look for savings on individual products. Click the New York Times Ad link for advertised specials. Click the Deal of the Week Specials link for limited-time bargains, updated each Tuesday. Click the Clearance link for closeout, discontinued, and refurbished merchandise. Click the Rebate Center for manufacturer rebates. Free shipping on selected items.

LetsTalk.com

www.letstalk.com (877.825.5460)

Cell phones and service plans.

BARGAIN HUNTER'S SECRETS: Search for savings on specific products and service plans. Click the Rebate Center link for manufacturer rebates.

OneCall

www.onecall.com (800.340.4770)

Home audio and video, telephones, and accessories.

BARGAIN HUNTER'S SECRETS: Look for savings on individual products. Click the Clearance tab for discontinued and open-box specials. Click the Package Specials link for bargains on bundles. Click the Promotions link for current sales and promotions. Click the Rebates link for manufacturer rebates.

Outpost.com

www.outpost.com (877.688.7678)

Home audio and video, portable audio, and small electronics. (Owned by Fry's Electronics.)

BARGAIN HUNTER'S SECRETS: Look for savings on individual products. Click the Advertised Specials link for current sale items.

PlanetDTV.com

www.planetdtv.com (800.851. 1356)

Plasma, LCD, and projection TVS.

BARGAIN HUNTER'S SECRETS: Look for savings on individual products.

Plasma.com Best Bargain

www.plasma.com (877.722.8948)

Plasma, LCD, and projection TVs.

BARGAIN HUNTER'S SECRETS: Look for savings on individual products. Click the Featured Items link for best deals. Free shipping.

PlasmaTVs.com Best Bargain

www.plasmatvs.com (900.923.8007)

Plasma, LCD, and projection TVs.

BARGAIN HUNTER'S SECRETS: Look for savings on individual products.

Radio Shack

www.radioshack.com (800.843.7422)

Cables, accessories, batteries, telephones, satellite systems, small electronics, and gadgets.

BARGAIN HUNTER'S SECRETS: Click the What's On Sale link for sale items. Click the Coupons link for print coupons (not good online).

Sears

www.sears.com (800.349.4358)

Home audio and video, portable audio, car audio, telephones, and accessories. (Click the Electronics tab.)

BARGAIN HUNTER'S SECRETS: Click the Reconditioned and Auctions item link for closeout and refurbished items. See the Now On Sale section for sale merchandise. Low-price guarantee.

The Sharper Image

www.sharperimage.com (800.344.5555)

Small electronics and gadgets.

BARGAIN HUNTER'S SECRETS: Click the Outlet Store link for closeout and reconditioned merchandise.

Simply Wireless

www.simplywireless.com (888.449.8484)

Cell phones and service plans.

BARGAIN HUNTER'S SECRETS: Search for savings on specific products and service plans.

Sony

www.sonystyle.com (877.865.7669)

Home audio and video, portable audio, and car audio. Manufacturer direct.

BARGAIN HUNTER'S SECRETS: Look for savings on individual products. Click the Clearance links on category pages for closeout and reconditioned merchandise; click the Great Deals link for sales and promotions.

ThinkGeek

www.thinkgeek.com (888.433.5788)

Gadgets, gizmos, small electronics, and computer accessories.

BARGAIN HUNTER'S SECRETS: Click the Clearance link for closeout and sale merchandise.

Zbattery.com

www.zbattery.com (800.624.8681)

Batteries for laptop PCs, cordless phones, cell phones, cameras, and camcorders.

BARGAIN HUNTER'S SECRETS: Click the Sale Items link for sale and clearance merchandise.

EYEWEAR

Although you can't get your eyes examined over the Internet (no Web-based opticians yet!), you *can* buy your glasses online—as long as you already know your prescription. (Most prescription items are sold on a nonreturnable basis.) The Web is especially good for buying contacts; buy in volume to get even greater discounts.

Of course, the Web is also a great place to shop for sunglasses. There are many sites online that specialize in both bargain and fashion shades. You'll also find a bigger selection online that what you're used to with traditional outlets. Just remember to shop around; the sites with the most expensive brands often don't have the lowest prices.

You can also find eyewear products at many of the retailers in the Apparel section of this directory, as well as at several sites in the Department Stores and Mass Merchants category.

A Pair of Shades

www.apairofshades.com (888.742.3370)

Sunglasses, frames, prescription glasses, and contact lenses.

BARGAIN HUNTER'S SECRETS: Look for savings on individual items.

Coastal Contacts

www.coastalcontacts.com (866.333.6888)

Contact lenses.

BARGAIN HUNTER'S SECRETS: Look for savings on individual items. Free shipping on orders of more than $89.

Eyeglasses.com

www.eyeglasses.com (888.896.3885)

Sunglasses, frames, prescription glasses, reading glasses, and contact lenses.

BARGAIN HUNTER'S SECRETS: Look for savings on individual items. Free shipping.

FramesDirect.com

www.framesdirect.com (800.248.9427)

Sunglasses, frames, prescription glasses, and contact lenses.

BARGAIN HUNTER'S SECRETS: Look for savings on individual items. Click the Coupons link for manufacturer promotions.

Lens.com

www.lens.com (800.536.7266)

Contact lenses.

BARGAIN HUNTER'S SECRETS: Look for savings on individual items.

Lenses for Less

www.lensesforless.com (800.211.9806)

Contact lenses.

BARGAIN HUNTER'S SECRETS: Click the Specials link for free shipping on large quantity orders.

Lensmart

www.lensmart.com (800.693.8246)

Contact lenses.

BARGAIN HUNTER'S SECRETS: Look for savings on individual items.

LensQuest

www.lensquest.com (888.867.4209)

Contact lenses.

BARGAIN HUNTER'S SECRETS: Look for savings on individual items. Free shipping on orders of $99 or more.

Peepers Contacts

www.peeperscontacts.com (800.988.4790)

Contact lenses and sunglasses.

BARGAIN HUNTER'S SECRETS: Look for savings on individual items.

Sport Eyes

www.sporteyes.com (888.223.2669)

Sports eyewear and sunglasses.

BARGAIN HUNTER'S SECRETS: Click the Closeouts or Bargain Bin link for clearance and discontinued items. Free shipping on orders of more than $75.

Sunglass City

www.thesunglasscity.com (888.822.7297)

Sunglasses.

BARGAIN HUNTER'S SECRETS: Look for links to close-out specials on the home page.

Sunglass Hut

www.sunglasshut.com (800.786.4527)

Sunglasses.

BARGAIN HUNTER'S SECRETS: Go to the Sunglasses page and click the Great Value link for discounted merchandise.

FLOWERS, CANDLES, AND GIFTS

This category demonstrates that you can buy virtually anything online. Fresh flowers? No problem. Gift baskets? Lots of 'em. Fancy candles? You betcha—and at pretty good prices, besides.

But here's the thing. When you're shopping for flowers online, you won't find a lot of bargains. When you visit an online florist, there likely isn't a sale section on the site. Prices end up being pretty much the same from one site to another, and very close to what you find at traditional florist shops. After all, it's difficult to offer "clearance" flowers—this is the type of product that literally dies when it gets old.

Note that the first merchant in this category, 1-800-FLOWERS.com, was the #4 online merchant overall on the 2003 American Customer Satisfaction Index, with a 76% satisfaction rating. 1-800-FLOWERS.com also earns my Best Selection citation, which no doubt corresponds to the site's high satisfaction level.

1-800-FLOWERS.com

www.1800flowers.com (800.356.9377)

Flowers, candy, and gifts.

BARGAIN HUNTER'S SECRETS: See the By Price section of the home page to shop for low-priced items. Click the Special Savings links on category pages for sale items.

AKA Gourmet

www.akagourmet.com (800.735.3284)

Gift baskets.

BARGAIN HUNTER'S SECRETS: Click the Specials link for sale items. Click the Shop by Price link to shop for low-priced items.

Amazon.com

www.amazon.com (800.201.7575)

Gift baskets and chocolates. (Click the Gourmet Food tab.) Many items offered by third-party partners, such as Hickory Farms and Harry and David.

BARGAIN HUNTER'S SECRETS: Look for discounts on individual product pages.

Candlemart.com

www.candlemart.com (877.352.6353)

Candles, bath and body, and accessories.

BARGAIN HUNTER'S SECRETS: Click the Specials link for sale items; on the Specials page, click the Daily Deal graphic for limited-time offers. Click the Clearance link for closeouts and discontinued items.

CandlesForever.com

www.candlesforever.com (800.316.4925)

Candles, bath and body, and accessories.

BARGAIN HUNTER'S SECRETS: Free shipping on all orders of more than $50.

CardStore.com

www.cardstore.com (510.595.6702)

Custom greeting cards.

BARGAIN HUNTER'S SECRETS: Buy in quantity for larger savings.

cardSupply

www.cardsupply.com (800.444.2273)

Greeting cards, invitations, and stationery.

BARGAIN HUNTER'S SECRETS: Click the Special Deals link for sale items.

Casa de Fruta

www.casadefruta.com (800.543.1702)

Gift baskets, fruit baskets, nuts, and chocolates.

BARGAIN HUNTER'S SECRETS: Click the Specials link for sale items.

Coast to Coast Flowers

www.coasttocoastflowers.com (888.269.5297)

Flowers, gourmet baskets, cookies, and candles.

BARGAIN HUNTER'S SECRETS: Use the Pick Your Price section to shop for low-priced items. Join the Petal Rewards program to earn points with every purchase.

Cookie Bouquets

www.cookiebouquets.com (800. 233.2171)

Cookies and gift baskets.

BARGAIN HUNTER'S SECRETS: Click the Specials! link for sale items.

Florist.com

www.florist.com (800.709.9622)

Flowers, fruit baskets, and cookies.

BARGAIN HUNTER'S SECRETS: Click the Flowers Under $45 link for low-priced items.

FTD

www.ftd.com (800.736.3383)

Flowers, gourmet gifts, gift baskets, fruit baskets, and gifts.

BARGAIN HUNTER'S SECRETS: See the Shop by Price links to shop for low-priced items.

Gifts in 24

www.giftsin24.com (800.244.5232)

Notes, cards, memos, and gifts.

BARGAIN HUNTER'S SECRETS: Click the Specials link for sale items.

GiftTree

www.gifttree.com (800.931.3620)

Flowers, wine gifts, gift baskets, candy, fruit baskets, and balloons.

BARGAIN HUNTER'S SECRETS: See the Gifts by Price links to shop for low-priced items.

Hallmark

www.hallmark.com (877.490.2355)

Greeting cards, flowers, and gifts.

BARGAIN HUNTER'S SECRETS: Click the Sales and Specials link for sale items and promotions. On category pages, click the Weekly Specials link for limited-time offers; use the Price links to shop for low-priced items.

Harry and David Best Bargain

www.harryanddavid.com (877.456.7700)

Gift baskets, fresh fruit, chocolates, gourmet foods, and floral gifts.

BARGAIN HUNTER'S SECRETS: Click the Sale link for discounted items. Look for savings on individual items.

Illuminations Best Selection

www.illuminations.com (800.621.2998)

Candles, gifts, and home décor.

BARGAIN HUNTER'S SECRETS: Click the Sale link for weekly specials and other sale merchandise. Click the Clearance link for closeout items. Free shipping on orders of $50 or more.

KaBloom Best Bargain

www.kabloom.com (800.522.5666)

Flowers, cookies, candy, gourmet baskets, and gifts.

BARGAIN HUNTER'S SECRETS: Click the Special Discounts link for notification of special savings.

Nationwide Florist

www.nationwideflorist.com (888.701.3500)

Flowers, cheesecakes, cookies, and gifts.

BARGAIN HUNTER'S SECRETS: Use the Pick Your Price links to shop for low-priced items.

papercards.com

www.papercards.com (716.837.7256)

Greeting cards.

BARGAIN HUNTER'S SECRETS: Free shipping on orders of more than $3. Discounted prices on multiple card orders. Look for sale notices on the home page.

Personal Creations

www.personalize.com (800.326.6626)

Personalized gifts.

BARGAIN HUNTER'S SECRETS: Click the Sales & Clearance link for discounted and discontinued items.

ProFlowers.com

www.proflowers.com (888.373.7437)

Flowers, gift baskets, chocolates, and gourmet desserts.

BARGAIN HUNTER'S SECRETS: Click the Special Savings link for limited-time offers.

SF Music Box Company

www.sfmusicbox.com (800.635.9064)

Music boxes.

BARGAIN HUNTER'S SECRETS: Use the Gifts by Price links to shop for low-priced items.

Things Remembered

www.thingsremembered.com (866.902.4438)

Personalized gifts.

BARGAIN HUNTER'S SECRETS: First-time buyers save 10%. Click the Price link to shop for low-priced items.

Vermont Teddy Bear Company

www.vermontteddybear.com (800.829.2327)

Gift bears.

BARGAIN HUNTER'S SECRETS: Join the PreFUR'd Member program for special monthly offers.

Wine Country Gift Baskets

www.winecountrygiftbaskets.com (800.324.2793)

Wine baskets, gourmet food baskets, gift baskets, and chocolate.

BARGAIN HUNTER'S SECRETS: Click the Specials link for discounted items.

FOOD AND DRINK

It might seem odd to buy food online, just because of the freshness challenges involved. But it ends up not being a big problem, for a number of reasons.

First, most food items available online are nonperishable. And it's no problem shipping a nonperishable item—just put it in a box and ship it out. You don't have to worry about a box of crackers spoiling before it gets to your door.

Second, technology now exists to safely ship many perishable items. In most instances, the food (meats, cheeses, and so on) is placed in an insulated container, along with some sort of high-tech ice pack. (Much more effective than old-fashioned dry ice.) Shipping is typically via a next-day delivery service, so the food is cool and fresh when it gets to you.

In addition, there are some online groceries that actually deliver from local stores direct to your door. Admittedly, this type of service hasn't proven to be overly popular with consumers, but you can still find a few national services (such as NetGrocer and Peapod), as well as some regional grocery chains, that offer local delivery. The big problem with this type of online grocery delivery service is that it's not a bargain; instead of saving money by shopping online, you typically pay extra, in the form of a delivery fee. And some online grocers don't accept coupons, which makes your final bill that much higher. So, use these services for their convenience, not for price. (And always check with your local grocery stores to see what delivery services they offer.)

While we're on the topic of bargain hunting, know that any food bargains you might find—at any type of online merchant—are apt to be few and far between. Most online merchants tend to specialize in gourmet foods, and they don't like to discount that type of product. You have to really look hard for big savings, even at the merchants listed here.

A.G. Ferrari Foods

www.agferrari.com (877.878.2783)

Italian foods.

BARGAIN HUNTER'S SECRETS: Pull down the Our Products menu and click the Sale link for sale items.

Adagio Teas

www.adagio.com

Teas.

BARGAIN HUNTER'S SECRETS: Free shipping on orders of more than $75.

Allen Brothers

www.allenbrothers.com (800.957.0111)

Steaks, beef, and meat.

BARGAIN HUNTER'S SECRETS: Pull down the What's New menu and select Specials for promotional items.

alltea.com Best Selection

www.alltea.com (415.382.1146)

Teas.

BARGAIN HUNTER'S SECRETS: 10% discount on orders of $100 or more.

Amazon.com

www.amazon.com (800.201.7575)

Coffees, teas, chocolate, meat, seafood, cheese, low-carb food, and ethnic food. (Click the Gourmet Food tab.) Many items offered by third-party partners, such as Hickory Farms and Harry and David.

BARGAIN HUNTER'S SECRETS: Look for discounts on individual product pages.

Ambrosia

www.ambrosiawine.com (800.435.2225)

Wine (Napa and Sonoma).

BARGAIN HUNTER'S SECRETS: Join an Ambrosia monthly wine club to receive 15% off all wine purchases.

AULSuperStore.com

www.aulsuperstore.com (800.791.2114)

Groceries. ($25 minimum purchase)

BARGAIN HUNTER'S SECRETS: Discount prices. Click the Super Specials link for sale items. Free delivery.

Basic Ingredients

www.basic-ingredients.com (440.964.2002)

Bulk foods, candy, chocolate, coffees, teas, grains, nuts, jams, soups, spices, and snacks.

BARGAIN HUNTER'S SECRETS: Bulk pricing.

Beer on the Wall

www.beeronthewall.com (888.840.2337)

Beer (microbreweries).

BARGAIN HUNTER'S SECRETS: Look for Sale icons next to individual items.

BevMo! Best Selection Best Bargain

www.bevmo.com (877.772.3866)

Beer, wine, and spirits.

BARGAIN HUNTER'S SECRETS: All items discounted. Click the Clearance tab for special savings.

Bulk Candy Store Best Bargain Best Selection

www.bulkcandystore.com (561.615.8646)

Candy.

BARGAIN HUNTER'S SECRETS: Bulk pricing.

Burgers' Smokehouse

www.smokehouse.com (800.624.5426)

Hickory-smoked meats.

BARGAIN HUNTER'S SECRETS: Free gifts with purchases of more than $50. Click the Two for One Specials link for sale items.

Cheese Express

www.cheeseexpress.com (888.530.0505)

Gourmet cheeses.

BARGAIN HUNTER'S SECRETS: Click the Promotions & Hot Picks link for special purchases.

Chefshop.com

www.chefshop.com (877.337.2491)

Gourmet food, chocolate, meat, cheese, teas, coffees, and condiments.

BARGAIN HUNTER'S SECRETS: Click the Sale link for limited-stock specials.

D'Italia Foods

www.ditalia.com (888.260.2192)

Italian food and gifts.

BARGAIN HUNTER'S SECRETS: Click the Specials tab for discounted items.

Dean & Deluca Best Selection

www.deandeluca.com (877.826.9246)

Gourmet foods, meat, cheese, chocolate, teas, coffees, and wine.

BARGAIN HUNTER'S SECRETS: Click the Sale link for sale items.

Earthy Delights

www.earthy.com (800.367.4709)

Gourmet foods, cheese, caviar, pasta, produce, fruits, nuts, chocolate, spices, and condiments.

BARGAIN HUNTER'S SECRETS: Look for specials throughout the site. Go to the Seasonal/Gifts/New page for sale items. Free shipping on orders of $125 or more.

EthnicGrocer.com

www.ethnicgrocer.com (866.438.4642)

Ethnic foods.

BARGAIN HUNTER'S SECRETS: Click the Specials link for sale items.

Fine Wine House

www.finewinehouse.com (877.981.6555)

Wine.

BARGAIN HUNTER'S SECRETS: All items discounted.

Flying Noodle

www.flyingnoodle.com (800.566.0599)

Pasta, sauces, and oils.

BARGAIN HUNTER'S SECRETS: Click the Sale Items link for specials.

FreshPasta.com

www.freshpasta.com (800.747.2782)

Pasta and sauces.

BARGAIN HUNTER'S SECRETS: Look for specials on home page.

iGourmet.com

www.igourmet.com (877.446.8763)

Gourmet foods, meat, seafood, cheese, sauces, dry goods, coffees, teas, desserts, and gifts.

BARGAIN HUNTER'S SECRETS: Click the On Sale Now link for sale items.

LowCarbChocolates

www.lowcarbchocolates.com (888.267.2065)

Low-carb, Atkins-friendly candy and chocolates.

BARGAIN HUNTER'S SECRETS: All items discounted.

MexGrocer.com

www.mexgrocer.com (877.463.9476)

Mexican food.

BARGAIN HUNTER'S SECRETS: Click the Hot Specials link for sale items.

NetGrocer

www.netgrocer.com

Groceries.

BARGAIN HUNTER'S SECRETS: Look for the checkmark icon for savings on individual products.

Omaha Steaks

www.omahasteaks.com (800.960.8400)

Steaks, meat, seafood, and sauces.

BARGAIN HUNTER'S SECRETS: Look for savings on individual items. Look for sale items on the home page. Click the Overstocks link for discounted items.

OnlineFoods.net

www.onlinefoods.net (239.348.0747)

Groceries.

BARGAIN HUNTER'S SECRETS: Look for savings on individual items.

Peapod

www.peapod.com (800.573.2763)

Groceries (local delivery to Chicago, New York, Connecticut, Massachusetts, Rhode Island, and Washington, D.C. only).

BARGAIN HUNTER'S SECRETS: Look for savings on individual items.

SeafoodS.com

www.seafoods.com (877.710.3467)

Seafood and caviar.

BARGAIN HUNTER'S SECRETS: Look for specials on the home page.

SpecialTeas

www.specialteas.com (888.365.6983)

Teas.

BARGAIN HUNTER'S SECRETS: Click the Special Offers link for sale items.

WeGoShop.com

www.wegoshop.com

Groceries (local delivery in selected areas).

BARGAIN HUNTER'S SECRETS: Look for savings on individual items.

Wine.com Best Selection

www.wine.com (877.665.3213)

Wine.

BARGAIN HUNTER'S SECRETS: Click the Great Wines Under $25 link for low-priced items. On the Wine Shop tab, click the Wines on Sale This Month link for sale items.

Zenobia Nuts on the Net (866.936.6242)

www.nutsonthenet.com

Nuts.

BARGAIN HUNTER'S SECRETS: Free delivery. See the Buy by the Case page for bulk savings.

HEALTH AND BEAUTY

There are many online merchants selling cosmetics, perfume, skin care products, and other health and beauty items. Some merchants specialize in high-end products; others go with a more affordable product selection. Whatever type of product you're interested in, do your investigative shopping and you're bound to find some bargains.

The same can be said for prescription medicine. Many legitimate pharmacies enable you to fill your prescriptions online; some even enable you to buy certain types of drugs, such as Viagra, without a prescription—although they might tack on a consultation fee to your initial order. (Make sure you shop around for the lowest consultation fee; some sites waive this fee, which can save you a few bucks.) Pricing on medicine is all over the place, so you might want to use the Price RX comparison engine (**www.price-rx.com**) to shop for the lowest prices.

For general health and beauty items, you can supplement the sites listed here with those merchants in the Department Store and Mass Merchants category, who often have extensive selections of this type of product. In addition, many women's apparel merchants also carry perfume and cosmetic items.

Abbeys Perfume Best Bargain Best Selection

www.abbeysperfume.com (303.985.2879)

Perfumes, body lotion, candles, and gift baskets.

BARGAIN HUNTER'S SECRETS: Discount pricing. Click the Clearance Sale link for closeout bargains.

Amazon.com

www.amazon.com (800.201.7575)

Health care, cosmetics, personal care, bath and beauty, nutrition, and medical supplies and equipment. (Click the Health & Personal Care tab.) Many items offered by third-party partners.

BARGAIN HUNTER'S SECRETS: Look for discounts on individual product pages.

Apothia

www.apothia.com (877.276.8442)

Cosmetics, perfume, and candles.

BARGAIN HUNTER'S SECRETS: Look for savings on individual products.

Avon

www.avon.com (800.527.2866)

Cosmetics, perfume, bath and beauty, and jewelry.

BARGAIN HUNTER'S SECRETS: Look for specials on main shopping page. Click the Specials links for additional sale items. Free gift with qualifying purchase; see the Free Gift tab for details.

Ball Beauty Supply

www.ballbeauty.com (323.655.2330)

Cosmetics, hair care, nail care, skin care, small appliances, and accessories.

BARGAIN HUNTER'S SECRETS: All items discounted. Click the Monthly Specials link for limited-time specials.

Beauty.com Best Selection

www.beauty.com (800.378.4786)

Cosmetics, perfume, hair care, skin care, bath and beauty, and accessories.

BARGAIN HUNTER'S SECRETS: Click the Steals & Deals link for sale items.

BeautyHabit.com

www.beautyhabit.com (800.377.8771)

Cosmetics, perfume, hair care, skin care, bath and beauty, aromatherapy, candles, and baby care.

BARGAIN HUNTER'S SECRETS: Look for the Monthly Specials link on the home page. Free shipping on orders of $100 or more.

BeautySampling.com

www.beautysampling.com (877.726.7591)

Perfume.

BARGAIN HUNTER'S SECRETS: Save money by sampling miniature sizes.

ClickPharmacy Best Selection

www.clickpharmacy.com (800.838.9525)

Prescription drugs, health and wellness.

BARGAIN HUNTER'S SECRETS: Look for savings on individual products.

Condomania

www.condomania.com (800.926.6366)

Condoms, lubricants, and bath and massage.

BARGAIN HUNTER'S SECRETS: Look for savings on individual products. Click the Clearance link for sale and discounted items.

CosmeticMall.com Best Selection

www.cosmeticmall.com (631.262.9302)

Cosmetics, perfume, bath and body, skin care, hair care, and gifts.

BARGAIN HUNTER'S SECRETS: Click the On Sale link for sale merchandise. Click the Promotions link for current manufacturer promotions.

Crabtree and Evelyn

www.crabtreeandevelyn.com (800.272.2873)

Cosmetics, perfume, bath and beauty, skin care, and hair care.

BARGAIN HUNTER'S SECRETS: Free shipping on orders of $60 or more.

CVS Online Pharmacy

www.cvs.com (888.607.4287)

Prescription drugs, health and wellness, vitamins, cosmetics, hair care, and baby care.

BARGAIN HUNTER'S SECRETS: Look for discounts on individual items. Click the Super Savers link for sale items. Click the More Special Offers link for manufacturer promotions. Click the Weekly Store Ads link for advertised specials. Click the ExtraCare link to get 2% off most purchases.

DentalDepot.com

www.dentaldepot.com (978.681.1170)

Dental supplies.

BARGAIN HUNTER'S SECRETS: Look for savings on individual items.

DERMAdoctor.com

www.dermadoctor.com (877.337.6237)

Skin care.

BARGAIN HUNTER'S SECRETS: Click the Special Offers link for promotional items. Free shipping on orders of more than $49.

DermStore.com Best Bargain

www.dermstore.com (800.213.3376)

Skin care.

BARGAIN HUNTER'S SECRETS: Look for savings on individual products. See the Clearance Specials section of the home page for closeout items. Free shipping on orders of more than $75.

Diamond Beauty

www.diamondbeauty.com (800.669.6638)

Cosmetics and skin care.

BARGAIN HUNTER'S SECRETS: All items discounted.

Dr. Leonard's Healthcare

www.drleonards.com (800.455.1918)

Healthcare, cosmetics, and skin care.

BARGAIN HUNTER'S SECRETS: All items discounted.

Drugstore.com Best Selection

www.drugstore.com (800.378.4786)

Cosmetics, skin care, perfume, bath and beauty, nutrition and wellness, vitamins, and prescription drugs.

BARGAIN HUNTER'S SECRETS: Free shipping on orders of $49 or more. Join the drugstore.com dollar program to earn 5% off nonprescription purchases.

eBubbles.com

www.ebubbles.com (888.403.8701)

Bath and beauty and skin care.

BARGAIN HUNTER'S SECRETS: From the Shop page, click the Clearance link for closeout merchandise; click the Specials link for sale items.

eCondoms.com

www.econdoms.com (253.351.5001)

Condoms and lubricants.

BARGAIN HUNTER'S SECRETS: All items discounted. Click the Sale Items link for discounted merchandise.

eDrugnet

www.edrugnet.com (786.551.6174)

Prescription drugs.

BARGAIN HUNTER'S SECRETS: Look for savings on individual products.

folica.com

www.folica.com (888.919.4247)

Hair care, nail care, and health and beauty.

BARGAIN HUNTER'S SECRETS: All items discounted. Click the Clearance Sale link for sale items. Free shipping on orders of more than $75.

Fragrance.net

www.fragrance.net (800.987.3738)

Perfume, skin care, aromatherapy, and candles.

BARGAIN HUNTER'S SECRETS: See the Clearance Outlet section of the home page for sale and closeout items.

GLOSS

www.gloss.com (888.550.4567)

Cosmetics and skin care.

BARGAIN HUNTER'S SECRETS: Free shipping on orders of $100 or more.

Go Soak

www.gosoak.com (877.968.7625)

Bath and body.

BARGAIN HUNTER'S SECRETS: Free shipping on orders of $50 or more.

Imagination Perfumery Best Bargain

www.imaginationperfumery.com (866.338.8376)

Perfume and bath and body.

BARGAIN HUNTER'S SECRETS: Most items heavily discounted. Click the Specials link for limited-time bargains. Free shipping for orders of more than $75.

Med-Pharmacy-Online.com

www.med-pharmacy-online.com (888.557.1872)

Prescription drugs.

BARGAIN HUNTER'S SECRETS: Look for savings on individual products.

National Allergy Supply

www.nationalallergysupply.com (800.522.1448)

Asthma and allergy relief medications and products.

BARGAIN HUNTER'S SECRETS: Look for savings on individual products.

Omnivit

www.omnivit.com (877.231.3588)

Vitamins and supplements.

BARGAIN HUNTER'S SECRETS: Look for savings on individual products.

Perfumania.com

www.perfumania.com (800.927.1777)

Perfume, cosmetics, skin care, and bath and body.

BARGAIN HUNTER'S SECRETS: Look for savings on individual products. Free shipping on orders of $59 or more.

Perfume Emporium

www.perfumeemporium.com (877.782.6580)

Perfume, skin care, candles, and jewelry.

BARGAIN HUNTER'S SECRETS: Look for savings on individual products. Sign up for the Beauty Bucks program to accumulate bonus points on all purchases.

The Perfume Spot

www.perfumespot.com (866.289.6776)

Perfume and bath and body.

BARGAIN HUNTER'S SECRETS: All items heavily discounted. Click the Clearance Items link for additional savings.

Perfume Station

www.perfumestation.com (866.576.7748)

Perfume, cosmetics, skin care, bath and body, candles, and gifts.

BARGAIN HUNTER'S SECRETS: Click the Clearance! tab for sale items. Free shipping with purchase of $100 or more.

PrescriptionDrugs.com

www.prescriptiondrugs.com (888.557.1872)

Prescription drugs.

BARGAIN HUNTER'S SECRETS: All items discounted. Look for This Month's Specials on the home page.

Priority Pharmacy

www.prescriptionpharmacy.com (800.487.7115)

Prescription drugs.

BARGAIN HUNTER'S SECRETS: Look for savings on individual items. Free shipping.

Relax the Back

www.relaxtheback.com (800.222.5728)

Back-related products: chairs, pillows, lotions, and accessories.

BARGAIN HUNTER'S SECRETS: Look for savings on individual products.

Rx.com

www.rx.com

Prescription drugs (online ordering in partnership with local pharmacies).

BARGAIN HUNTER'S SECRETS: Look for savings at individual pharmacies.

Scentiments.com

www.scentiments.com (800.685.7321)

Perfume and skin care.

BARGAIN HUNTER'S SECRETS: Click the Great Deals link for sale items. Click the Clearance link for closeout products.

SelectRX.com

www.selectrx.com (877.638.6337)

Prescription drugs.

BARGAIN HUNTER'S SECRETS: Look for savings on individual items.

Sephora

www.sephora.com (877.737.4672)

Cosmetics, perfume, skin care, bath and body, hair care, and gifts.

BARGAIN HUNTER'S SECRETS: Free shipping on orders of more than $75.

Skin-Etc.

www.skin-etc.com (817.488.9227)

Skin care and hair care.

BARGAIN HUNTER'S SECRETS: Look for savings on individual products. Free delivery on orders of $200 or more.

Sneeze.com

www.sneeze.com (800.469.6673)

Asthma and allergy relief medications and products.

BARGAIN HUNTER'S SECRETS: Look for savings on individual products.

VitaCost

www.vitacost.com (800.793.2601)

Vitamins and supplements.

BARGAIN HUNTER'S SECRETS: All items heavily discounted.

Vitamin Shoppe

www.vitaminshoppe.com (800.223.1216)

Vitamins and supplements.

BARGAIN HUNTER'S SECRETS: Look for savings on individual products. Click the Money Saving Offers link for sales and promotions. Click the Clearance Center link for closeout items. 99-cent shipping on orders of $99 or more.

Walgreens

www.walgreens.com (877.250.5823)

Prescription drugs, health care, baby care, vitamins, cosmetics, and bath and beauty.

BARGAIN HUNTER'S SECRETS: Look for savings on individual items. Click the Online Savings ad for sale items. Click the Your Local Weekly ad link for limited-time offers. Click the Rebates & More link for manufacturer rebates and promotions.

HOBBIES AND COLLECTIBLES

In the right hands, just about anything is "collectible"—and just about any type of collectible is available online. Are you interested in model trains? Figurines? Animation cels? Comic books? Barbie dolls? It doesn't matter; you can probably find what you want online.

The problem with shopping for collectibles online isn't the selection, it's the price. As with artwork and antiques, you're often dealing with rare and one-of-a-kind items—and the rarer the item, the less likely it is to be discounted. In fact, it's darned near impossible to compare prices on one-of-a-kind items, which makes that aspect of online shopping somewhat moot.

The best advice I can give you is to shop around and try to determine a reasonable price for the general type of item you're looking for. Even if you can't find that item heavily discounted, at the very least you shouldn't overpay.

As to where to look, I've included a sampling of sites for different types of collectibles. There are more out there; use Froogle (or even Google) to search for a specific type of collectible. And don't forget eBay (**www.ebay.com**); it's often the best place to find all types of collectible items.

AllPosters.com

www.allposters.com (888.654.0143)

Art prints and posters.

BARGAIN HUNTER'S SECRETS: Look for sale items on the home page. For low-priced items, click the Art Prints Under $12.99 link.

Animation Art Gallery Best Selection

www.animationartgallery.com (310.623.1833)

Animation art.

BARGAIN HUNTER'S SECRETS: Look for savings on individual items.

Animation Celection

www.animationcelection.com (800.223.5328)

Animation art.

BARGAIN HUNTER'S SECRETS: Look for savings on individual items.

Animation Royal Arts

www.ara-animation.com (800.888.9449)

Animation art.

BARGAIN HUNTER'S SECRETS: Look for savings on individual products.

Art Rock

www.artrock.com (415.777.5736)

Rock and roll collectibles.

BARGAIN HUNTER'S SECRETS: Look for savings on individual items. Click the Sale Items, Yeah! link for bargains.

Bob's Comic Books Best Bargain

www.bobscomics.com

Comic books and collectibles.

BARGAIN HUNTER'S SECRETS: All items discounted. Click the Bargain Bin link for discounted items. Free shipping on orders of more than $10.

Cheap Seats Sports Cards

www.cheapseatscards.com (219.473.0022)

Sports cards.

BARGAIN HUNTER'S SECRETS: Look for savings on individual items.

Chisholm Larsson Gallery

www.chisholm-poster.com (212.741.1703)

Vintage posters.

BARGAIN HUNTER'S SECRETS: Look for savings on individual items.

ClassicPhotos.com

www.classicphotos.com (218.365.6219)

Vintage pictures.

BARGAIN HUNTER'S SECRETS: Look for savings on individual items.

CoinLand.com

www.coinland.com (866.327.2165)

Coins.

BARGAIN HUNTER'S SECRETS: Look for savings on individual products.

CoinWire.com

www.coinwire.com (877.415.4435)

Coins.

BARGAIN HUNTER'S SECRETS: Look for savings on individual products. Click the Closeout link for discounted and discontinued items.

CollectiblesToday.com Best Selection

www.collectiblestoday.com (877.268.6638)

Dolls, figurines, plates, music boxes, sports, die-cast cars, and collectible art.

BARGAIN HUNTER'S SECRETS: Look for savings on individual items.

Collector Online

www.collectoronline.com (800.546.2941)

Coins, stamps, comics, glass, dolls, figurines, toys, and collectible art.

BARGAIN HUNTER'S SECRETS: Look for Store Specials on the home page. Use the Browse by Price section to search for low-priced items.

Crafts Etc!

www.craftsetc.com (800.888.0321)

Crafts, art supplies, sewing, candles, projects, and accessories. (Affiliated with the Hobby Lobby retail chain.)

BARGAIN HUNTER'S SECRETS: Look for savings on individual products.

David Hall Rare Coins

www.davidhall.com (800.759.7575)

Coins.

BARGAIN HUNTER'S SECRETS: Look for savings on individual items.

Do Wah Diddy

www.dowahdiddy.com (602.957.3874)

Pop culture collectibles; movie, television, and rock and roll memorabilia.

BARGAIN HUNTER'S SECRETS: Look for savings on individual items.

eHobbies Best Bargain

www.ehobbies.com (877.346.2243)

Radio control airplanes and cars, die-cast cars, slot cars, model trains, toys, rockets, science kits, and astronomy.

BARGAIN HUNTER'S SECRETS: Look for savings on individual items. Click the Free Shipping link for items with free shipping. Click the Scratch & Dent Sale link for additional bargains. Click the Auctions link to bid on auction items on eBay.

Entertainment Earth

www.entertainmentearth.com (818.255.0095)

Action figures, toys, and collectibles.

BARGAIN HUNTER'S SECRETS: Click the Clearance tab for closeout merchandise.

Franklin Mint

www.franklinmint.com (877.843.6468)

Die-cast models, dolls, bears, sculpture, knives, watches and clocks, and jewelry.

BARGAIN HUNTER'S SECRETS: Click the Specials link for promotional items. Click the Under $100 link for low-priced items. Become a registered user for additional savings.

FritzGifts.com

www.fritzgifts.com (800.266.8029)

Figurines, bears, porcelain, and crystal.

BARGAIN HUNTER'S SECRETS: Click the Current Specials link for discounted items. Free shipping on all orders of more than $75.

Gremlin Fine Arts Gallery

www.thegremlin.com (877.473.6546)

Animation and comic art.

BARGAIN HUNTER'S SECRETS: Look for savings on individual items.

Hall of Fame Memorabilia

www.halloffamememorabilia.com (800.980.3263)

Sports memorabilia.

BARGAIN HUNTER'S SECRETS: Look for savings on individual items.

Heritage Rare Coins and Currency

www.heritagecoin.com (800.872.6467)

Coins.

BARGAIN HUNTER'S SECRETS: Bid on auction items. Click the Weekly Specials link for limited-time offers.

HeritageComics.com

www.heritagecomics.com (800.872.6467)

Comics, comic art, and posters.

BARGAIN HUNTER'S SECRETS: Bid on auction items.

Herrick Stamp Company

www.herrickstamp.com (516.569.3959)

Stamps.

BARGAIN HUNTER'S SECRETS: Click the Special Offers link for discounted items. Click the Large Lots link for savings on collections and large lots.

Hobby-Lobby International

www.hobby-lobby.com (615.373.1444)

Radio control airplanes, helicopters, and boats. (Not affiliated with the Hobby Lobby chain of craft stores.)

BARGAIN HUNTER'S SECRETS: Click the Sale Items & Specials link for discounted items.

HobbyTown USA

www.hobbytown.com

Plastic models, radio control airplanes and cars, rockets, model trains, and accessories.

BARGAIN HUNTER'S SECRETS: Look for savings on individual items.

Pop House

www.pophouse.com (888.515.2327)

Pop culture memorabilia.

BARGAIN HUNTER'S SECRETS: Look for savings on individual items.

James T. McCusker, Inc.

www.jamesmccusker.com (800.852.0076)

Stamps.

BARGAIN HUNTER'S SECRETS: Bid on auction items. Look for reduced-priced items on the home page.

Lilliput

www.lilliputmotorcompany.com (800.846.8697)

Die-cast models.

BARGAIN HUNTER'S SECRETS: Click the Sale Items link for bargains.

Megahobby.com

www.megahobby.com (888.642.0093)

Plastic models and accessories.

BARGAIN HUNTER'S SECRETS: Click the Super Sale Items link for discounted items.

Michaels

www.michaels.com (800.642.4235)

Crafts, art supplies, sewing, candles, projects, and accessories.

BARGAIN HUNTER'S SECRETS: Look for savings on individual products.

Mile High Comics

www.milehighcomics.com (800.676.6423)

Comic books and collectibles.

BARGAIN HUNTER'S SECRETS: Look for savings on individual comics.

MisterArt.com

www.misterart.com (866.672.7811)

Crafts, art supplies, and original artwork.

BARGAIN HUNTER'S SECRETS: Look for savings on individual items. Click the Special Deals link for sale items.

Movie Goods

www.moviegoods.com (866.279.2403)

Movie memorabilia, posters, photographs, lobby cards, and scripts.

BARGAIN HUNTER'S SECRETS: Look for savings on individual items. Look for links to eBay auctions.

Night Owl Books

www.nightowlbooks.com (703.590.2966)

Movie posters and memorabilia.

BARGAIN HUNTER'S SECRETS: Look for savings on individual products.

The Oddball Mall

www.oddball-mall.com

Sports cards.

BARGAIN HUNTER'S SECRETS: Look for savings on individual items.

OnlineSports.com

www.onlinesports.com (800.856.2638)

Sports memorabilia.

BARGAIN HUNTER'S SECRETS: Look for savings on individual items.

Pro Sports Memorabilia

www.prosportsmemorabilia.com (888.950.5399)

Sports memorabilia.

BARGAIN HUNTER'S SECRETS: Look for savings on individual items.

Shop 4 Collectibles

www.shop4collectibles.com (212.430.6520)

Dolls, bears, figurines, glass, and gifts.

BARGAIN HUNTER'S SECRETS: Look for savings on individual items.

Vintage Vending

www.vintagevending.com (888.242.6633)

Pop culture memorabilia, furniture, and vending machines.

BARGAIN HUNTER'S SECRETS: Look for savings on individual items.

HOME AND GARDEN

The Home and Garden category is a bit of a catch-all category. It's home to major appliances (refrigerators, microwave ovens, and so on), small appliances (blenders, toasters, and the like), gas grills, cookware, dinnerware, silverware, cutlery, vacuum cleaners, bedding, furniture, lighting, home décor, home repair and building supplies, plants and seeds, gardening tools, power tools, hand tools, hardware, you name it.

Some online merchants carry all these different items; most specialize in some subset of the above. When you're dealing with larger items, make sure to factor shipping into your total costs. With all items, take the time to look for manufacturer rebates, which are common in this category. And make sure that you shop at more than one store; the selection varies considerably from merchant to merchant.

In addition to the merchants listed here, make sure that you look at those in the Department Stores and Mass Merchants category. And if you're looking for appliances, some of the stores in the Electronics category are likely to carry some selection.

Abed.com

www.abed.com (800.977.5337)

Mattresses, beds, waterbeds, and pillows.

BARGAIN HUNTER'S SECRETS: Look for savings on individual items. Look for specials on home page.

ABT Electronics

www.abtelectronics.com (888.228.5800)

Major appliances and small appliances.

BARGAIN HUNTER'S SECRETS: Most items discounted; look for savings on individual product pages. Click the Clearance Center link for closeout merchandise.

Amazon.com

www.amazon.com (800.201.7575)

Click the Home and Garden tab for bed and bath, lighting, kitchen items, small appliances, grills, lawn and garden, plants and seeds, personal care, and floor care. Click the Kitchen & Housewares tab for cookware, cutlery, housewares, dinnerware, flatware, and stemware. Click the Tools & Hardware tab for power tools, hand tools, lawn and garden tools, and job site equipment. Click the Furniture & Décor tab for bedroom, dining room, home entertainment, home office, living room, and patio furniture. Click the Outdoor Living tab for gardening tools, grills, lawn and landscaping, and outdoor décor.

BARGAIN HUNTER'S SECRETS: On the Home and Garden and Tools & Hardware pages, click the Today's Deals tab for sale and promotional items; click the Outlet, Used & Reconditioned tab for clearance and refurbished items. Look for additional bargains during the sitewide Friday Sale. Look for bargains on used and new items from third-party merchants in the More Buying Choices section of each product page. Free shipping on orders of $25 or more.

American Blinds, Wallpaper & More

www.decoratetoday.com (800.575.8016)

Blinds, shutters, wallpaper, curtains, rugs, lighting, bedding, home accents, framed art, and paint.

BARGAIN HUNTER'S SECRETS: Look for savings on individual items. Click the Hot Deals graphic for sale items. Look for sale and closeout links on the home page. Free shipping.

American LightSource

www.americanlightsource.com (800.741.0571)

Lighting, fixtures, chandeliers, wall sconces, lamps, exterior lighting, and mirrors.

BARGAIN HUNTER'S SECRETS: Look for savings on individual items.

Appliance Accessories

www.applianceaccessories.com (888.222.8608)

Appliance parts and accessories (vents, cords, filters, and so on).

BARGAIN HUNTER'S SECRETS: Look for savings on individual items.

Appliances.com

www.appliances.com (888.543.8345)

Major appliances and small appliances.

BARGAIN HUNTER'S SECRETS: Click the Overstocks link for clearance items. Click the Rebates & Specials link for manufacturer rebates and promotions.

Bed Bath and Beyond

www.bedbathandbeyond.com (800.462.3966)

Bed and bath, kitchen items, dining, home décor, and small appliances.

BARGAIN HUNTER'S SECRETS: Look for savings on individual products. Click the Clearance link for end-of-season bargains.

Bedsheet.com

www.bedsheet.com (800.965.5558)

Bedding, sheets, and comforters.

BARGAIN HUNTER'S SECRETS: Click the On Sale link for sale items. Flat $5.99 shipping on all purchases.

Blankets.com

www.blankets.com (888.248.7568)

Blankets, pillows, and bedding.

BARGAIN HUNTER'S SECRETS: Click the On Sale links on category pages for sale items.

Blindsgalore

www.blindsgalore.com (877.702.5463)

Blinds, shades, and draperies.

BARGAIN HUNTER'S SECRETS: Click the Special Offers tab for sale items. Look for the Best Buys section of the home page. Free shipping.

The Bombay Company

www.bombayco.com (800.829.7789)

Furniture, accessories, wall décor, bedding, and lighting.

BARGAIN HUNTER'S SECRETS: Click the Specials link for sale items. See the This Week's Feature Promotions section of the home page for limited-time bargains.

Brent and Becky's Bulbs

www.brentandbeckysbulbs.com (804.693.3966)

Flower bulbs.

BARGAIN HUNTER'S SECRETS: Look for savings on individual items.

BuilderDepot

Best Selection

www.builderdepot.com (866.843.7687)

Home improvement, building materials, power tools, hand tools, hardware, electrical supplies, plumbing, lawn and garden, appliances, home security, floor covering, heating and cooling, and lighting.

BARGAIN HUNTER'S SECRETS: Look for savings on individual items. New customers get 10% off first order.

Burpee

www.burpee.com (888.333.5808)

Plants and seeds.

BARGAIN HUNTER'S SECRETS: Click the Internet Specials graphic for online-only bargains. Click the Seed Shop Bargains graphic for sale items.

Carol Wright Gifts

www.carolwrightgifts.com (732.287.8833)

Home furnishings, housewares, and health and beauty.

BARGAIN HUNTER'S SECRETS: Most items discounted. Click the Clearance Items link for closeout merchandise.

Celebrity Cookware.com

www.celebritycookware.com (888.366.7440)

Small appliances, housewares, kitchen and cooking, and health and beauty.

BARGAIN HUNTER'S SECRETS: Look for savings on individual items. Sign up for special offers via email.

Chef Store

www.chefstore.com

Small appliances, cookware, housewares, tools and gadgets, knives, tableware, and bar accessories.

BARGAIN HUNTER'S SECRETS: Look for savings on individual items. Free shipping on orders of more than $25.

Coastal Tool

Best Selection

www.coastaltool.com (877.551.8665)

Power tools and hand tools.

BARGAIN HUNTER'S SECRETS: Look for savings on individual items. Shipping based on total cost, not on weight; that makes it a good place to buy heavy power tools.

CompactAppliance.com

www.compactappliance.com (800.297.6076)

Major appliances, small appliances, and housewares.

BARGAIN HUNTER'S SECRETS: Look for savings on individual products.

The Company Store

www.thecompanystore.com (800.323.8000)

Bed and bath, bedding, home accessories, and sleepwear.

BARGAIN HUNTER'S SECRETS: Click the Clearance link for closeout items. Look for sale items on the home page.

Container Store

Best Selection

www.containerstore.com (888.266.8246)

Storage, shelving, and boxes.

BARGAIN HUNTER'S SECRETS: Click the Special Savings link for sale items.

Cooking.com

www.cooking.com (800.663.8810)

Cookware, cutlery, small appliances, tableware, and barware.

BARGAIN HUNTER'S SECRETS: Click the Clearance link for closeout merchandise. Click the Special Values link for manufacturer rebates and promotions. Look for sales and promotions on the home page. Free shipping on orders of more than $99.

CornerHardware.com

www.cornerhardware.com (800.361.1787)

Hardware, power tools, hand tools, kitchen and bath, rugs, flooring, blinds, lighting, housewares, lawn and garden, heating and cooling, electrical, and plumbing.

BARGAIN HUNTER'S SECRETS: Click the Blowout Items link for sale merchandise.

Crate & Barrel

www.cratebarrel.com (800.967.6696)

Dinnerware, drinkware, kitchen, furniture, rugs, lighting, and bed and bath.

BARGAIN HUNTER'S SECRETS: Click the Outlet link for clearance items. Click the Sale link for sale merchandise.

CutleryAndMore.com

www.cutleryandmore.com (800.650.9866)

Cutlery, cookware, and kitchen gadgets.

BARGAIN HUNTER'S SECRETS: Look for savings on individual items. Free shipping on orders of more than $99.

DreamRetail

www.dreamretail.com (250.382.1538)

Small appliances, housewares, kitchenware, lawn and garden, home security, home furnishings, and tools.

BARGAIN HUNTER'S SECRETS: All items discounted.

DynaDirect.com

www.dynadirect.com (877.438.3962)

Major appliances, small appliances, floor care, furniture, garden tools, home décor, home security, home improvement, kitchen, outdoor living, personal care, and gadgets. (Click the Household tab.)

BARGAIN HUNTER'S SECRETS: All items discounted. Click the Special Offers link for manufacturer promotions. Click the Current Rebates link for manufacturer rebates. Click the Free Shipping link for all items with free shipping.

Eddie Bauer

www.eddiebauer.com (800.625.7935)

Click the Home Store link for bedding, lighting, bath, furniture, and window coverings.

BARGAIN HUNTER'S SECRETS: Click the Sale link on the Home Store page for sale items. Go to **www.eddiebaueroutlet.com** for clearance merchandise.

Efendos

www.efendos.com (877.644.0784)

Small appliances, house and garden, kitchen and housewares, and health and beauty.

BARGAIN HUNTER'S SECRETS: Look for savings on individual items. Free shipping.

eFunctional.com

www.efunctional.com (435.752.1992)

Small appliances, gardening, tools, camping supplies, outdoor furniture, and health and beauty.

BARGAIN HUNTER'S SECRETS: Look for savings on individual products.

Family on Board

www.familyonboard.com (800.793.2075)

Family and children's travel gear.

BARGAIN HUNTER'S SECRETS: Click the Bargains Online! link for discontinued items, overstocks, and sale merchandise.

FaucetDirect

www.faucetdirect.com (800.864.2555)

Plumbing supplies, faucets, and bath and shower accessories.

BARGAIN HUNTER'S SECRETS: Look for savings on individual items.

FineGardenProducts.com

www.finegardenproducts.com (888.949.2999)

Outdoor accessories, bird feeders, fountains, outdoor furniture, lighting, mail boxes, sprinklers, and wind chimes.

BARGAIN HUNTER'S SECRETS: Look for savings on individual products.

Fingerhut

www.fingerhut.com (800.208.2500)

Small appliances, bed and bath, lawn and garden, hardware, home furnishings, kitchen, and health and beauty.

BARGAIN HUNTER'S SECRETS: Look for savings on individual items. Look for bargains in the Hot Deals section of the home page.

Frontgate

www.frontgate.com (800.263.9850)

Bed and bath, home furnishings, kitchen, home care, patio and garden, outdoor furniture, grills, and pool and spa.

BARGAIN HUNTER'S SECRETS: Click the Frontgate Outlet link for clearance and sale merchandise.

Gardener's Supply Company

www.gardeners.com (888.833.1412)

Gardening, landscaping, greenhouses, pest control, tools, and watering.

BARGAIN HUNTER'S SECRETS: Click the Outlet link for clearance and sale items.

The Giving Tree

www.givingtreeonline.com (888.678.0068)

Luxury linens.

BARGAIN HUNTER'S SECRETS: Click the Specials! Link for sale items.

GoodCatalog.com

www.goodcatalog.com (831.649.2489)

Home improvement, garden, outdoor living, home décor, and pet care.

BARGAIN HUNTER'S SECRETS: Click the Outlets links on the home page for deals, discounts, and closeouts.

Great Windows

www.greatwindows.com (800.556.6632)

Blinds, shades, shutters, and window treatments.

BARGAIN HUNTER'S SECRETS: Click the Specials & Promotions link for sale items.

Home Decorators Collection

www.homedecorators.com (800.240.6047)

Home décor, rugs, furniture, bath, lighting, and outdoor.

BARGAIN HUNTER'S SECRETS: Look for savings on individual items. Click the Outlet Site link for sale and clearance items.

Home Depot

www.homedepot.com (800.430.3376)

Building supplies, remodeling, home décor, lighting, outdoor living, tools, hardware, major appliances, and home security.

BARGAIN HUNTER'S SECRETS: Click the Promotions links for sales and promotions.

HomeClick.com *Best Bargain*

www.homeclick.com (800.643.9990)

Bath, kitchen, hardware, lighting, outdoor, and tableware.

BARGAIN HUNTER'S SECRETS: All items heavily discounted. Click the Outlet link for liquidation specials. Free shipping on orders of more than $99.

iFLOOR.com

www.ifloor.com (800.454.3941)

Flooring, carpet, rugs, tile, and linoleum.

BARGAIN HUNTER'S SECRETS: Click the Blowouts link for sale items.

iGadgets.com *Best Bargain*

www.igadgets.com (877.775.7779)

Small appliances, electronics, gadgets, home and garden, kitchen, tools, hardware, health and beauty, and home security. (Also operates as **www.igadget.com** and **www.bioarmed.com**.)

BARGAIN HUNTER'S SECRETS: Most items heavily discounted. Click the Buy 1 Get 1 Free link for special offers. Look for sales and specials on the home page. Click the Free shipping link for items with free shipping.

internetfloors.com *Best Bargain*

www.internetfloors.com (888.872.1555)

Flooring.

BARGAIN HUNTER'S SECRETS: Outlet pricing. Look for sales and specials links on the home page.

Kitchen Collection

www.kitchencollection.com (888.548.2651)

Bakeware, cookware, cutlery, small appliances, and gadgets.

BARGAIN HUNTER'S SECRETS: Look for savings on individual items. See the Hot Deals section of the home page for additional bargains. Click the Closeouts link for clearance merchandise.

Kitchen Etc. *Best Selection*

www.kitchenetc.com (800.232.4070)

Dinnerware, glassware, housewares, cookware, cutlery, and gadgets.

BARGAIN HUNTER'S SECRETS: Click the Hot Prices link for discounted merchandise. Click the Clearance link for closeout items. Click the This Week's Specials link for limited-time offers.

LampStore.com

www.lampstore.com (888.874.3676)

Lighting, lamps, and fixtures.

BARGAIN HUNTER'S SECRETS: Look for savings on individual items.

LightingCenter.com

www.lightingcenter.com (888.815.4519)

Lighting, lamps, fixtures, ceiling fans, home décor, and furniture.

BARGAIN HUNTER'S SECRETS: Look for savings on individual items.

Linenplace.com

www.linenplace.com (866.629.0300)

Bed and bath, sheets, blankets, pillows, towels, shower curtains, bath and body, and accessories.

BARGAIN HUNTER'S SECRETS: Look for savings on individual items.

Lowes

www.lowes.com (800.445.6937)

Major appliances, small appliances, cabinets, cleaning supplies, doors and windows, electrical, flooring, hardware, heating and cooling, home décor, lawn and garden, lighting, plumbing, building supplies, power tools, hand tools, paint, plumbing, and home security.

BARGAIN HUNTER'S SECRETS: Look for savings in the This Week section of the home page. Click the Weekly Ads link for limited-time offers. Click the Rebates link for manufacturer rebates.

Mellinger's

www.mellingers.com (800.321.7444)

Seeds, bulbs, plants, and lawn and garden supplies.

BARGAIN HUNTER'S SECRETS: Look for savings on individual items.

Organize Everything

www.organize-everything.com (800.600.9817)

Storage, shelving, and boxes.

BARGAIN HUNTER'S SECRETS: Look for savings on individual items.

Orvis

www.orvis.com (888.235.9763)

Click the Country Home link for furniture, bedding, floor coverings, lighting, candles, dining and kitchen, yard and garden, and fireplace and hearth.

BARGAIN HUNTER'S SECRETS: Click the Sale Room link for sale items.

PartSelect Best Selection

www.partselect.com (888.895.1535)

Appliance parts and accessories (vents, cords, filters, and so on).

BARGAIN HUNTER'S SECRETS: Look for savings on individual items.

Pier 1

www.pier1.com (800.245.4595)

Bed and bath, candles, home décor, kitchen, tableware, and outdoor living.

BARGAIN HUNTER'S SECRETS: Click the Sales & Events link for sale merchandise and promotions. Click the Clearance Store link for closeout items.

Plow & Hearth

www.plowhearth.com (800.494.7544)

Home décor, fireplace and hearth, rugs, furniture, outdoor furniture, gardening, landscaping, and bird feeders.

BARGAIN HUNTER'S SECRETS: Click The Outlet link for clearance and sale merchandise.

Pool Warehouse

www.poolwarehouse.com (800.609.4917)

Pools, spas, saunas, and supplies.

BARGAIN HUNTER'S SECRETS: Look for savings on individual items.

PotsAndPans.com Best Bargain

www.potsandpans.com (800.450.0156)

Cookware.

BARGAIN HUNTER'S SECRETS: All items discounted. Click the Hot Deals! link for sale merchandise. Click the Monthly Specials link for limited-time offers.

Pottery Barn

www.potterybarn.com (866.472.4001)

Bed and bath, pillows, rugs, furniture, lighting, tableware, home décor, and accessories.

BARGAIN HUNTER'S SECRETS: Click the Sale link for sale merchandise. Free shipping on selected items.

RepairClinic.com

www.repairclinic.com (800.269.2609)

Appliance parts and accessories (vents, cords, filters, and so on).

BARGAIN HUNTER'S SECRETS: Look for savings on individual items.

Replacements, Ltd. Best Selection

www.replacements.com (800.737.5223)

China, crystal, silver, and collectibles. (Specializes in replacing broken or missing pieces.)

BARGAIN HUNTER'S SECRETS: Click the Specials! tab for sale merchandise.

Restoration Hardware

www.restorationhardware.com (800.762.1005)

Bed and bath, lighting, home décor, furniture, windows, floors, and hardware.

BARGAIN HUNTER'S SECRETS: Click the Sale link for sale items.

Safety Central

www.safetycentral.com (406.222.3171)

Home security and safety.

BARGAIN HUNTER'S SECRETS: Look for savings on individual items.

Sears Best Selection

www.sears.com (800.349.4358)

Major appliances, small appliances, housewares, bed and bath, lawn and garden, tools, and hardware.

BARGAIN HUNTER'S SECRETS: Click the Clearance link for closeout and discontinued items. Click the Auctions on eBay link to bid on auction items. Look for sale items on main category pages.

Specialty Pool Products

www.poolproducts.com (888.764.7665)

Pools, spas, hot tubs, saunas, and supplies.

BARGAIN HUNTER'S SECRETS: Look for savings on individual items. Click the Clearance link for closeout merchandise. Click the Auctions link to bid on auction items.

Stacks and Stacks

www.stacksandstacks.com (800.761.5222)

Shelving, bed and bath, home furnishings, kitchen, laundry, outdoor living, and home security.

BARGAIN HUNTER'S SECRETS: Look for savings on individual items.

Sur La Table

www.surlatable.com (866.328.5412)

Small appliances, bakeware, barware, cookware, glassware, housewares, and knives.

BARGAIN HUNTER'S SECRETS: Click the Special Offers link for manufacturer promotions. Click the Sale Items link for sale merchandise.

TableTools.com

www.tabletools.com (888.211.6603)

Dinnerware, flatware, bakeware, cookware, barware, drinkware, knives, and linens.

BARGAIN HUNTER'S SECRETS: Look for savings on individual items. Click the Clearance Section link for closeout merchandise.

Target

www.target.com (800.591.3869)

Bed and bath, small appliances, kitchenware, lighting, home décor, outdoor living, window coverings, and rugs.

BARGAIN HUNTER'S SECRETS: Click the Clearance link for closeout merchandise. Click the Weekly Ad link for limited-time offers. Look for sale items on home page and category pages.

Too Home

www.toohome.com (800.878.6021)

Bed and bath, small appliances, kitchenware, outdoor living, patio and garden, fireplaces, spas, lighting, and storage.

BARGAIN HUNTER'S SECRETS: Discount pricing on all items. Click the Sales & Deals link for additional savings.

Tools-Plus

www.toolsplus.com (800.222.6133)

Hand tools, power tools, outdoor power equipment, and woodworking machinery.

BARGAIN HUNTER'S SECRETS: All items discounted. Click the Rebates, Bonuses, and Closeouts links for sales, promotions, and clearance merchandise. Flat $6.50 per order shipping—great for heavy items.

Universal Appliance and Kitchen Center

store.universal-akb.net (800.464.9429)

Major appliances, small appliances, and vacuums.

BARGAIN HUNTER'S SECRETS: Look for specials on category pages. Click the Rebates & Promotions link for manufacturer rebates and promotions.

US Appliance

www.us-appliance.com (800.259.3603)

Major appliances and small appliances.

BARGAIN HUNTER'S SECRETS: Click the Clearance Deals link for closeout and refurbished items. Click the Rebates link for manufacturer rebates and promotions.

Wholesalerug.com

www.wholesalerug.com (800.346.7847)

Rugs and accessories.

BARGAIN HUNTER'S SECRETS: All items discounted.

Williams-Sonoma

www.williams-sonoma.com (877.812.6235)

Bakeware, barware, cookware, dinnerware, cutlery, flatware, glassware, home furnishings, linens, storage, and outdoor living.

BARGAIN HUNTER'S SECRETS: Pull down the Shop menu and select Sale Items for sale merchandise.

JEWELRY AND WATCHES

There aren't quite as many jewelry merchants online as you might expect. I'm not sure why this is the case; perhaps expensive jewelry is one item many people need to see in person before they buy. Or perhaps some folks just aren't comfortable laying out that kind of money online.

For whatever reason, then, when you're shopping for jewelry on the Web, there aren't a lot of merchants to choose from. And you won't always find big bargains online—although there are bargains to be found. But if you take your time and shop at multiple stores, you should end up saving some money.

The same is true with buying watches online. In fact, there are some big bargains to be had at online watch stores. Just make sure that you insure any big-ticket items you purchase. (The same goes when you buy expensive jewelry.)

In addition to the stores listed here, you can often find jewelry and watches at those merchants in the Department Stores and Mass Merchants category. It's also worth your while to shop eBay (**www.ebay.com**), and the sites in the Wholesale Clubs and Shopping Networks category.

The $5.00 Jewelry Store

www.5dollarjewelrystore.shoppingcartsplus.com (248.545.6092)

Bracelets and necklaces.

BARGAIN HUNTER'S SECRETS: All items priced at $5.

Amazon.com

www.amazon.com (800.201.7575)

Fine jewelry, fashion jewelry, wedding and engagement, men's jewelry, children's jewelry, and watches. (Click the Jewelry & Watches tab.)

BARGAIN HUNTER'S SECRETS: Look for savings on individual product pages. Free shipping on orders of more than $25.

Antique Jewelry Exchange

www.antiquejewelryexch.com (800.809.4190)

Diamonds, gemstones, cameos, men's jewelry, and watches. Specializes in antique and rare rings.

BARGAIN HUNTER'S SECRETS: Click the Clearance link for closeout bargains.

Ashford

www.ashford.com (888.922.9039)

Diamonds, jewelry, watches, handbags, and sunglasses. Offers "build your own" service.

BARGAIN HUNTER'S SECRETS: Click the Ashford Outlet link for discounted items and closeouts.

Atlantic Time

www.atlantictime.com (949.470.4545)

Jewelry, gold, watches, crystal and glass, and fine art.

BARGAIN HUNTER'S SECRETS: Look for clearance and sale links on the home page.

Blue Nile

www.bluenile.com (800.242.2728)

Diamonds, engagement rings, wedding and anniversary rings, earrings, necklaces, pendants, bracelets, and watches. Offers "build your own" option.

BARGAIN HUNTER'S SECRETS: Use the Start with the Budget section to shop for low-priced items.

BlueDial.com

www.bluedial.com (866.831.3564)

Watches.

BARGAIN HUNTER'S SECRETS: Look for savings on individual items. Click the Sort By Price link to shop for low-priced items. Free shipping.

Boucher Gemstone Jewelry

www.boucherjewelry.com (866.623.9269)

Gemstone jewelry: bracelets, earrings, necklaces, and lariats.

BARGAIN HUNTER'S SECRETS: Click the Specials link for sale items.

Goldspeed.com

www.goldspeed.com (800.465.3340)

Wedding rings, engagement rings, gold chains, diamond jewelry, platinum jewelry, silver jewelry, and watches.

BARGAIN HUNTER'S SECRETS: Many items heavily discounted. Click the Clearance! link for closeout items. Free shipping on orders of $250 or more.

Ice

www.ice.com (800.539.3580)

Rings, earrings, bracelets, pendants, necklaces, and watches.

BARGAIN HUNTER'S SECRETS: Look for sale items on the home page. Free shipping on orders of more than $150.

JEGEM.com

www.jegem.com

Bracelets, earrings, necklaces, pendants, rings, hair jewelry, and belt buckles.

BARGAIN HUNTER'S SECRETS: Click the Daily Special graphic for limited-time offers. Use the Browse by Price link to shop for low-priced items. Free shipping on orders of more than $250.

Jemznjewels

www.jemznjewels.com (800.488.8265)

Fashion rings, bracelets, and earrings.

BARGAIN HUNTER'S SECRETS: Click the On Sale link for sale items. Click the Under $400 link for lower-priced merchandise.

Jest Jewels

www.jestjewels.com (415.563.8839)

Girls' and teens' jewelry and accessories.

BARGAIN HUNTER'S SECRETS: Look for savings on individual items. Look for sale links on the home page.

Jewelry Discount Network

www.jewelrydiscount.net (800.498.7302)

Engagement rings, anniversary rings, wedding rings, diamond rings, earrings, necklaces, and bracelets.

BARGAIN HUNTER'S SECRETS: All items discounted.

Jewelry Mall

www.jewelrymall.com

Online mall of jewelry merchants.

BARGAIN HUNTER'S SECRETS: Click the Exclusive Jewelry Specials link for sale items. Look for bargains at individual stores.

JewelryWeb.com

www.jewelryweb.com (800.955.9245)

Fine jewelry, chains, and gold.

BARGAIN HUNTER'S SECRETS: Look for savings on individual items. Look for sale links on the home page.

Jewelryzone.com

www.jewelryzone.com (800.431.3377)

Loose diamonds, wedding bands, engagement rings, gemstones, and watches.

BARGAIN HUNTER'S SECRETS: Look for savings on individual items.

justMetal

www.justmetal.com (876.270.7886)

Rings, bracelets, earrings, necklaces, pendants, and men's jewelry.

BARGAIN HUNTER'S SECRETS: Look for savings on individual items. Free shipping on orders of $95 or more.

Lawson Watch & Clock

www.lawsonwatch.com (866.427.5456)

Watches, clocks, and weather stations.

BARGAIN HUNTER'S SECRETS: Click the Clearance Watches & Clocks link for closeout and sale items.

Princeton Watches

www.princetonwatches.com (800.572.8263)

Watches and clocks.

BARGAIN HUNTER'S SECRETS: Click the Bargain Center link for overstock bargains.

SteelNavel.com

www.steelnavel.com (818.293.0472)

Body jewelry.

BARGAIN HUNTER'S SECRETS: See the Sales & Discounts! section on the home page. Free shipping on orders of more than $100.

USA WatchCo.com

www.usawatchco.com (800.394.4446)

Wrist watches, pocket watches, and clocks.

BARGAIN HUNTER'S SECRETS: Click the Go to Specials link for sale items.

The Watch Company

www.watchco.com (800.584.1618)

Watches.

BARGAIN HUNTER'S SECRETS: Click the Clearance link for closeout and sale items. Free shipping.

WatchZone Best Bargain

www.watchzone.com (800.521.5568)

Watches.

BARGAIN HUNTER'S SECRETS: Click the Hot Deals tab for sale items. Become a member (free) for additional savings.

Worldlux Watches

www.worldlux-watches.com (888.721.7367)

Watches, pens, and men's jewelry.

BARGAIN HUNTER'S SECRETS: Use the On Sale and Clearance options when searching for watches.

WorldOfWatches.com Best Bargain

www.worldofwatches.com (800.222.0077)

Watches.

BARGAIN HUNTER'S SECRETS: Search for specials by brand. Free shipping on orders of $150 or more.

WristWatch.com

www.wristwatch.com (800.974.7892)

Watches and clocks.

BARGAIN HUNTER'S SECRETS: Click the Specials link for sale items. Free shipping on orders of $50 or more.

Zales

www.zales.com (800.311.5393)

Jewelry, wedding rings, pearls, men's jewelry, and watches.

BARGAIN HUNTER'S SECRETS: Click the Advertised Items link for limited-time offers. Click the Clearance link for closeout and sale items.

LUGGAGE

There aren't a whole lot of dedicated online luggage merchants, but the ones that do exist offer some great bargains. Take into account, however, that shipping luggage (even empty luggage) is often costly, due to the bulk. Remember to factor in shipping charges to your total costs.

In addition to the merchants listed here, most of the stores in the Department Stores and Mass Merchants category also offer luggage for sale online. There are also some merchants in the Apparel category—especially those that specialize in handbags and accessories—with decent luggage selections.

When shopping for new luggage, look for items with rollers, to make it easier to roll through the airport. Even better are retractable rollers that can't be pulled off by the automated machinery. And when you're shopping for carry-on luggage, make sure it's small enough to fit within the airlines' more restrictive new size limits. Where the airlines used to allow you to carry on fairly big items, they've really cracked down, size-wise. Buy accordingly.

Bag King

www.bagking.com (888.655.2247)

Backpacks, computer bags, camera bags, and briefcases.

BARGAIN HUNTER'S SECRETS: Click the Close Outs & Specials link for sale and clearance items.

eBags Best Selection

www.ebags.com (800.820.6126)

Luggage, backpacks, handbags, and travel accessories.

BARGAIN HUNTER'S SECRETS: Look for savings on individual items. Look for sale links on the home page.

GoingInStyle.com

www.goinginstyle.com (800.637.8953)

Luggage and travel accessories.

BARGAIN HUNTER'S SECRETS: Click the Special Offers link for sale items.

Irv's Luggage Warehouse Best Bargain

www.irvs.com (888.300.4787)

Luggage, backpacks, and handbags.

BARGAIN HUNTER'S SECRETS: All items heavily discounted. Click the Discount Specials link for sale items. Free shipping on orders of more than $100.

Lazar's Luggage Superstore

www.lazarsluggage.com (877.728.3660)

Luggage, briefcases, and backpacks.

BARGAIN HUNTER'S SECRETS: Click the Closeout Bin link for clearance items. See the Picks of the Month on the home page.

LeTravelStore.com

www.luggage.com (800.713.4260)

Luggage, backpacks, briefcases, shoulder bags, and travel accessories.

BARGAIN HUNTER'S SECRETS: Look for savings on individual items. Look for sale links on the home page.

Luggage Online Best Bargain

www.luggageonline.com (888.958.4424)

Luggage, briefcases, backpacks, and travel accessories.

BARGAIN HUNTER'S SECRETS: Click the Best Buys tab for sale items. Look for sale items on the home page. Free shipping on orders of more than $100. Low price guarantee.

Magellan's

www.magellans.com (800.962.4943)

Luggage and travel accessories.

BARGAIN HUNTER'S SECRETS: Click the Specials link for sale items.

Mori Luggage & Gifts

www.moriluggage.com (800.678.6674)

Luggage, briefcases, and travel accessories.

BARGAIN HUNTER'S SECRETS: Look for savings on individual items.

Samsonite

www.samsonitecompanystores.com (800.262.8282)

Luggage, backpacks, computer bags, and accessories. Manufacturer direct.

BARGAIN HUNTER'S SECRETS: Look for sale and clearance items on the home page.

Suitcase.com Best Selection

www.suitcase.com (888.627.3887)

Luggage, backpacks, briefcases, and travel accessories.

BARGAIN HUNTER'S SECRETS: All items discounted. Click the Sales & Promotions link for sale items.

Travel Smith

www.travelsmith.com (800.995.7010)

Luggage and travel accessories.

BARGAIN HUNTER'S SECRETS: Look for savings on individual items. Look for links to clearance items on the home page.

WorldTraveler

www.worldtraveler.com (800.314.2247)

Luggage, backpacks, briefcases, handbags, and computer bags.

BARGAIN HUNTER'S SECRETS: All items discounted. Click the Specials link for sale items. Free shipping on all orders of more than $100.

MOVIES, MUSIC, AND VIDEOGAMES

Entertainment is a big category for online merchants. Whether you're looking for CDs, DVDs, videotapes, or videogames, you'll find a big selection online, along with significantly discounted prices.

These items are particularly suited for online shopping because they're small and easy (and cheap) to ship. If you order a few items at a time, chances are you'll offset the small shipping charge by the savings in sales tax. And most online merchants offer a much wider selection than you'll find in any "bricks and mortar" store!

Most of the sites in this category offer all types of entertainment products; some specialize in specific products, like videogames. Interestingly, some of the lowest prices come at traditional mass merchants, Wal-Mart especially. This is one category where using a price comparison site really helps; there are even a few entertainment-oriented comparison shopping sites, such as Best Web Buys (**www.bestwebbuys.com**), DVD Price Search (**www.dvdpricesearch.com**), Game Pricezone (**www.gamepricezone.com**), MetaPrices (**www.metaprices.com**), Price.com (**www.price.com**), and ShoppingAisles.com (**www.shoppingaisles.com**).

Afterburner Games

www.afterburnergames.com

Videogames. Also offers videogame rentals.

BARGAIN HUNTER'S SECRETS: Look for savings on individual items. First-time customers get $10 off their first order.

Amazon.com Best Bargain Best Selection

www.amazon.com (800.201.7575)

Click the DVD tab for DVDs. Click the Video tab for videotapes. Click the Music tab for CDs. Click the Computer & Video Games tab for videogames.

BARGAIN HUNTER'S SECRETS: All items discounted. In each category, click the Today's Deals tab for sale items. On the DVD page, click the Used DVDs tab for bargains on used merchandise. On the Video page, click the Used Videos tab for bargains on used merchandise. On the Music page, click the Used Music tab for bargains on used merchandise. On the Computer & Video Games page, click the Used & Rare tab for bargains on used and hard-to-find games; click the Outlet tab for clearance merchandise. Look for additional savings on new or used products from third-party merchants in the More Buying Choices section of each product page. Look for limited-time savings during the sitewide Friday Sale. Free shipping on orders of $25 or more.

AnimeDVDStore.com

www.animedvdstore.com

DVDs. (Specializes in Japanese anime.)

BARGAIN HUNTER'S SECRETS: Look for savings on individual items.

Barnes & Noble

www.barnesandnoble.com (877.275.2626)

Click the DVD & Video tab for DVDs and videotapes. Click the Music tab for CDs.

BARGAIN HUNTER'S SECRETS: All items discounted; see individual product pages for savings. On each category page, click the On Sale links for sale merchandise. Free shipping on orders of $25 or more.

Blockbuster.com

www.blockbuster.com (972.683.5959)

DVDs, videotapes, and videogames.

BARGAIN HUNTER'S SECRETS: Look for savings on individual items. Look for "free rental" deals with selected purchases. Look for bargains on pre-viewed movies and games.

Bop Shop.com

www.bopshop.com (585.271.3354)

Vinyl LPs.

BARGAIN HUNTER'S SECRETS: Click the Internet Specials link for sale items.

CafeDVD

www.cafedvd.com

DVD rentals online. Also sells used DVDs.

BARGAIN HUNTER'S SECRETS: Earn 5% in CafeDVD Reward Points with every rental. Look for bargains when purchasing previously viewed DVDs.

CD Universe Best Bargain

www.cduniverse.com (800.231.7937)

CDs, DVDs, and videogames.

BARGAIN HUNTER'S SECRETS: All items discounted. Click the Bargain Bin link for discounted items.

CDconnection.com

www.cdconnection.com (408.985.7905)

CDs.

BARGAIN HUNTER'S SECRETS: All items discounted.

CDSource

www.cdsource.com

CDs, DVDs, and videogames.

BARGAIN HUNTER'S SECRETS: All items discounted.

Cheap-CDs.com Best Bargain

www.cheap-cds.com

CDS.

BARGAIN HUNTER'S SECRETS: All items heavily discounted; "91% new CDs under $12.99."

Christianbook.com

www.christianbook.com (800.247.4784)

Religious CDs, DVDs, and videotapes.

BARGAIN HUNTER'S SECRETS: Look for savings on individual titles.

Collector's Choice Music

www.ccmusic.com (800.993.6344)

CDs. Specializes in imports and hard-to-find titles.

BARGAIN HUNTER'S SECRETS: All items discounted. Click the Closeouts link for clearance items. Free shipping on orders of $50 or more.

Critic's Choice Video

www.ccvideo.com (800.993.6357)

DVDs and videotapes.

BARGAIN HUNTER'S SECRETS: All items discounted. Click the Bargains link for sale items. Click the DVDs Under $10 link for low-priced titles.

DVD Empire

www.dvdempire.com (888.383.1880)

CDs, DVDs, and videogames. Also offers used DVDs.

BARGAIN HUNTER'S SECRETS: All items discounted. See the Bargains section of the home page for sale merchandise. See the Sales & Promos section of the home page for manufacturer promotions. Click the Used tab for bargains on used movies. Free shipping on three or more titles.

DVDPlanet

www.dvdplanet.com (800.624.3078)

DVDs.

BARGAIN HUNTER'S SECRETS: All items discounted. Free shipping on orders of $25 or more. See the DVD Deals section of the home page for low-priced titles.

EB Games

www.ebgames.com (877.432.9675)

Videogames, computer games, and DVDs.

BARGAIN HUNTER'S SECRETS: All items discounted. Look for savings on pre-played games. Trade in old games for credit.

fye.com

www.fye.com

CDs, DVDs, videotapes, and videogames.

BARGAIN HUNTER'S SECRETS: All items discounted. Click the Specials link for sale items. Click the Hot Deals link for promotional items. Free shipping on orders of more than $49.

Game Quest

www.gamequestdirect.com (714.572.9022)

Videogames and DVDs.

BARGAIN HUNTER'S SECRETS: All items discounted. Click the Specials link for sale items.

GameStop.com

www.gamestop.com (817.424.2200)

Videogames. Also sells used games.

BARGAIN HUNTER'S SECRETS: Look for savings on individual items. Click the Preowned link for bargains on used games. Click the Price Drops link for discounted items. Click the Stopwatch Sale link for limited-time bargains.

GoGamer.com

www.gogamer.com (888.948.9661)

Videogames and computer games.

BARGAIN HUNTER'S SECRETS: Look for savings on individual items. Look for the Blow-Out Deals link on the home page for discounted items.

GospelDirect.com

www.gospeldirect.com (800.467.7353)

Religious CDs, DVDs, and videotapes.

BARGAIN HUNTER'S SECRETS: Click the Hot Deals link for sale items. Click the Closeouts link for clearance items.

KB Toys

www.kbtoys.com

Videogames. (Also operates as **www.etoys.com**.)

BARGAIN HUNTER'S SECRETS: Look for savings on individual items. See the Great Values section of the Video Games page for sale items.

Laser's Edge

www.lasersedge.com (317.848.2088)

DVDs. Also offers used DVDs.

BARGAIN HUNTER'S SECRETS: All items discounted. Look for savings on used movies.

MoviesUnlimited.com

www.moviesunlimited.com (800.668.4344)

DVDs.

BARGAIN HUNTER'S SECRETS: All items discounted. Look for sale items on the home page.

Netflix

www.netflix.com

DVD rentals online.

BARGAIN HUNTER'S SECRETS: Flat monthly fee for unlimited rentals.

SecondSpin.com

www.secondspin.com (800.962.6445)

Used CDs, DVDS, and videotapes.

BARGAIN HUNTER'S SECRETS: Look for bargains on used merchandise. Will also buy your used items.

VideoGameCentral.com

www.videogamecentral.com (877.426.3769)

Videogames and computer games. Also sells used games.

BARGAIN HUNTER'S SECRETS: Look for savings on individual items. Click the Game Trade-Ins link for bargains on used games.

Wal-Mart Best Bargain

www.walmart.com

CDs, DVDs, videotapes, and videogames.

BARGAIN HUNTER'S SECRETS: All items heavily discounted.

YesAsia.com

www.yesasia.com (888.716.5753)

CDs, DVDs, videotapes, and videogames. Specializes in anime and other Japanese, Korean, and Chinese entertainment.

BARGAIN HUNTER'S SECRETS: Look for savings on individual items.

MUSICAL INSTRUMENTS

Buying a musical instrument online is sometimes more costly than it appears, especially with big items such as drum sets and keyboards, where the high shipping costs get you. Shipping aside, there are bargains to be found online, along with a bigger selection than you find at your local "mom and pop" music store.

Don't expect immediate shipment on all items, however, because many online music merchants don't carry all items listed in stock. They might have to get what you ordered from the factory, which could take awhile. Still, if the price is right, it might be worth the wait—which you'd probably experience at a traditional retailer, too.

American Musical Supply

www.americanmusical.com (800.458.4076)

Guitars, keyboards, drums, recording, and live sound.

BARGAIN HUNTER'S SECRETS: Look for savings on individual items. Click the See Weekly Deals link for limited-time bargains. Click the Outlet Zone link for closeout and refurbished merchandise.

Brook Mays Music Company Best Bargain

www.brookmays.com (800.637.8966)

Guitars, keyboards, drums, recording, and live sound.

BARGAIN HUNTER'S SECRETS: Click the Clearance link for closeout items. Free shipping on orders of more than $99.

Elderly Instruments

www.elderly.com (888.473.5810)

Guitars. Specializes in vintage and used instruments.

BARGAIN HUNTER'S SECRETS: Look for savings on pre-owned instruments. Click the Cheapo Depot link for closeout items.

Giardinelli

www.giardinelli.com (800.249.8361)

Band and orchestra instruments—trumpets, trombones, woodwinds, violins, and so on.

BARGAIN HUNTER'S SECRETS: Click the Clearance Center graphic for closeout items. Free shipping on orders of more than $299.

GuitarTrader.com

www.guitartrader.com (888.424.8482)

Guitars, recording, and live sound.

BARGAIN HUNTER'S SECRETS: Click the 50% Off and On Sale links for sale merchandise. Click the Scratch & Dent link for bargains on damaged items. Click the Package Deals link for guitar/amplifier packages. Free shipping on orders of more than $150.

Interstate Music Best Selection

www.interstatemusic.com (877.213.2580)

Guitars, keyboards, drums, band and orchestra instruments, recording, and live sound.

BARGAIN HUNTER'S SECRETS: Look for savings on individual items. Look for sale items on the home page and category pages. Free shipping on orders of more than $99.

Musician's Friend Best Selection

www.musiciansfriend.com (800.391.8762)

Guitars, keyboards, drums, band and orchestra instruments, recording, and live sound.

BARGAIN HUNTER'S SECRETS: Look for savings on individual items. Look for weekly specials on the home page. Click the Clearance Center graphic for closeout and refurbished merchandise. Free shipping on orders of more than $299.

Sam Ash Best Selection Best Bargain

www.samash.com (800.472.6274)

Guitars, keyboards, drums, recording, band and orchestra instruments, and live sound.

BARGAIN HUNTER'S SECRETS: Look for savings on individual items. Click the Today's Deals link for sale items. Click the Closeout Items link for clearance and refurbished merchandise. Free shipping on orders of more than $99.

SameDayMusic.com

www.samedaymusic.com (866.744.7736)

Guitars, keyboards, drums, recording, and live sound.

BARGAIN HUNTER'S SECRETS: Look for savings on individual items. Free shipping on selected items.

Sweetwater Sound

www.sweetwater.com (800.222.4700)

Keyboards, recording, and live sound.

BARGAIN HUNTER'S SECRETS: Look for savings on individual items. Click the Rebates link for manufacturer rebates. Click the Trading Post link to buy and sell used equipment. Free shipping on most items.

Woodwind and Brasswind

www.wwbw.com (800.348.5003)

Band and orchestra instruments—trumpets, trombones, clarinets, saxophones, violins, and so on.

BARGAIN HUNTER'S SECRETS: Look for savings on individual items. See the home page for sales and promotions. Free shipping on most items.

zZounds

www.zzounds.com (800.996.8637)

Guitars, keyboards, recording, and live sound.

BARGAIN HUNTER'S SECRETS: Look for savings on individual items. Free shipping on most items.

OFFICE SUPPLIES

It should come as no surprise that the market for office supplies online is dominated by the same "big box" superstores that dominate the retail landscape: Office Depot, Office Max, and Staples. These stores have set up online operations that mirror their retail operations, so whatever you can find in their stores (or in their catalogs) you can find online—and have delivered directly to your door.

There are also a handful of online-only office supply superstores that are worth checking out, as well as a number of stores that specialize in specific types of office products, such as writing supplies, stationery, or ink and toner. Discounts are abundant, which makes this an ideal category to shop for online.

The best bargains in this category come when you buy in bulk. Don't order just a single package of paper; order a whole box. And while you're at it, stock up on pens and paper clips and rubber bands. The more you include on a single order, the more you'll save on shipping costs. So don't make this an impulse buying category; instead, stock up on your most-used supplies at regular intervals.

Amazon.com

www.amazon.com (800.201.7575)

Click the Office Products tab for office supplies, paper and envelopes, ink and toner, writing instruments, office furniture, telephones, and accessories.

BARGAIN HUNTER'S SECRETS: Click the Today's Deals tab for sale and promotional items. Click the Outlet tab for closeout and refurbished merchandise.

American Printing & Envelope

www.apec-usa.com (800.221.9403)

Paper and envelopes.

BARGAIN HUNTER'S SECRETS: Click the Special Items link for sale and closeout items.

Business-Supply.com

www.business-supply.com (800.676.0180)

Office supplies, paper and envelopes, art supplies, writing instruments, shipping supplies, and office furniture.

BARGAIN HUNTER'S SECRETS: Click the Specials links for sale items. Free shipping for all orders of more than $25.

Collage

www.collagecatalog.com (800.343.3529)

Stationery, writing instruments, and paper products.

BARGAIN HUNTER'S SECRETS: Look for savings on individual items.

DiscountOfficeSupplies.com

www.discountofficesupplies.com (800.734.6020)

Office supplies, art supplies, paper and envelopes, writing instruments, office furniture, and ink and toner.

BARGAIN HUNTER'S SECRETS: All items discounted. Click the On Sale link for sale items. Look for other bargains on the home page. Free shipping on orders of more than $50.

FJAproduct.com

www.fjaproducts.com (800.982.9989)

Ink and toner and fax supplies.

BARGAIN HUNTER'S SECRETS: Look for savings on individual items. Free shipping on all orders of more than $30.

FineStationery.com

www.finestationery.com (888.808.3465)

Stationery and invitations.

BARGAIN HUNTER'S SECRETS: Look for savings on individual items.

FLAX Art & Design

www.flaxart.com (800.343.3529)

Art supplies and stationery.

BARGAIN HUNTER'S SECRETS: Look for savings on individual items. Sign up for email offers.

GreenLightOffice.com

www.greenlightoffice.com (800.536.6789)

Office supplies, art supplies, writing instruments, office furniture, filing and storage, and shipping supplies.

BARGAIN HUNTER'S SECRETS: Look for the green light icons for lowest prices on specific products. Free shipping on orders of more than $50.

Ink Oasis

www.inkoasis.com (800.455.5987)

Toner and ink and fax supplies.

BARGAIN HUNTER'S SECRETS: Look for savings on individual items. Free shipping on orders of more than $50.

Levenger

www.levenger.com (800.545.0242)

Writing instruments, stationery, desk accessories, and office furniture.

BARGAIN HUNTER'S SECRETS: Click the Outlet graphic for clearance merchandise.

Office Depot

www.officedepot.com (888.284.3638)

Office supplies, paper and envelopes, writing instruments, desk accessories, ink and toner, filing and storage, school supplies, and office furniture.

BARGAIN HUNTER'S SECRETS: Look for savings on individual items. See the Rebate Center section of the home page for manufacturer rebates. See the Advertised Specials and Seasonal Specials sections for limited-time offers.

OfficeMart.com

www.officemart.com (800.657.7907)

Office supplies, art supplies, paper and envelopes, office furniture, filing and storage, shipping supplies, writing instruments, desk accessories, and ink and toner.

BARGAIN HUNTER'S SECRETS: Look for savings on individual items. Click the Specials tab for sale items. Free delivery for orders of more than $50.

OfficeMax Best Selection

www.officemax.com (800.283.7674)

Office supplies, art supplies, paper and envelopes, writing instruments, desk accessories, ink and toner, filing and storage, school supplies, and office furniture.

BARGAIN HUNTER'S SECRETS: Look for savings on individual items. Look for specials and sales on the home page. Click the Rebate Center link for manufacturer rebates. Click the Weekly In-Store Specials link for store specials.

OfficeWorld.com

www.officeworld.com

Office supplies, paper and envelopes, writing instruments, shipping supplies, office furniture, filing and storage, and ink and toner.

BARGAIN HUNTER'S SECRETS: Look for savings on individual items. Free shipping on orders of $49 or more.

OnlineLabels.com

www.onlinelabels.com (888.575.2235)

Labels.

BARGAIN HUNTER'S SECRETS: Look for savings on individual items.

Paper Mart Packaging Store

www.papermart.com (800.745.8800)

Boxes, bags, shipping supplies, and gift wrap.

BARGAIN HUNTER'S SECRETS: Look for savings on individual items.

Price-Less Inkjet Cartridge

www.priceless-inkjet.com (877.408.3652)

Ink and toner and paper.

BARGAIN HUNTER'S SECRETS: Look for savings on individual items. See Specials section of home page for limited-time offers.

Shoplet

www.shoplet.com

Office supplies, paper and envelopes, desk accessories, and office furniture.

BARGAIN HUNTER'S SECRETS: Free shipping.

Staples Best Selection

www.staples.com (800.378.2753)

Office supplies, art supplies, paper and envelopes, writing instruments, desk accessories, ink and toner, filing and storage, school supplies, office furniture, and custom printing and stationery.

BARGAIN HUNTER'S SECRETS: Click the Weekly Specials link for limited-time savings. Click the Paper Deals link for savings on paper products. Click the Clearance Center link for closeout and refurbished items. Click the Rebate Center link for manufacturer rebates.

Viking Office Products

www.vikingop.com (800.711.4242)

Business supplies, desktop accessories, filing and storage, shipping supplies, paper and envelopes, writing instruments, ink and toner, office furniture, and school supplies.

BARGAIN HUNTER'S SECRETS: Click the Monthly Deals & Specials link for limited-time bargains. Click the Rebates link for manufacturer rebates. Click the Clearance Center link for closeout and refurbished merchandise. Free shipping on orders of more than $25.

ONLINE AUCTIONS

You learned all about online auctions in Chapter 9, "Hunting for Bargains at eBay and Other Online Auctions." These sites are great in that you can find bargains on both new and used products, in almost all product categories, offered by both individuals and retailers. For many savvy shoppers, eBay is *the* place to shop online—a one-stop shop for everything they buy.

In terms of customer satisfaction, eBay was ranked as the #1 online auction site in the 2003 American Customer Satisfaction Index, with an 84% satisfaction rating. Interestingly, uBid, a business-to-consumer auction site, ranked #2 in the category, with a 73% rating.

Remember, when you make a purchase at an online auction site, you're not purchasing from the auction site itself, you're purchasing from another user, either an individual or a merchant. The auction site only facilitates the purchase, which means that any issues you have regarding the transaction have to be worked out between you and the seller.

One last thing. If you need something right away, you might not have time to wait out the entire auction process, nor risk losing the auction. If offered, you might want to take advantage of the "buy it now" option, which lets you purchase the item for a fixed price and get it shipped immediately. This might not give you best possible price (you might have won the auction with a lower bid), but does take the guesswork out of the process.

Amazon.com Auctions

auctions.amazon.com

Consumer-to-consumer and retailer-to-consumer auctions. All major product categories.

eBay

www.ebay.com

Consumer-to-consumer and retailer-to-consumer auctions. All major product categories.

uBid

www.ubid.com

Retailer-to-consumer auctions. Specializes in computer and electronics products.

Yahoo! Auctions

auctions.yahoo.com

Consumer-to-consumer and retailer-to-consumer auctions. All major product categories.

ONLINE MALLS AND DIRECTORIES

Before there were comparison shopping sites, there were online malls (sometimes called online directories). As you learned in Chapter 7, "Hunting for Bargains at Online Malls, Catalogs, and Department Stores," these are sites that amalgamate dozens of smaller merchants together into a single virtual shopping mall. Visit one site, and get access to dozens (or hundreds) more. Many of these online malls enable you to search for products across multiple merchants, and some even integrate all their merchants into a common shopping cart and checkout system.

Most of these online malls are general interest, in that they feature merchants in a variety of product categories. Some malls focus on merchants that offer a specific type of product. And some share merchants with other sites; there's little exclusivity involved, these days.

Any bargains you find at an online mall aren't the result of the mall itself, but rather of the individual mall merchant. While some malls offer comparison shopping services, most don't. So you'll need to find the merchant you want first, and then search that merchant's site for the best bargains.

@InterMall
www.1mall.com
Wide selection of stores in all categories.

African American Shopping Mall
www.aasm.com
Afrocentric products.

All-Internet Shopping Directory
www.all-internet.com
Wide selection of stores in all categories.

Antique and Collectible Mall
www.tias.com
Antiques, art, and collectibles.

Buyer's Index
www.buyersindex.com
Wide selection of stores in all categories.

Cybershopping.ca
www.cybershopping.ca
Canadian merchants.

Craft Ireland
www.craftireland.com
Irish crafts and gifts.

Crafty Crafters
www.craftycrafters.com
Crafts and gifts.

digiCHOICE
www.digichoice.com
Customizable products.

Elegant-Lifestyle.com
www.elegant-lifestyle.com
Luxury and high-end items.

ePlanetShopping.com
www.eplanetshopping.com
Wide selection of stores in all categories.

FingerTipShopper
www.fingertipshopper.com
Wide selection of stores in all categories.

Hippy Buggs Shopping Mall
www.hippybuggs.com
Hippy-oriented merchandise.

Internet Store List
www.internetstorelist.com
Wide selection of stores in all categories.

InternetMall
www.internetmall.com
Wide selection of stores in all categories.

Jewelry Mall
www.jewelrymall.com
Jewelry and watches.

OddSpot.com
www.oddspot.com
Hard-to-find merchandise.

Shop Reach
www.shopreach.com
Wide selection of stores in all categories.

Shopping A to Z
www.shoppingatoz.co.uk
British merchants.

Shopping-Headquarters
www.shopping-headquarters.com
Wide selection of stores in all categories.

ShoppingAide.com
www.shoppingaide.com
Wide selection of stores in all categories.

ShoppingTrolley.net
www.shoppingtrolley.net
British merchants.

ShopStiX Consumer Mall
www.shopstix.com
Canadian merchants.

SkyMall
www.skymall.com
Wide selection of stores in all categories.

Wired Seniors
www.wiredseniors.com
Products for seniors.

WebSquare.com
www.websquare.com
Wide selection of stores in all categories.

PET SUPPLIES

Despite the well-publicized failure of dot-com pioneer Pets.com, the market for pet supplies online has somehow managed to survive—and thrive. (The Pets.com URL, by the way, now redirects to the PetSmart site.) Whatever type of pet product you're looking for—food, toys, medications, you name it—it's available online, and often at a considerable savings.

One of the things that doomed Pets.com was the idea that shipping heavy bags of dog food cross-country was too costly to be a bargain. There's some truth to that; you definitely need to watch the shipping costs if you're buying bulk food from one of today's pet supply sites. But there are still bargains to be had, and some sites offer deals on shipping that can help reduce your total cost.

Also useful for pet-loving bargain hunters is the ability to buy pet medications online, without a prescription. The online pricing is considerably less than what you're likely to get from your local veterinarian.

As you might expect, the big "bricks and mortar" retailers are also big players online. They have lots of competition, however, so don't limit your shopping to the name sites. Especially check out the pet medication sites, which typically offer considerable savings over what you pay at the vet's office.

1-800-PetMeds

www.1800petmeds.com (800.738.6337)

Pet medications and gifts.

BARGAIN HUNTER'S SECRETS: Get $5 off orders of $100 or more; get $10 off orders of $150 or more. Click the Today's Specials link for sale items. Free shipping on orders of more than $49.

Allpets.com

www.allpets.com (888.738.6388)

Dog and cat supplies.

BARGAIN HUNTER'S SECRETS: All items discounted. See the Weekly Specials section of home page for limited-time bargains.

BestNest.com

www.bestnest.com (877.369.5446)

Wild bird baths, feeders, houses, and seed.

BARGAIN HUNTER'S SECRETS: All items discounted.

Doctors Foster & Smith

www.drsfostersmith.com (800.381.7179)

Dog, cat, fish, bird, reptile, and small pet supplies. Pet medications.

BARGAIN HUNTER'S SECRETS: Click the Specials link for sale items.

Duncraft Wild Bird Central

www.duncraft.com (800.593.5656)

Wild bird baths, feeders, houses, and seed.

BARGAIN HUNTER'S SECRETS: Click the Special Offers link for sale items. Click the Clearance Outlet link for closeout merchandise.

FerretStore.com

www.ferretstore.com (888.833.7738)

Dog, cat, bird, ferret, and small pet supplies. (Not just for ferrets!)

BARGAIN HUNTER'S SECRETS: Click the Sale Items link for discounted merchandise. Free shipping on orders of $35 or more.

JeffersPet.com

www.jefferspet.com (800.533.3377)

Dog, cat, reptile, bird, ferret, and horse supplies.

BARGAIN HUNTER'S SECRETS: Click the Bargains link for sale items.

Little River Pet Shop

www.pet-shop.net (408.541.1300)

Dog, cat, ferret, and small pet supplies.

BARGAIN HUNTER'S SECRETS: All items discounted. Click the Sales links for discounted items.

MarineDepot.com

www.marinedepot.com (714.385.0080)

Aquarium supplies and live fish (at **www.marinedepotlive.com**)

BARGAIN HUNTER'S SECRETS: All items discounted.

MyPetPrescriptions.com

www.mypetprescriptions.com (877.666.2501)

Pet medications.

BARGAIN HUNTER'S SECRETS: Look for savings on individual items.

Pet Care Central

www.petcarecentral.com (888.833.7738)

Dog, cat, bird, ferret, and small pet supplies.

BARGAIN HUNTER'S SECRETS: Click the Sale link for sale items. Free shipping on orders of $49.99 or more.

Pet Food Express

www.petfoodexpress.com (877.472.7777)

Dog, cat, bird, fish, reptile, and small pet supplies.

BARGAIN HUNTER'S SECRETS: All items discounted. Look for clearance and sale links on home page.

Petguys.com

www.petguys.com (800.360.4144)

Dog, cat, fish, bird, reptile, and small pet supplies.

BARGAIN HUNTER'S SECRETS: Wholesale prices. Click the Blowouts! link for sale and clearance items.

Pet Rx

www.petrx.com (888.889.1814)

Pet medications.

BARGAIN HUNTER'S SECRETS: Look for savings on individual items.

PetCareRx.com

www.petcarerx.com (800.844.1427)

Dog, cat, bird, fish, and small pet supplies. Pet medications.

BARGAIN HUNTER'S SECRETS: Look for specials on the home page. Look for savings on individual items.

PETCO.com Best Selection

www.petco.com (877.738.6742)

Dog, cat, fish, bird, reptile, and small pet supplies.

BARGAIN HUNTER'S SECRETS: See the Online Specials section of the home page for sale items and promotions. Click the Free Shipping Store link for items with free shipping.

PetFoodDirect.com Best Selection

www.petfooddirect.com (800.865.1333)

Dog, cat, bird, fish, reptile, and small pet supplies.

BARGAIN HUNTER'S SECRETS: Look for special offers on the home page. Click the Free Shipping link for items with free shipping. Click the Red Tag link for clearance, overstock, and sale items.

PetMarket.com Best Bargain

www.petmarket.com (888.738.6758)

Dog, cat, bird, horse, and small pet supplies.

BARGAIN HUNTER'S SECRETS: All items discounted. Click the Specials link for weekly sale items. Click the Clearance link for closeout items. Click the Coupons and Rebates link for manufacturer savings.

Pets-Warehouse Best Selection

www.pets-warehouse.com (800.991.3299)

Dog, cat, bird, fish, reptile, and small pet supplies.

BARGAIN HUNTER'S SECRETS: All items discounted.

PetShed Best Bargain

www.petshed.com (866.430.2823)

Pet medications.

BARGAIN HUNTER'S SECRETS: All items heavily discounted.

PetSmart Best Selection

www.petsmart.com (888.839.9638)

Dog, cat, bird fish, reptile, and small pet supplies.

BARGAIN HUNTER'S SECRETS: Look for savings on individual products.

PetStreetMall

www.petstreetmall.com (800.957.5753)

Dog, cat, bird, fish, reptile, and small pet supplies.

BARGAIN HUNTER'S SECRETS: All items discounted. Look for sale links on home page. Free shipping on orders of more than $40.

ThatPetPlace.com

www.thatpetplace.com (800.733.3829)

Dog, cat, fish, bird, reptile, and small pet supplies. Live fish and reptiles.

BARGAIN HUNTER'S SECRETS: Look for savings on individual items. Click the Bargain Counter link for sale items.

WorldPetStore.com

www.worldpetstore.com (800.569.3397)

Dog, cat, bird, fish, reptile, and small pet supplies.

BARGAIN HUNTER'S SECRETS: Get $5 off orders of $50 or more; get $10 off orders of $100 or more. Click the Monthly Specials link for limited-time bargains. Free shipping on orders of $125 or more.

SHOES

Shoes are big online—and I'm not just talking extra-large widths! Whether you're an obsessive shoe shopper or just looking for a bargain on a new pair of loafers, the selection online is tremendous and the bargains equally so. This category is one of the largest categories for online shoppers, which has attracted all manner of merchants to the show. You'll find discount shoe stores, manufacturer-direct stores and clearance outlets, and any number of designer boutiques.

In addition to the shoe merchants listed here, shoes are a big part of the mix for most stores in the Apparel and Department Stores and Mass Merchants sections of this directory. Along these lines, special attention should be paid to Nordstrom, which is a very large player in this category.

When you're shopping for shoes online, look for the sale and clearance sections. With so many bargains available online, there's no reason to pay full retail price! And don't forget to examine the returns policy, especially if your feet are a little hard to fit.

Birkenstock Central

www.birkenstockcentral.com (800.247.5748)

Men's and women's shoes, sandals, and clogs.

BARGAIN HUNTER'S SECRETS: Click the Bargains link for sale items. Look for additional bargains on home page. Free shipping on all items of more than $100.

ClassicSportsShoes.com

www.classicsportsshoes.com (888.266.5295)

Retro athletic shoes.

BARGAIN HUNTER'S SECRETS: Click the Sale Shoes link for sale items.

Cole Haan

www.colehaan.com (800.695.8945)

Men's and women's shoes and accessories.

BARGAIN HUNTER'S SECRETS: Click the Sale link for discounted items.

DesignerShoes.com

www.designershoes.com (888.371.7463)

Women's shoes, boots, sandals, and athletic shoes.

BARGAIN HUNTER'S SECRETS: Click the Sale link for discounted items.

eWeddingShoes.com

www.eweddingshoes.com (877.823.1500)

Women's wedding shoes and accessories.

BARGAIN HUNTER'S SECRETS: Click the Sale link for discounted items.

FamousFootwear.com

www.famousfootwear.com (866.432.6687)

Men's, women's, and children's shoes, boots, sandals, and athletic shoes.

BARGAIN HUNTER'S SECRETS: Click the Sale link for discounted items.

Florsheim

www.florsheim.com (800.843.7463)

Men's dress and casual shoes and boots. Manufacturer direct for Florsheim, Imperial, FLS, Comfortech, and Nunn Bush brands.

BARGAIN HUNTER'S SECRETS: Click the Clearance link for closeout and sale items. Free shipping on orders of $100 or more.

Foot Locker

www.footlocker.com (800.991.6815)

Men's and women's athletic shoes.

BARGAIN HUNTER'S SECRETS: Look for sale links on the home page.

J-Ray Shoes

www.jrayshoes.com (800.342.6321)

Children's and baby shoes.

BARGAIN HUNTER'S SECRETS: Click the Sale Shoes link for discounted items.

Johnston & Murphy

www.johnstonmurphy.com (888.324.6189)

Men's dress and casual shoes. Manufacturer direct.

BARGAIN HUNTER'S SECRETS: Click the Clearance link for sale and closeout items.

Journeys

www.journeys.com (888.324.6356)

Teens' shoes, boots, sandals, and athletic shoes.

BARGAIN HUNTER'S SECRETS: Click the Sale Stuff link for discounted items.

Keds

www.keds.com (800.428.6575)

Women's and children's casual and athletic shoes. Manufacturer direct.

BARGAIN HUNTER'S SECRETS: Click the Sale link for discounted items. Look for clearance links on the home page.

My Glass Slipper

www.myglassslipper.com (866.933.7463)

Women's wedding shoes and accessories.

BARGAIN HUNTER'S SECRETS: Click the Under $100 link for low-priced items.

Nike

www.niketown.com (800.806.6453)

Men's, women's, and children's athletic shoes. Manufacturer direct.

BARGAIN HUNTER'S SECRETS: Click the Clearance links for closeout and sale items.

Nine West

www.ninewest.com (800.999.1877)

Women's shoes, sandals, and boots.

BARGAIN HUNTER'S SECRETS: Click the Shop Sale link for discounted items.

Nordstrom Best Selection

www.nordstrom.com (888.282.6060)

Men's, women's, and children's shoes, sandals, and boots. Offers extended sizes.

BARGAIN HUNTER'S SECRETS: Look for savings on individual items.

Oddball Shoe Company

www.oddballshoe.com (800.884.4046)

Men's large-size shoes.

BARGAIN HUNTER'S SECRETS: Click the Specials link for sale items. Click the Clearance link for closeout merchandise.

Onlineshoes.com Best Bargain

www.onlineshoes.com (800.786.3141)

Men's and women's shoes, sandals, boots, and athletic shoes.

BARGAIN HUNTER'S SECRETS: Click the Sale Shoes link for discounted items. See the Promotions section of the home page for additional savings.

Payless

www.payless.com (877.474.6379)

Men's, women's, and children's shoes, boots, sandals, athletic shoes, and accessories.

BARGAIN HUNTER'S SECRETS: Buy 3 pairs get 1 free. Look for sale items on the home page.

Shoebuy.com Best Bargain Best Selection

www.shoebuy.com (888.200.8414)

Men's, women's, teens', and children's shoes, sandals, boots, athletic shoes, and accessories.

BARGAIN HUNTER'S SECRETS: All items discounted. Click the Sale Center link for discounted items. Free shipping on all orders.

Shoes.com Best Selection

www.shoes.com (888.233.6743)

Men's, women's, and children's shoes, sandals, boots, athletic shoes, and accessories.

BARGAIN HUNTER'S SECRETS: Click the On Sale tab for discounted items. Free shipping on orders of $35 or more.

Davidson Shoes Plus

www.shoestoboot.com (877.427.9333)

Men's, women's, and children's shoes, sandals, boots, and athletic shoes.

BARGAIN HUNTER'S SECRETS: Click the On Sale! tab for discounted items. Free shipping on orders of $75 or more.

Soho Shoe Salon

www.sohoshoe.com (718.464.8603)

Women's shoes and boots in hard-to-find and large sizes.

BARGAIN HUNTER'S SECRETS: Click the Sale Shoes link for discounted items.

Road Runner Sports

www.roadrunnersports.com (800.636.3560)

Men's and women's running shoes.

BARGAIN HUNTER'S SECRETS: Click the Clearance Store link for closeout and sale items.

Zappos.com Best Bargain Best Selection

www.zappos.com (888.492.7767)

Men's, women's, and children's shoes, sandals, boots, and athletic shoes. Offers wide and narrow sizes.

BARGAIN HUNTER'S SECRETS: Free shipping on all orders. Click the Shoes on Sale links for discounted items.

SPORTING GOODS

This ended up being one of the largest sections of the directory, simply because there are so many different types of sports out there. What you end up with is a large number of sport-specific merchants, along with the expected sporting goods superstores.

As to which type of store offers the best bargains, there's no hard-and-fast rule. Some of the smaller stores offer prices that rival the big-box merchants. And the same goes with selection; although you might expect a sport-specific store to carry a wide selection of that sport's merchandise, the big superstores often carry just as many products in that category. In other words, it pays to shop around.

And while you're shopping, don't forget the merchants in the Department Stores and Mass Merchants category. Sears and Wal-Mart, especially, offer wide selections at decent prices.

One thing to watch out for in this category is shipping costs, especially if you're buying a big or heavy item. (Weight-lifting equipment is particularly problematic!) Shipping an air-filled basketball is one thing, but shipping an exercise bike can cost big bucks. Look for free- or reduced-shipping specials, and make sure to factor the shipping into your total expenditure.

ActionVillage.com

www.actionvillage.com (847.709.6100)

Skateboarding, snowboarding, paintball, and go-karting.

BARGAIN HUNTER'S SECRETS: Click the Specials links for sale items.

Active Mail Order

www.activemailorder.com (800.588.3911)

Skateboarding.

BARGAIN HUNTER'S SECRETS: Click the Sale tab for discounted items. Free shipping on all orders of more than $89.

Altrec.com

www.altrec.com (800.369.3949)

Camping, hiking, cycling, skiing, snowboarding, and running.

BARGAIN HUNTER'S SECRETS: Click the Clearance link for closeout merchandise. Look for sale links on the home page.

Amazon.com

www.amazon.com (800.201.7575)

Archery, badminton, baseball, basketball, billiards, boating, bowling, boxing, camping and hiking, cheerleading, climbing, cricket, cycling, darts, diving, equestrian, exercise and fitness, fishing, football, golf, gymnastics, hockey, hunting, kayaking, lacrosse, martial arts, paintall, racquetball, rugby, running, skateboarding, skating, sledding, skiing, snowboarding, soccer, surfing, swimming, tennis, track and field, volleyball, windsurfing, wrestling, and yoga. (Click the Sports & Outdoors tab.) Some items from third-party merchants.

BARGAIN HUNTER'S SECRETS: Look for savings on individual items. Look for the Great Deals sections on category pages. Look for used and new bargains from third-party merchants in the More Buying Choices section of product pages.

American Fly Fishing Company

www.americanfly.com (800.410.1222)

Fishing.

BARGAIN HUNTER'S SECRETS: Click the Closeouts link for clearance items.

Athleta

www.athleta.com (888.322.5515)

Women's athletic apparel: swimwear, tops, shorts, pants, sports bras, and running shoes.

BARGAIN HUNTER'S SECRETS: Click the Sale Outlet link for clearance merchandise.

Backcountrygear.com

www.backcountrygear.com (800.953.5499)

Camping, climbing, hiking, and backpacking.

BARGAIN HUNTER'S SECRETS: Click the Clearance link for closeout and sale items.

Balazs Boxing

www.balazsboxing.com (888.466.6765)

Boxing.

BARGAIN HUNTER'S SECRETS: Click the Balazs Bargains link for closeout items.

Barefoot Yoga Co.

www.barefootyoga.com (877.227.3366)

Yoga.

BARGAIN HUNTER'S SECRETS: Click the Sale Items link for discounted merchandise.

Bargainsports.net

www.bargainsports.net (888.271.7500)

Backpacking, baseball, cross country, golf, hockey, skating, skiing, snowboarding, swimming, and tennis.

BARGAIN HUNTER'S SECRETS: All items discounted.

Base Gear

www.basegear.com

Camping and hiking.

BARGAIN HUNTER'S SECRETS: Click the Sales and Hot Buys link for discounted and promotional items.

Big Toe Soccer

www.bigtoesports.com (800.244.8637)

Soccer.

BARGAIN HUNTER'S SECRETS: Click the Sale link for discounted merchandise.

BigFitness.com

www.bigfitness.com (800.731.0098)

Exercise and fitness, yoga.

BARGAIN HUNTER'S SECRETS: All items discounted. Look for savings on used equipment.

BikesDirect.com

www.bikesdirect.com

Biking.

BARGAIN HUNTER'S SECRETS: All items discounted. Free shipping on all orders.

BLADES Board and Skate

www.blades.com (888.552.5233)

Snowboarding, skateboarding, and inline skating.

BARGAIN HUNTER'S SECRETS: Click the Outlet link for clearance and sale items.

BoatersWorld.com

www.boatersworld.com (877.690.0004)

Boating, sailing, water sports, fishing, and fish finders.

BARGAIN HUNTER'S SECRETS: Click the Clearance link for closeout and sale items. Click the Rebates link for manufacturer rebates. Free shipping on orders of more than $100.

Bowler's Paradise Best Selection

www.bowlersparadise.com (888.969.2695)

Bowling.

BARGAIN HUNTER'S SECRETS: Click the Specials link for sale items.

Bowling.com

www.bowling.com (800.441.2695)

Bowling.

BARGAIN HUNTER'S SECRETS: Click the Closeouts link for clearance merchandise.

Cabela's Online Store

www.cabelas.com (800.237.4444)

Archery, boating, camping, fishing, and hunting.

BARGAIN HUNTER'S SECRETS: Click the Bargain Cave link for heavily discounted items. Click the Web Exclusives link for additional bargains.

Campmor

www.campmor.com (800.525.4784)

Camping, climbing, and hiking.

BARGAIN HUNTER'S SECRETS: Click the Hot Deals and Web Bargains links for discounted items.

Cascade Outfitters

www.cascadeoutfitters.com (800.223.7238)

Rafting, kayaking, and river equipment.

BARGAIN HUNTER'S SECRETS: Click the Sale links for discounted merchandise.

Century Martial Art Supply Best Selection

www.centuryfitness.com (800.626.2787)

Martial arts.

BARGAIN HUNTER'S SECRETS: Click the Outlet link for closeout and sale merchandise.

ClassicSportsShoes.com

www.classicsportsshoes.com (888.266.5295)

Retro athletic shoes.

BARGAIN HUNTER'S SECRETS: Click the Sale Shoes link for sale items.

Complete Sportswear

www.sportsteam.com (800.441.0618)

Cheerleading, team uniforms, and mascots.

BARGAIN HUNTER'S SECRETS: Click the Monthly Madness link for sale merchandise.

Cool Sports Equipment

www.csskiequipment.com (888.208.4770)

Camping, hiking, boating, fishing, swimming, sledding, and skateboarding.

BARGAIN HUNTER'S SECRETS: Click the Clearance Rack link for closeout and sale merchandise.

Dick's Sporting Goods Best Selection

www.dickssportinggoods.com (877.846.9997)

Baseball, basketball, camping and hiking, cycling, exercise, fishing, football, golf, hunting and archery, in-line skating, lacrosse, paintball, racquetball, running, skateboarding, skiing, snowboarding, soccer, tennis, water sports, and winter sports.

BARGAIN HUNTER'S SECRETS: Look for savings on individual items. See the As Advertised section of the home page for additional bargains. Free shipping on orders of $99 or more.

Divers Direct

www.diversdirect.com (800.348.3872)

Scuba diving.

BARGAIN HUNTER'S SECRETS: Click the Specials link for sale items.

eAngler

www.eangler.com (877.979.3474)

Fishing, boating.

BARGAIN HUNTER'S SECRETS: Look for savings on individual items.

eSpikes

www.espikes.com (800.676.7463)

Track and field.

BARGAIN HUNTER'S SECRETS: Click the Sale Items! link for discounted merchandise.

Fogdog Sports

www.fogdog.com (800.624.2017)

Baseball, basketball, boating, bowling, camping, cycling, fishing, fitness, football, golf, hiking and climbing, hockey, hunting and archery, lacrosse, paintball, racquetball, running, skateboarding, skiing, snowboarding, soccer, softball, surfing, swimming, tennis, track and field, volleyball, and wrestling.

BARGAIN HUNTER'S SECRETS: Click the Outlet tab for closeout and sale items.

Foot Locker

www.footlocker.com (800.991.6815)

Men's and women's athletic shoes.

BARGAIN HUNTER'S SECRETS: Look for sale links on the home page.

G.I. Joe's

www.gijoes.com (800.578.5637)

Baseball, basketball, boating, camping and hiking, cycling, exercise, fishing, football, go-karts, golf, hunting and archery, hockey, paintball, running, skateboarding, skiing, snowboarding, soccer, tennis, water sports, winter sports, and yoga.

BARGAIN HUNTER'S SECRETS: Click the Clearance Camp link for closeout and sale merchandise.

Getboards.com

Best Bargain

www.getboards.com (800.754.2627)

Snowboarding, skiboarding, skateboarding, and wakeboarding.

BARGAIN HUNTER'S SECRETS: All items discounted. Click the Clearance Items link for closeout merchandise. Free shipping.

GigaGolf

www.gigagolf.com (800.724.3085)

Golf.

BARGAIN HUNTER'S SECRETS: Look for savings on individual items. Click the Close Outs link for clearance merchandise.

GolfDiscount.com

Best Bargain

www.golfdiscount.com (888.394.4654)

Golf.

BARGAIN HUNTER'S SECRETS: All items discounted. Click the Closeouts tab for clearance items. See the Bargain Seekers section of the home page for additional savings. Free shipping on many items.

GolfOutlet.com

www.golfoutlet.com

Golf.

BARGAIN HUNTER'S SECRETS: All items discounted. Click the Clearance Center link for closeout merchandise.

KarateDepot.com

www.karatedepot.com (877.216.2669)

Martial arts.

BARGAIN HUNTER'S SECRETS: Look for savings on individual items.

LeisurePro

www.leisurepro.com (888.805.3600)

Scuba diving.

BARGAIN HUNTER'S SECRETS: Click the Current Specials link for sale items. Click the Clearance Items link for closeout merchandise.

Liquid Golf

Best Selection

www.liquidgolf.com (800.903.6376)

Golf.

BARGAIN HUNTER'S SECRETS: Click the Sale Products link for discounted items. Click the Used tab for bargains on used equipment. Free shipping on orders of more than $100.

Modell's Sporting Goods

www.modells.com (866.835.9129)

Baseball, basketball, boxing and martial arts, camping and hiking, cycling, fishing, fitness, football, golf, hockey, lacrosse, paintball, racquetball, running, skateboarding, snowboarding, soccer, squash, tennis, water sports, winter sports, wrestling, and yoga.

BARGAIN HUNTER'S SECRETS: Click the Outlet link for closeout and sale merchandise.

MonsterSkate.com

www.monsterskate.com (866.287.8337)

Skateboarding.

BARGAIN HUNTER'S SECRETS: Look for savings on individual items. Click the On Sale link for discounted items.

Mountain Gear

www.mgear.com (800.829.2009)

Climbing, backpacking, and snow sports.

BARGAIN HUNTER'S SECRETS: Click the On Sale link for discounted items. Free shipping on orders of more than $50.

The Movement Connection

www.movementconnection.com (877.326.2300)

Dance, gymnastics, yoga, and cheerleading.

BARGAIN HUNTER'S SECRETS: Click the Specials tab for sale items.

Nike

www.niketown.com (800.806.6453)

Men's, women's, and children's athletic shoes and apparel. Manufacturer direct.

BARGAIN HUNTER'S SECRETS: Click the Clearance links for closeout and sale items.

Overtons.com Best Selection

www.overtons.com (800.334.6541)

Boating, water sports.

BARGAIN HUNTER'S SECRETS: Click the Overton's Outlet link for closeout and sale merchandise.

Peter Glenn Ski & Sports

www.peterglenn.com (800.818.0946)

Skiing, snowboarding, and winter sports.

BARGAIN HUNTER'S SECRETS: Click the Clearance links for closeout items.

Plaine's

www.plaines.com (888.216.7122)

Cycling, skiing, and snowboarding.

BARGAIN HUNTER'S SECRETS: Click the Specials tab for sale items.

RingSide.com

www.ringside.com (877.426.9464)

Boxing.

BARGAIN HUNTER'S SECRETS: Click the Closeouts link for clearance items. Click the Web Specials link for sale merchandise.

Riverwire.com

www.riverwire.com (888.606.5279)

Fishing.

BARGAIN HUNTER'S SECRETS: Look for savings on individual items. Free shipping.

Road Runner Sports Best Selection

www.roadrunnersports.com (800.636.3560)

Running.

BARGAIN HUNTER'S SECRETS: Click the Clearance Store link for closeout merchandise.

SailNet

www.sailnet.com (800.234.3220)

Sailing.

BARGAIN HUNTER'S SECRETS: Click the SailNet Outlet link for overstock and clearance merchandise.

Skateboard.com

www.skateboard.com (866.752.3266)

Skateboarding.

BARGAIN HUNTER'S SECRETS: Click the Closeouts and Overstock link for clearance items.

Soccer.com Best Selection

www.soccer.com (800.950.1994)

Soccer.

BARGAIN HUNTER'S SECRETS: Click the Sale! link for discounted items.

Sport Eyes

www.sporteyes.com (888.223.2669)

Sports eyewear and sunglasses.

BARGAIN HUNTER'S SECRETS: Click the Closeouts or Bargain Bin links for clearance and discontinued items. Free shipping on orders of more than $75.

Sports 4 Kids

www.sports4kids.com (800.864.0080)

Children's sports—baseball, basketball, bicycles, boating, boxing, cheerleading, field hockey, football, golf, gymnastics, hockey, kids fitness, lacrosse, pedal cars, scooters, skateboarding, sledding, snowboarding, soccer, softball, tennis, toboggans, track and field, tricycles, tumbling, volleyball, water sports, and wrestling.

BARGAIN HUNTER'S SECRETS: Look for clearance and sale links on the home page.

Springco Athletics

www.springcoathletics.com (800.383.0305)

Track and field.

BARGAIN HUNTER'S SECRETS: Click the Closeouts and Overstocked Items link for clearance and sale merchandise.

Supergo Bike Shops

www.supergo.com (800.326.2453)

Bicycling.

BARGAIN HUNTER'S SECRETS: Click the Hottest Deals link for sale merchandise.

TackleDirect

www.tackledirect.com (888.354.7335)

Fishing.

BARGAIN HUNTER'S SECRETS: Click the Promotions link for special savings. Free shipping on orders of more than $150.

The Tennis Company

www.tenniscompany.com (888.276.1727)

Tennis.

BARGAIN HUNTER'S SECRETS: Click the Specials link for sale merchandise. Look for bargains on used items.

Tennis Warehouse

www.tenniswarehouse.com (800.883.6647)

Tennis.

BARGAIN HUNTER'S SECRETS: Look for savings on individual items. Look for sale and liquidation links on the home page.

TheTentStore.com

www.thetentstore.com (800.873.6072)

Camping and backpacking.

BARGAIN HUNTER'S SECRETS: Click the Specials link for sale items.

Title Boxing

www.titleboxing.com (800.999.1213)

Boxing.

BARGAIN HUNTER'S SECRETS: Click the Specials link for sale items.

Tour Line Golf

www.tourlinegolf.com (800.530.5767)

Golf. Specializes in used golf clubs.

BARGAIN HUNTER'S SECRETS: Save on used equipment.

TravelCountry.com

www.travelcountry.com (800.643.3629)

Camping, hiking, and backpacking.

BARGAIN HUNTER'S SECRETS: Pull down the What's On Sale list for discounted items. Free shipping on most items.

VolleyHut

www.volleyhut.com (858.486.3307)

Volleyball.

BARGAIN HUNTER'S SECRETS: Click the On Sale link for discounted items.

West Marine

www.westmarine.com (800.262.8464)

Boating, sailing, and fishing.

BARGAIN HUNTER'S SECRETS: Click the Specials link for sale items. Click the Clearance Outlet link for closeout and refurbished items. Click the Rebates link for manufacturer rebates.

workoutwarehouse.com

www.workoutwarehouse.com (800.999.3756)

Fitness and exercise.

BARGAIN HUNTER'S SECRETS: Look for savings on individual items.

Worldwaters.com

www.worldwaters.com (541.383.0696)

Fishing.

BARGAIN HUNTER'S SECRETS: Click the Closeouts links on category pages for clearance merchandise.

Worldwide Sport Supply

www.wwsport.com (800.756.3555)

Wrestling, volleyball, and track and field.

BARGAIN HUNTER'S SECRETS: Click the Deals links on category pages for sales merchandise.

Yoga Zone

www.yogazone.com (800.264.9642)

Yoga.

BARGAIN HUNTER'S SECRETS: Look for sale items on the home page.

TICKETS

This is one of the newer categories of online shopping, and I include it here not because there are huge bargains to be found (there typically aren't), but because of the convenience factor. It's great to be able to order your movie tickets online before you leave home, and thus avoid long lines when you get to the theater. The same with tickets to sporting events and concerts; it's actually faster to order off a Web site than it is to wait on hold over the phone.

But, as I said, don't expect any bargains from these services. In fact, you might even find a small service charge added to the ticket price. The exceptions are the ticket broker sites, such as GreatTickets and Preferred Tickets, which sometimes offer tickets at a discount. (They sometimes offer tickets at a premium, too, if the event is sold out.) As with anything, make sure that you shop around.

Fandango

www.fandango.com (866.857.5191)

Movie tickets.

GreatTickets

www.greattickets.com (800.701.6561)

Sports, concert, and events tickets.

BARGAIN HUNTER'S SECRETS: Ticket broker.

MovieTickets.com

www.movietickets.com (888.440.8457)

Movie tickets.

Preferred Tickets

www.preferredtickets.com (916.774.0000)

Sports, concert, and events tickets.

BARGAIN HUNTER'S SECRETS: Ticket broker.

Stub Hub

www.stubhub.com (866.788.2482)

Concert and sports tickets.

BARGAIN HUNTER'S SECRETS: Ticket broker.

The Ticket Machine

www.theticketmachine.com (888.887.4411)

Sports, concert, and events tickets.

BARGAIN HUNTER'S SECRETS: Ticket broker.

Ticketmaster

www.ticketmaster.com (213.639.6100)

Concert, sports, and event tickets.

TicketWeb

www.ticketweb.com

Concert and event tickets.

TOYS AND GAMES

Even though the toy category is a big one, there aren't a lot of toy merchants online. That's partly a reflection of the overall toy market, which in the "bricks and mortar" world is dominated by three retailers—Wal-Mart, Toys 'R' Us, and KB Toys. These same three players dominate the online toy market (Toys 'R' Us through its association with Amazon.com), which means these are the sites to go to for both selection and bargains.

That doesn't mean you should ignore the smaller toy sites. In particular, the Web is a great place to find those games, puzzles, and educational toys not typically carried by the big three. As with all things, make sure that you shop around; pricing varies a lot from retailer to retailer.

As you might imagine, this becomes a very popular category during the holiday shopping season. It's not uncommon for these sites to slow down under the heavy holiday traffic, and for shipping to take a day or two longer than normal. That means you should shop early, not only to avoid the rush but also to get first shot at the most popular toys and games. Even online, the season's hottest toys tend to sell out fast, so don't be caught short!

Active Toys

www.activetoys.com (877.858.8697)

Toy trucks.

BARGAIN HUNTER'S SECRETS: Click the Toy Specials link for sale items. Click the Shipping Specials link for shipping promotions.

AllAboardToys.com

www.allaboardtoys.com (800.416.7155)

Thomas the Tank Engine, Bob the Builder, Jay Jay the Jet Plane, and similar toys.

BARGAIN HUNTER'S SECRETS: Click the Now on Sale link for discounted items. Free shipping for orders of more than $69.

Amazon.com Best Selection

www.amazon.com (800.201.7575)

Toys for all ages, offered in association with Toys 'R' Us. (Click the Toys & Games tab or go directly to **www.toysrus.com**.)

BARGAIN HUNTER'S SECRETS: Look for savings on individual items. Click the Toys Outlet tab for clearance and sale merchandise.

American Girl

www.americangirlstore.com (800.845.0005)

American Girl dolls and accessories. Manufacturer direct.

BARGAIN HUNTER'S SECRETS: Click the Sale link for discounted items.

AreYouGame.com

www.areyougame.com (800.471.0641)

Games and puzzles.

BARGAIN HUNTER'S SECRETS: Click the Deals & Steals links for sale items.

Bits and Pieces

www.bitsandpieces.com (800.884.2637)

Games and puzzles.

BARGAIN HUNTER'S SECRETS: Click the Outlet Store tab for clearance and sale merchandise.

Boardgames.com

www.boardgames.com (908.429.0202)

Games and puzzles.

BARGAIN HUNTER'S SECRETS: Look for savings on individual items.

DiscoverThis

www.discoverthis.com (866.438.8697

Science toys and kits.

BARGAIN HUNTER'S SECRETS: Click the Sale! link for discounted merchandise. Free shipping on orders of more than $100.

Edu4Fun

www.edu4fun.com (888.338.4386)

Educational toys and puzzles.

BARGAIN HUNTER'S SECRETS: Click the Clearance Sale link for closeout and sale items.

eLearningToys

www.elearningtoys.com (800.283.8155)

Wooden educational toys.

BARGAIN HUNTER'S SECRETS: Use the Toys by Price section to shop for low-priced items. Free shipping on orders of more than $75.

Fisher-Price

www.fisher-pricestore.com (608.831.5210)

Infant and pre-school toys. Manufacturer direct.

BARGAIN HUNTER'S SECRETS: Click the Now on Sale link for discounted items.

Free Bears

www.freebears.com (866.340.2327)

Teddy bears and stuffed animals.

BARGAIN HUNTER'S SECRETS: Click the Sale Items tab for discounted merchandise. Get a free bear with $50 order.

HearthSong

www.hearthsong.com (888.623.6557)

Toys and crafts.

BARGAIN HUNTER'S SECRETS: Click the On Sale link for sale merchandise.

Imagine Toys

www.imaginetoys.com (888.777.1641)

Toys for all ages.

BARGAIN HUNTER'S SECRETS: Click the Bargain Bin link for clearance and sale merchandise.

KB Toys Best Selection

www.kbtoys.com

Toys for all ages. (Also operates as **www.etoys.com**.)

BARGAIN HUNTER'S SECRETS: Look for savings on individual items. Click the Clearance tab for sale and closeout items.

kidsurplus.com

www.kidsurplus.com (866.543.3325)

Toys, games, and puzzles.

BARGAIN HUNTER'S SECRETS: Surplus pricing.

Lego

www.lego.com (800.453.4652)

Lego sets. Manufacturer direct.

BARGAIN HUNTER'S SECRETS: Click the Sales and Deals link for special savings.

PuzzleHouse.com

www.puzzlehouse.com (877.924.6895)

Jigsaw puzzles.

BARGAIN HUNTER'S SECRETS: Free shipping on orders of more than $125.

RecRooms Direct

www.recrooms.com (800.890.3010)

Air hockey, foosball, dart boards, ping pong tables, and other recreation equipment.

BARGAIN HUNTER'S SECRETS: Subscribe to the First Notice List for bargains on closeouts and specials.

Red Wagons

www.redwagons.com

Sleds and wagons.

BARGAIN HUNTER'S SECRETS: Look for savings on individual items. Free shipping.

RoboToys

www.robotoys.com (818.769.5563)

Robots, science, and educational toys.

BARGAIN HUNTER'S SECRETS: Look for savings on individual items.

Small Blue Planet Toys

www.smallblueplanet.com (800.320.0890)

Action figures, dolls, sports, and plush toys.

BARGAIN HUNTER'S SECRETS: Click the What's On Sale link for sale items.

Smarter Kids

www.smarterkids.com (800.293.9314)

Educational toys.

BARGAIN HUNTER'S SECRETS: Click the Clearance Center tab for closeout and sale items.

Spilsbury

www.spilsbury.com (800.285.8619)

Games and puzzles.

BARGAIN HUNTER'S SECRETS: Click the Clearance tab for closeout and sale items. See the Online Specials section of the home page for additional savings.

Toyscamp.com

www.toyscamp.com (908.272.8806)

Toys for all ages.

BARGAIN HUNTER'S SECRETS: All items discounted. Click the Clearance tab for closeout and sale items. Click the Free Shipping tab for items with shipping promotions.

Wal-Mart

www.walmart.com

Toys for all ages. (Click the Toys tab.)

BARGAIN HUNTER'S SECRETS: Look for savings on individual items.

TRAVEL

The Internet has long been a locus for savvy travelers. Online travel is a big business, and that means there are some big players vying for your travel dollar—along with a lot of smaller competitors.

The big players are three in number: Expedia, Orbitz, and Travelocity. Expedia and Travelocity both act as agents in the transaction; they pass a customer's reservation to the travel supplier in return for a commission, and purchase rooms, seats, and so on from suppliers at negotiated rates, reselling that inventory to consumers at discount prices. Orbitz offers direct booking for the nation's biggest airlines; the company is owned by American, Continental, Delta, Northwest, and United Airlines, and has the greatest access to airline Internet-only fares.

Right behind the big three are two sites that take a bit different approach. Both Hotwire and Priceline operate a little like online auctions. You pick a destination and name a price, and then these sites try to find an airline or hotel to accept your offer. No supplier is obligated to accept, so you can always end up out in the cold. But if your offer is matched, you'll get some of the best prices available in the travel business. Know, however, that after you've accepted a deal, your tickets are nonrefundable, nonchangeable, and do not earn frequent flyer miles. These sites are a good deal if your travel plans are extremely flexible—and if you don't mind some rather bizarre multi-stop routing on occasion. If you're locked into a specific time of day for travel—and want to get there via the fastest, most direct route—then skip Priceline and Hotwire and use one of the big three travel sites instead.

Of course, not even the big three sites are perfect. That's because any given site might not offer all the flights and hotels available for a particular destination, or offer the same pricing. In fact, you'll frequently find that your results differ considerably from site to site; it's not unusual to find different availability and pricing information *on the same flights and hotels* at different travel sites. That's because different travel sites work from different database systems, and the different systems aren't always in synch.

For that reason, smart online travel shoppers will visit several Web sites in their quest to find the perfect fares, flights, and lodging. See what Expedia offers, and then go to Travelocity or Orbitz or one of the smaller sites. Use whichever site gives you the best deal.

Of course, you can also book your reservations direct with most airline, hotel, and rental car companies. I don't list all these sites here (they're easy enough to find) because you don't often find the best bargains there. (That's right—it's generally cheaper to go through a third-party reservations site.) The major exceptions are the low-fare airlines, such as Southwest (**www.southwest.com**) and JetBlue (**www.jetblue.com**), which offer online-only fare specials. Check these sites out to see what's available.

By the way, the big three travel sites were all given high scores on the 2003 American Consumer Satisfaction Index. Expedia and Orbitz both scored 77% satisfaction ratings, and Travelocity scored a 76% rating. Priceline also scored high on the index, with a 71% rating.

1800Cheapseats.com

www.1800cheapseats.com (800.243.2773)

Flights, hotels, rental cars, cruises, and vacations.

BARGAIN HUNTER'S SECRETS: Click the Hot Deals tab for package deals.

1800USAHotels.com

www.1800usahotels.com (800.872.4683)

Hotels and rental cars.

BARGAIN HUNTER'S SECRETS: Low rate guarantee.

4Airlines.com

www.4airlines.com (800.910.1240)

Flights, hotels, and rental cars.

BARGAIN HUNTER'S SECRETS: Click the Hot Deals link for package deals.

A1 Discount Hotels

www.a1-discount-hotels.com (888.511.5743)

Hotels, rental cars, flights, vacation rentals, and cruises.

BARGAIN HUNTER'S SECRETS: Low hotel rate guarantee.

Accommodation Search Engine

www.ase.net

Hotels, bed & breakfasts, and holiday rentals.

BARGAIN HUNTER'S SECRETS: Search for best deals.

AirGorilla.com

www.airgorilla.com

Flights, hotels, rental cars, vacations, and cruises.

BARGAIN HUNTER'S SECRETS: See the Hot Deals section of the home page for package deals.

Airline Consolidator.com

www.airlineconsolidator.com (888.468.5385)

Flights, car rentals, hotels, and cruises.

BARGAIN HUNTER'S SECRETS: Specializes in discount international airline tickets.

airtreks.com

www.airtreks.com (877.247.8735)

Flights.

BARGAIN HUNTER'S SECRETS: Specializes in around-the-world and multi-stop international flights.

All-Hotels

www.all-hotels.com

Hotels, bed and breakfasts, and flights.

BARGAIN HUNTER'S SECRETS: Click the Promotions & Deals tab for package deals.

American Express Travel

travel.americanexpress.com (800.346.3607)

Flights, hotels, and rental cars.

BARGAIN HUNTER'S SECRETS: See the Vacations & Last Minute Specials section for package deals.

CheapRooms.com

www.cheaprooms.com (800.311.5192)

Hotels, flights, rental cars, and vacation rentals.

BARGAIN HUNTER'S SECRETS: Click the Hot Deals link for the best hotel bargains.

CheapTickets.com

www.cheaptickets.com (888.922.8849)

Flights, hotels, condo rentals, rental cars, cruises, and vacation packages.

BARGAIN HUNTER'S SECRETS: Click the Specials tab for deals and bargains.

EconomyTravel.com

www.economytravel.com (888.222.2110)

Flights, hotels, and rental cars. Specializes in international travel.

BARGAIN HUNTER'S SECRETS: Click the Airfare Sales links for best deals.

Expedia Best Selection

www.expedia.com (800.397.3342)

Flights, hotels, rental cars, vacation packages, and cruises.

BARGAIN HUNTER'S SECRETS: Click the Deals tab for specials and deals. See the Today's Deals section of the home page for current bargains.

Findmyroom

www.findmyroom.com

Hotels.

BARGAIN HUNTER'S SECRETS: Search for best deals.

HotelDiscounts.com

www.hoteldiscounts.com (800.715.7666)

Hotels and vacation packages.

BARGAIN HUNTER'S SECRETS: See the Today's Specials section of the home page for current deals.

Hotels.com Best Selection

www.hotels.com (800.246.8357)

Hotels and vacation packages.

BARGAIN HUNTER'S SECRETS: Click the Deals & Specials link for discounted rates and last-minute deals.

HotWire

Best Bargain

www.hotwire.com (877.468.9473)

Flights, hotels, car rentals, cruises, and packages.

BARGAIN HUNTER'S SECRETS: Bid for low-priced flights and rooms. Click the Deals & Destinations tab for bargains and package deals. See the This Week's Best Deals section of the home page for other bargains.

iCruise.com

www.i-cruise.com (866.942.7847)

Cruises.

BARGAIN HUNTER'S SECRETS: See the Hot Specials section of the home page for last-minute bargains.

Lodging.com

www.lodging.com (888.563.4464)

Hotels and packages.

BARGAIN HUNTER'S SECRETS: Click the Hot Hotel Rates link for best bargains.

OneTravel.com

www.onetravel.com (866.567.3594)

Flights, hotels, rental cars, vacations, and condos.

BARGAIN HUNTER'S SECRETS: Click the Specials tab for package deals.

Orbitz

Best Selection

www.orbitz.com (888.656.4546)

Flights, hotels, rental cars, cruises, and vacations.

BARGAIN HUNTER'S SECRETS: Click the Deals tab for bargains and packages. See the Flight Deals and Other Travel Deals sections of the home page for additional savings.

PlacesToStay.com

www.placestostay.com (866.224.9765)

Hotels.

BARGAIN HUNTER'S SECRETS: Click the Discounts button for lowest hotel rates.

Priceline

Best Bargain

www.priceline.com (800.774.2354)

Flights, hotels, rental cars, vacation packages, and cruises.

BARGAIN HUNTER'S SECRETS: Bid for low-priced flights and rooms. See the Deals section of the home page for additional savings.

Qixo.com

www.qixo.com

Flights, hotels, rental cars, and cruises.

BARGAIN HUNTER'S SECRETS: Click the Hot Travel Deals link for best bargains.

Quickbook

www.quickbook.com (800.789.9887)

Hotels.

BARGAIN HUNTER'S SECRETS: Click the Limited-Time Specials link for sale prices.

Site59

www.site59.com (800.845.0192)

Vacation packages.

BARGAIN HUNTER'S SECRETS: Search for best bargains.

TravelNow.com

www.travelnow.com (866.476.8771)

Flights, hotels, rental cars, vacation packages, vacation rentals, and cruises.

BARGAIN HUNTER'S SECRETS: Click the Hotel Deals link for lodging bargains.

Travelocity

Best Selection

www.travelocity.com (888.709.5983)

Flights, hotels, rental cars, vacations, and cruises.

BARGAIN HUNTER'S SECRETS: Click the Last Minute Deals tab for special savings. See the Travel Deals section of the home page for more bargains.

TravelWeb

www.travelweb.com (866.437.8132)

Hotels.

BARGAIN HUNTER'S SECRETS: Click the Deals link for the best savings.

Uniglobe.com

www.uniglobe.com

Flights, rental cars, hotels, cruises, vacations, and vacation rentals.

BARGAIN HUNTER'S SECRETS: Click the Hot Deals tab for the best bargains.

VacationOutlet.com

www.vacationoutlet.com

Vacations, cruises, and car rentals.

BARGAIN HUNTER'S SECRETS: See the Today's Special Offers section of the home page for current bargains.

WEDDINGS

Getting married? On a budget? Then use the Internet to find the best bargains on all manner of wedding items—for both the ceremony and reception. You can even shop for wedding dresses online, if that's your style. (And if you're shopping for wedding dresses, don't forget to check out the women's apparel stores listed elsewhere in this directory.)

The big consideration when shopping for wedding items online is time. Make sure that you shop far enough in advance to allow for any necessary personalization, as well as the customary shipping time. And don't expect to find generous returns policies!

By the way, it's unlikely that you'll be able to do all your wedding shopping at a single site, as most of these retailers specialize in just part of the entire matrimonial experience. You may need to pick one site for the wedding reception, another for invitations, a third for guest gifts, and a final site for the wedding dress. Even online, there's a large amount of coordination involved in planning everything out!

1stExpressions.com

www.1stexpressions.com (888.732.3560)

Invitations.

BARGAIN HUNTER'S SECRETS: Click the Weekly Specials link for sale items.

American Bridal

www.americanbridal.com (800.568.3398)

Invitations, reception items, ceremony items, and accessories.

BARGAIN HUNTER'S SECRETS: Click the Specials link for sale items.

BachelorettePartyShop.com

www.bachelorettepartyshop.com (847.622.4317)

Bachelorette party games, favors, gifts, and decorations.

BARGAIN HUNTER'S SECRETS: Look for savings on individual items.

BestBridesmaid.com

www.bestbridesmaid.com (888.217.5655)

Bridesmaid dresses.

BARGAIN HUNTER'S SECRETS: Look for savings on individual items.

Bridalink Store

www.bridalink.com (800.725.6763)

Reception items, ceremony items, party favors, gifts, and accessories.

BARGAIN HUNTER'S SECRETS: Low price guarantee.

BridalPeople.com

www.bridalpeople.com (877.520.0259)

Wedding shoes, bridal headpieces and veils, bridal jewelry, ceremony items, bridal party gifts, and accessories.

BARGAIN HUNTER'S SECRETS: Look for savings on individual items. Free shipping for orders of more than $250.

BrideSave.com

www.bridesave.com (888.321.4696)

Bridal gowns, bridesmaid dresses, veils and headpieces, shoes, handbags, wedding supplies, and accessories.

BARGAIN HUNTER'S SECRETS: Look for savings on individual items.

eWeddingShoes.com

www.eweddingshoes.com (877.823.1500)

Women's wedding shoes and accessories.

BARGAIN HUNTER'S SECRETS: Click the Sale link for discounted items.

Exclusively Weddings

www.exclusivelyweddings.com (800.759.7666)

Invitations, reception items, ceremony items, wedding party gifts, guest favors, and accessories.

BARGAIN HUNTER'S SECRETS: Click the What's On Sale? link for sale items.

Forever & Always Company

www.foreverandalways.com (800.404.4025)

Wedding favors, gifts, and accessories.

BARGAIN HUNTER'S SECRETS: Click the Clearance Items link for sale merchandise.

GroomStop.com

www.groomstop.com (214.747.1270)

Best man and groomsmen gifts.

BARGAIN HUNTER'S SECRETS: Look for savings on individual items.

The Knot

www.theknot.com (877.843.5668)

Ceremony items, reception items, favors, gifts, and accessories. (Click the Wedding Shop tab.)

BARGAIN HUNTER'S SECRETS: Click the On Sale link for discounted items.

Marilyn's Wedding Keepsakes

www.marilynskeepsakes.com (800.263.5808)

Wedding favors, gifts, and accessories.

BARGAIN HUNTER'S SECRETS: Click the Special Promotions link for sale items.

My Glass Slipper

www.myglassslipper.com (866.933.7463)

Women's wedding shoes and accessories.

BARGAIN HUNTER'S SECRETS: Click the Under $100 link for low-priced items.

Romantic Headlines

www.romanticheadlines.com (972.769.8432)

Bridal veils, headpieces, tiaras, lingerie, and accessories.

BARGAIN HUNTER'S SECRETS: Click the On Sale link for bargain basement merchandise. Free shipping on orders of $100 or more.

Wedding Expressions

Best Selection

www.weddingexpressions.com (888.659.5085)

Wedding gowns, favors, ceremony items, reception items, and accessories.

BARGAIN HUNTER'S SECRETS: Click the Closeouts link for clearance items.

The Wedding Helpers

www.weddinghelpers.com (800.274.0675)

Invitations, favors, and accessories.

BARGAIN HUNTER'S SECRETS: Look for savings on individual items.

The Wedding Shopper

www.theweddingshopper.com

Bridal shower items, ceremony items, reception items, favors, gifts, bridal jewelry, and accessories.

BARGAIN HUNTER'S SECRETS: See the Sale, Sale, Sale links for discounted items.

WHOLESALE CLUBS AND SHOPPING NETWORKS

The final category in this directory encompasses two different types of online merchants. Wholesale club sites are the online arms of traditional members-only wholesale clubs; after you've joined, you can shop from a variety of discounted merchandise, often in bulk. Shopping network sites enable you to order the same merchandise you find on the television shopping networks, as well as browse the closeout items available in their clearance stores.

Learn more about these sites in Chapter 7, "Hunting for Bargains at Online Malls, Catalogs, and Department Stores."

Costco

www.costco.com (800.774.2678)

Members-only wholesale club.

BARGAIN HUNTER'S SECRETS: Wholesale prices.

Home Shopping Network

www.hsn.com (800.933.2887)

Shopping network.

BARGAIN HUNTER'S SECRETS: Click the Clearance tab for closeout and sale merchandise.

QVC

www.iqvc.com (888.345.5788)

Shopping network.

BARGAIN HUNTER'S SECRETS: Click the Clearance link for closeout and sale merchandise.

Sam's Club

www.samsclub.com

Members-only wholesale club.

BARGAIN HUNTER'S SECRETS: Wholesale prices.

Shop At Home Network

www.shopathometv.com (866.366.4010)

Shopping network.

BARGAIN HUNTER'S SECRETS: Click the Clearance link for closeout and sale merchandise.

ShopNBC

www.shopnbc.com (800.884.2212

Shopping network.

BARGAIN HUNTER'S SECRETS: Click the Clearance link for closeout and sale merchandise.

INDEX

NUMBERS

A

C

D

E

F

G

H

I

J

K

L

M

P

Q-R

S

T

U

V

W

X-Z